Archaeology and Homeric Epic

SHEFFIELD STUDIES IN
AEGEAN ARCHAEOLOGY

Archaeology and Homeric Epic

edited by

Susan Sherratt and John Bennet

OXBOW | books
Oxford & Philadelphia

Published in the United Kingdom in 2017 by
OXBOW BOOKS
The Old Music Hall, 106–108 Cowley Road, Oxford OX4 1JE

and in the United States by
OXBOW BOOKS
1950 Lawrence Road, Havertown, PA 19083

Paperback Edition: ISBN 978-1-78570-295-2
Digital Edition: ISBN 978-1-78570-296-9 (epub)

A CIP record for this book is available from the British Library

Library of Congress Cataloging-in-Publication Data

Names: Sherratt, Susan, editor. | Bennet, John, editor.
Title: Archaeology and Homeric epic / edited by Susan Sherratt and John Bennet.
Description: Oxford & Philadelphia : Oxbow Books, 2016. | Series: Sheffield studies in Aegean archaeology | Includes bibliographical references.
Identifiers: LCCN 2016040020 (print) | LCCN 2016044861 (ebook) | ISBN 9781785702952 (pbk.) | ISBN 9781785702969 (epub) | ISBN 9781785702976 (mobi) | ISBN 9781785702983 (pdf)
Subjects: LCSH: Archaeology--Greece. | Homer--Influence. | Epic poetry, Greek--History and criticism. | Civilization, Homeric.
Classification: LCC DF78 .A644 2016 (print) | LCC DF78 (ebook) | DDC 938--dc23 LC record available at https://lccn.loc.gov/2016040020

For a complete list of Oxbow titles, please contact:

UNITED KINGDOM
Oxbow Books
Telephone (01865) 241249, Fax (01865) 794449
Email: oxbow@oxbowbooks.com
www.oxbowbooks.com

UNITED STATES OF AMERICA
Oxbow Books
Telephone (800) 791-9354, Fax (610) 853-9146
Email: queries@casemateacademic.com
www.casemateacademic.com/oxbow

Oxbow Books is part of the Casemate Group

Front cover: Reconstruction by Piet de Jong of battle scene in Hall 64 at Pylos (Lang 1969: col. pl. M). Courtesy of The Department of Classics, University of Cincinnati and American School of Classical Studies at Athens, Pylos Archive, Piet de Jong Collection of Watercolors. Photo Jennifer F. Stephens and Arthur E. Stephens.

Contents

List of Contributors

RODERICK BEATON
Centre of Hellenic Studies, King's College London

JOHN BENNET
Department of Archaeology, University of Sheffield

MARGARET H. BEISSINGER
Department of Slavic Languages and Literatures, Princeton University

STEPHANIE DALLEY
Oriental Institute, University of Oxford

JACK L. DAVIS
Department of Classics, University of Cincinnati

OLIVER DICKINSON
Department of Classics and Ancient History, University of Durham

PAUL HALSTEAD
Department of Archaeology, University of Sheffield

JOHANNES HAUBOLD
Department of Classics and Ancient History, University of Durham

SUSANNE HOFSTRA
Minneapolis, MN

KATHLEEN M. LYNCH
Department of Classics, University of Cincinnati

ALEXANDER MAZARAKIS AINIAN
Department of History, Archaeology and Social Anthropology, University of Thessaly

DIAMANTIS PANAGIOTOPOULOS
Institut für Klassische Archäologie, Ruprecht-Karls-Universität Heidelberg

SUSAN SHERRATT
Department of Archaeology, University of Sheffield

ANTHONY SNODGRASS
Clare College, Cambridge

Introduction

Susan Sherratt and John Bennet

The relationship between the Homeric epics and archaeology has suffered mixed fortunes over the course of the last century and a half, swinging between 'fundamentalist' attempts to use archaeology in order to demonstrate the essential historicity of the epics and their background at one extreme, and outright rejection of the idea that archaeology is capable of contributing anything at all to our understanding and appreciation of the epics at the other. Although narrow questions of historicity, particularly in relation to the Homeric Trojan War theme, have been revived in recent years (see especially Latacz 2004), we have chosen in this volume to concentrate rather on exploring a variety of other, perhaps sometimes more oblique, ways in which we can use archaeology, and also philology, anthropology and social history, to help offer insights into the epics, the contexts of their possibly prolonged creation (cf. Snodgrass, chapter 1), aspects of their 'prehistory' (Sherratt, Panagiotopoulos, Mazarakis-Ainian, chapters 4, 6–7), and what they may have stood for at various times in their long oral and written history (Dickinson and Davis and Lynch, chapters 2 and 5). The effects of the Homeric epics on the history and popular reception of archaeology, especially in the particular context of modern Germany, is also a theme that is explored here (Haubold, chapter 3).

We have thus, on the whole, attempted to move beyond the old dichotomies between historicity and irrelevance and to bring a multi-disciplinary approach to the Homeric epics (and in some cases other epics both ancient and more modern – see the contributions by Dalley, Beissinger and Beaton, chapters 8–10) by exploring not only their varied relationships to the archaeological record and the practice of archaeology, but also a variety of other issues, either explicitly or implicitly. These include such diverse questions as the relationships between visual and verbal imagery and the role of both of these in reflecting or enhancing elements of social and political ideology, the social contexts of epic (or sub-epic) creation or re-creation, the roles of bards and their relationships to different types of patrons and audiences, the ability of story-patterns, ideological elements and linguistic formulae to cross linguistic and/or cultural boundaries in general (and Near Eastern contributions to Homeric epic in particular), the construction and uses of 'history' as traceable through both epic and archaeology, the nature of 'historical memory' and its manipulation, linguistic and material-cultural stratigraphy as detectable in epic, composition-in-performance of oral history and its transmission and transformation, the relationship between 'prehistoric' (oral) and 'historical' (recorded in writing) periods, and the history of

'Homeric archaeology' and other 'epic archaeologies' in general. Throughout, our emphasis is above all on context and its relevance to the creation, transmission, re-creation and manipulation of epic in the present (or near-present) as well as in the ancient Greek past.

The Dating of Homer's Epics: Late 8th Century BC and Later

For long it was received wisdom among Classical scholars that the Homeric epics, whatever their earlier 'prehistory' (see below), were created, or at least emerged or crystallised in a more or less recognisable form, sometime around 700 BC, give or take a few decades on either side. This was despite the knowledge that the texts, as we know them, were divided into books and heavily edited by Alexandrian scholars. In recent decades, however, this view has been challenged - for example, by Minna Jensen (1980), who argued that the epics did not take on any recognisable form until they were written down in Athens in the Peisistratid period of the later sixth century BC, and by Gregory Nagy (e.g. 1995; 1996: 29–64), who sees the epics, as John Myres (1930) saw the Greeks themselves, as 'ever in the process of becoming' through several distinct stages of formation, from the Bronze Age right down to the Hellenistic period. The question of writing is often brought into this debate. There are some who believe that writing was essential for the 'crystallisation' of the epics, and that, if they were products of the late eighth century, they must have been written down at the first opportunity. Indeed, Barry Powell (1991) has argued that the Greek alphabet was adopted and adapted specifically to write down the Homeric epics in the later 8th century. Others (e.g. Kirk [1962]), by contrast, believe that it is not impossible to conceive of the epics being transmitted orally in comparatively stable form by rhapsodes for a couple of centuries before being committed to writing. In this volume, Snodgrass ('Homer, the moving target', chapter 1) argues that nothing recognisable as definitively 'Homeric' is likely to have emerged by the end of the eighth century, even if cycles of epic poetry, including some story-patterns of the sort familiar from the Homeric epics, were already in circulation. Fully accepting Nagy's long-term evolutionary model for the epics and its implications of a long period of fluidity of creation and re-creation, at least before commitment to writing in the sixth century BC, he suggests that looking for chronological correlates in the archaeological record for particular passages is the equivalent of shooting at a moving target over a very long run, in which widely separated chronological circumstances may have produced similar archaeological effects, particularly since many Homeric descriptions can in effect be interpreted in a variety of different ways. Nevertheless, the target (or rather, perhaps, a whole series of different targets) is an important one, and for individual passages or elements of these we should not give up the search to find some context or contexts that might explain what gave rise to these and their inclusion. This, in Snodgrass's words, may turn out to be a much more stimulating sport than tackling the 'stationary' target of an assumed late eighth century 'Homer'.

Archaeological Interpretation of Epic Content

However, even if we accept that the Homeric epics were essentially products of sometime around 700 BC and/or a succession of later periods, this does not mean that they were constructed entirely out of nothing in the eighth century or later, as both Nagy and Snodgrass concede. Objects such as Meriones' boar's tusk helmet (*Iliad* 10.261–7) or Ajax's 'shield like a tower' (e.g. *Iliad* 7.219; 11.485; 17.128), which appear to find best archaeological correlates in the Late Bronze Age (and often the early Late Bronze Age, c. 1650–1400 BC), have often since Schliemann been used as arguments for the original setting of the events and *personae* of the epics (if not their composition) in the 'Mycenaean' period. Ian Morris (1986), on the other hand, has argued that such objects play the part of 'epic distancing effects', deliberate archaisms introduced by an eighth century bard to convey the idea of a distant past to his audience. Here, Dickinson ('The will to believe: why Homer cannot be "true" in any meaningful sense', chapter 2) takes up and expands some of the spirit of Morris' viewpoint (including his idea of a wholly eighth century composition), arguing that not only do the epics not contain anything that could possibly be regarded as the real history of any period, but that the world and society the epics portray are entirely imaginary ones: purely poetic creations of what eighth century BC Greeks thought a bygone heroic world ought to have looked like.

The Homeric Epics, Homeric Archaeology and their Role in Modern Germany

The modern history of academic enquiries in western Europe into the Homeric epics as literary and historical works goes back to the eighteenth-nineteenth centuries, particularly in Germany, where the rather dry debate (the 'Homeric Question') between 'Unitarians' (who saw the epics as the work of a single author) and 'Analysts' (who regarded them as the products of a number of different authors, possibly of different periods) became the burning issue of the day among Homeric scholars. At the same time, any question of historical veracity contained in the epics was rejected by many philologists. As the nineteenth century progressed, however, but often now in less rarefied academic circles, interest arose in the question of the historicity of certain elements of the epics (which had never seriously been doubted in ancient or early modern times), particularly as possibly representing the earliest history of the Greeks, who had come to be widely regarded as the ancestors of modern Europeans and founders of their culture and values. Enter Heinrich Schliemann in the 1870s, a product in various ways of his own context in late nineteenth century Germany, who harnessed the emerging 'science' of archaeology to 'prove' that the Trojan War really took place before the era of historical Greece and that its Homeric participants were real people who lived in what we now call the Late Bronze Age. The effects of Schliemann's publicity machine were such that, for much of the twentieth century, the idea that the Trojan War really took place in the later part of the Late Bronze Age and that the epics were set (and probably also composed — at least in part) in this period remained the largely orthodox view, particularly among archaeologists (see e.g. Wace and Stubbings 1962; and cf. Snodgrass, chapter 1 in this volume). Schliemann's excavations at the site of Hisarlık (which he and others identified as Homer's Troy) also played a significant part in contributing to a sense of (bourgeois) German national identity and pride in the years around and following the first German unification in 1871, and Schliemann became — and in many ways has remained - a German national hero, with Hisarlık as in some senses a German 'national' site, embedded deep in the German popular psyche.

Here, in chapter 3 ('Dream and reality in the work of Heinrich Schliemann and Manfred Korfmann'), Haubold not only discusses the entirely manufactured 'dreams' which Schliemann claimed led him to Hisarlık in 1870, but also explores the peculiarly German context in which the late Manfred Korfmann's renewed excavations at Hisarlık took place from 1988 onwards, just a year before the Berlin Wall came down and the questions and problems surrounding German re-unification began to preoccupy German political, economic and (indeed) academic discourses. The iconic national status of Homer's Troy and its 'realities' as presented by Korfmann (whose excavations were largely funded not only by national funding bodies but also by Daimler-Benz) became the subject of a particularly vicious academic debate after the mounting of the exhibition *Troia - Traum und Wirklichkeit* in Stuttgart, Braunschweig and Bonn in 2001 (Latacz [ed.] 2001), in which the 'reality' of Troy and Homer's Trojan War, as spearheaded by Joachim Latacz (2001) in a book originally written quite undisguisedly for a German popular readership who already knew what they wanted to hear but were delighted to welcome 'new' archaeological evidence which appeared to support it, became a particularly hotly disputed issue.

What is particularly striking from the point of view of the relationship between Homer and archaeology is the way in which what was ostensibly a dry-as-dust archaeological debate also drew the interest of a much wider German public, in a way that one can hardly imagine happening in the twenty-first century in most other European countries in relation to a foreign archaeological site. Haubold explains this phenomenon in terms of the symbolic importance of Troy and its first excavator to German popular historical, social and institutional preoccupations in the period following re-unification after 1989, and points out the lessons it offers for the implications of the intellectual and historical contexts in which archaeology (above all where it involves Homer, creator of the first 'European' literature) takes place and is interpreted.

'Prehistory' of Homeric Epics

Varying Contexts of Creation and Transmission

There are problems with using objects like Meriones' helmet or Ajax's shield and their correlates in the archaeological record as support for the ideas, on the one hand, that the epics were originally composed in the Late Bronze Age or, on the other, that they were in some sense 'set' (even if imaginarily) in that period, some four or five centuries earlier than the eighth century BC. Instead, the general and specific patterns of datable material cultural references found in the epics appear to need some further explanation. Nor are such references confined just to items of material culture, but practices, attitudes and values, as well as some linguistic oddities, also show some interesting patterns which suggest that a long but unevenly punctuated 'prehistory' of heroic song lay behind and fed into what we know as the Homeric epics. Sherratt ('Homeric epic and contexts of bardic creation', chapter 4) looks briefly at some of these patterns and suggests that we should probably envisage them as the results of different chronological contexts of bardic creation in different circumstances and for different purposes, and that such different contexts may perhaps be identified by the different ways in which visual imagery is used at different times. In particular, a distinction between generic scenes apparently set in the present and portraying aspects of contemporary lifestyle, on the one hand, and scenes that seem to show specific narrative or story, whether or not obviously set in the past, on the other, may provide a clue as to the contexts in which bards are making active 'statements' on behalf of contemporary aspiring groups as opposed to recording the shared or accepted 'history' of wider collective societies.

The Past in the Past

Davis and Lynch ('Remembering and forgetting Nestor: Pylian pasts pluperfect?', chapter 5), in a different way, also tackle the question of collective memories of 'history', and ask what happened at the 'Palace of Nestor' at Ano Englianos in the periods following its destruction around 1200 BC. Did the Messenians of succeeding centuries associate these ruins with a Homeric Nestor who belonged to their renowned past? Their careful and critical analysis of the relatively few later artefacts and structures found at the site lead them to the conclusion that they did not. If so, this lessens the probability that persistent 'memories' of specific individual heroes firmly associated with particular locations inevitably survived from the Late Bronze Age into the Early Iron Age or Archaic periods, and perhaps rather gives some support to the possibility that heroes and/or their exploits and associations were 'invented' on the basis of particularly prominent ruins at some other sites.

In closely related mode, Panagiotopoulos ('In the grip of their past: tracing Mycenaean *memoria*', chapter 6), moves further back in time to collective 'memories' fostered in an earlier period. He asks whether we can detect acts of memorialising the past in the Mycenaean Late Bronze Age, whether these were planned or spontaneous, and how significant they may have been for different sections of society. Using the urban landscape of Mycenae, in particular, to shed light on Mycenaean mnemonic strategies, he argues that these changed according to their contexts over the passage of time, which itself may have implications for the study of the Homeric epics.

Finally, to come (as it were) full circle back to the eighth century, Mazarakis Ainian ('Heroes in Early Iron Age Greece and the Homeric epics', chapter 7) addresses the long-standing chicken-and-egg question of whether the rise of hero cults in Greece at this time was generated by the spread of the Homeric epics (or their cyclical forerunners) or whether the fashion for such cults within Greek society contributed to the creation, consolidation and spread of the epics (or epic cycles) themselves. Going back in time into the earlier centuries of the Early Iron Age, he traces a history of 'cults' honouring local (living or recently dead) heroes which eventually, by the eighth century, evolved into a trend of commemorating remote or mythical ancestors, perhaps as part of a political strategy of legitimation. Hero cults and epics (or their 'heroic song' forerunners) thus evolved organically and in parallel over a prolonged period, both becoming integral components of a new ideological nexus towards the end of the eighth century.

The Creation and Uses of Epic Traditions

Gilgamesh and the Homeric Epics

It has often been noticed that the *Iliad* and the *Odyssey* contain elements which appear to relate quite closely to literary elements or motifs found in ancient Near Eastern literature, and the question is by what means they reached the Greek world. Here, Dalley ('Gilgamesh and heroes at Troy: myth, history and education in the invention of tradition', chapter 8) addresses herself specifically to the evidence for the mechanisms of contact. She finds it in the education of scribes, who used literary texts, including epics such as *Gilgamesh*, as practice pieces, thus demonstrating how very widely known such literature was in the east. Eastern elements in the epics, Dalley argues, reached Greece primarily through literary media, incorporated into oral traditions probably mainly in Greece itself. Opportunities for transmission occurred first of all through direct contact in Anatolia and Syria in the Bronze Age, through Phoenician traders in the Early Iron Age, and finally through Greek-speakers living and working in the Assyrian empire. At the end of this chapter, Dalley addresses the question of how, and in what senses, we might regard the creation or elaboration of epics, such as *Gilgamesh* and the *Iliad*, as having some historical contexts and purposes, without this necessarily implying any historical content.

South Slavic Epic

In the 1920s and 1930s, the work of Milman Parry demonstrated the essentially oral nature of the Homeric epics (Parry 1971) and, together with Albert Lord's work on the methods and techniques of South Slavic traditional singers (Lord 1960), showed how what can be called a technique of oral composition-in-performance could be applied to them. This effectively brought an end to the old 'Unitarian' versus 'Analyst' debate, but opened up whole sets of new questions. These included such issues as the tension between the various forms of conservatism inherent in a technique which makes regular use of formulae at various levels and the freedom and incentive to innovate, the expectations of different types of audience in different types of setting, the nature of 'historical' memory, and how far one can expect recognisable history to be preserved over a long tradition of oral song creation and transmission. In chapter 9 ('History and the making of South Slavic epic'), Beissinger confronts all these issues, particularly the last. Returning to the South Slavic oral songs and epics that were the subject of Albert Lord's research in the mid-twentieth century, she explores the relationships between historical epic and history and the role of the former in generating nationalist (especially Serbian) sentiment, initially in opposition to the Ottoman empire but continuing in more recent Balkan conflicts. Her analysis provides a very good example of the power of epic to consolidate and disseminate national identities, ideas of national 'history' and nationalist aspirations in a much more direct and self-conscious fashion than is the case with Germany and the successive excavators of Homer's Troy, as discussed in chapter 3 by Haubold.

Digenis Akritis

Another example of what has come to be regarded by many as national epic can be seen in *Digenis Akritis*, discussed in chapter 10 ('*Digenes Akritis*, the Homeric question, and the making of a modern myth') by Beaton. Beaton recounts the discovery in the nineteenth century in a monastery in Trebizond of a twelfth century Byzantine poem about a hero of mixed Byzantine and Arab blood who fought (and engaged in other exploits) in the borderlands between Byzantium and Islam. The original poem was melded with oral folk-tales from various parts of Turkey to create an essentially modern collected confection that was hailed by many as a Greek national epic, at a time when the relatively new state of modern Greece had aspirations to recover the territories that had once been part of the Byzantine empire. Beaton makes the interesting point that *Digenis Akritis* represents the playing out of contemporary 'Analyst' views of the Homeric epics in reverse: rather than the constituent contributions of a number of different authors being separated out, they were instead put together and, precisely because of the currency of *Analyst* views of the ultimate prototype, the whole carried all the more impact as a 'modern' Greek epic.

Epics, the Past and Archaeology

The volume thus covers some very diverse terrain, from the question of at what point in time we can legitimately talk about what we now recognise as the Homeric epics, to that of how a modern Greek national epic, based on contemporary views of what the Homeric epics consisted of, was created. In between, there are discussions of how the epics relate to history, both in the form of how 'historical' their content is and in the form of their indirect relationship, through the activities of successive excavators of Troy, with modern German history and national identity. There are also investigations into the different kinds of material cultural contexts in which bards may have operated in different ways, either propagating the image of contemporary individuals or groups or emphasising a 'history' that wider communities felt able to share, into the extent to which Homeric heroes were recognised and commemorated in the places they have been supposed to inhabit, into how Late Bronze Age centres created and memorialised their own past, and into the roles and reputations of heroes and a 'heroic' way of life in Early Iron Age Greece and the interplay of these with the spread of epic. Finally, there are questions concerning Mesopotamian and South Slavic epic: in the former case the relationships of *Gilgamesh* to the Homeric epics, and the mechanisms and routes through which these were effected; and in the latter case (again) the question of historical content and its repeated role in the creation and maintenance of Slav nationalism.

The more general messages which arise from these diverse contributions are perhaps equally diverse and diffuse. Perhaps the main one, however, is that epic (above all, national epic - as the Homeric epics without doubt were), like the Bible (which started life as another national epic and formed the other major object of the new 'science' of philology in the late 18th-century German academy), have the power to be all things to all people, susceptible to an endless variety of approaches or interpretations depending on the questions asked, not least when juxtaposed to the archaeological record with its own varieties of potential, limitations and ambiguities. Like the Bible, epics such as the Homeric epics, South Slavic epic and even *Digenis Akritis*, still have political resonances or echoes of political resonances today, sometimes in unexpected places. They illustrate how powerful an inherited past (whether real or imaginary) can be in creating the identities of groups of people.

Archaeology can, and often has been, harnessed in support of such epic-derived pasts. Nonetheless, over the last 150 years the engagement of epic with archaeology has swung between a kind of fundamentalism, in an attempt to use the archaeological record to verify the written word, and a profound scepticism which sees epic as no more than a product of imagination, dreamed up for purposes of social advantage or political cohesion or even simply entertainment. In between, it has been used in attempts to anchor epic, or elements of epic, chronologically. As archaeology's own self-consciousness has developed, however, and as it has retreated from subservience to the ethnocentric European privilege accorded to the written word, a more equal weight given to both archaeology and literature as separate but complementary products of the same societies has allowed us to glimpse some of the subtleties and complexities of context which informed both, and to guess at the kinds of economic, social, political and other very human impulses which lay behind epic creation, transmission, re-creation and dissemination. Through such means reality and myth, truth and invention seem to dissolve into irrelevance as both epic and archaeology can be seen to be intertwined, both of them 'real' in some respects and 'unreal' in others, and with neither having a monopoly of power to shed light on the other.

Bibliography

Cottrell, L.

1984 *The Bull of Minos. The discoveries of Schliemann and Evans* (revised edn, with introduction by P. Levi). London: Bell & Hyman.

Jensen, M. S.

1980 *The Homeric Question and the Oral-Formulaic Theory* (Opuscula Graecolatina 20). Copenhagen: Museum Tusculanum Press.

Kirk, G. S.

1962 *The Songs of Homer*. Cambridge: Cambridge University Press.

Latacz, J.

2001 *Troia und Homer: der Weg zur Lösung eines alten Rätsels*. München: Koehler & Amelang.

2004 *Troy and Homer: Towards a Solution of an Old Mystery* (translated by K. Windle and R. Ireland). Oxford: Oxford University Press.

Latacz, J. (ed.)

2001 *Troia - Traum und Wirklichkeit*. Stuttgart: K. Theiss.

Lord, A. B.

1960 *The Singer of Tales* (Harvard Studies in Comparative Literature 24). Cambridge, MA.: Harvard University Press.

Morris, I.

1986 The use and abuse of Homer. *Classical Antiquity* 5: 81–138.

Myres, J. L.

1930 *Who were the Greeks?* (Sather Classical Lectures 6). Berkeley: University of California Press.

Nagy, G.

1995 An evolutionary model for the making of Homeric poetry: comparative perspectives. In J. B. Carter and S. P. Morris (eds.), *The Ages of Homer: A Tribute to Emily Townsend Vermeule*: 163–79. Austin, TX: University of Texas Press.

1996 *Homeric Questions*. Austin, TX: University of Texas Press.

Parry, M.

1971 *The Making of Homeric Verse: the Collected Papers of Milman Parry* (ed. A. Parry). Oxford: Clarendon Press.

Powell, B. B.

1991 *Homer and the Origin of the Greek Alphabet*. Cambridge: Cambridge University Press.

Wace, A. J. B. and F. H. Stubbings (ed.)

1962 *A Companion to Homer*. London: Macmillan.

Chapter 1

Homer, the Moving Target

Anthony Snodgrass

The topic chosen for this Round Table may have been more welcome to me than to most other participants. I apologise in advance if some of the content of my paper seems immaterial to the concerns of many readers. Yet even among those Aegean prehistorians who disclaim any interest whatever in the Homeric poems, there may lurk a sneaking suspicion that they have an indirect obligation to him, for the original creation of the posts that they hold.

Forty years ago, when I began doing research in the field of pre-Classical Greece, there was an assumption shared by all archaeologists on whose work the evidence of the Homeric epics had any bearing. This was, that any possibility of major extension in the evidence, or of major shifts in opinion consequent on this, lay entirely in the hands of us as archaeologists. We and our colleagues might make new discoveries which would change the whole balance of the archaeological background to Homer, or we might make new observations from the existing evidence, but there remained one constant in the picture: the texts themselves. This was not, of course, because Homeric textual scholarship had fallen into stagnation: on the contrary, its practitioners were heatedly debating all manner of issues of relatively recent growth, such as the nature of oral transmission, or the relationship of Homeric language to the Mycenaean dialect of the Late Bronze Age. But there was one thing on which they were broadly agreed: the process of the formation of the epics, into much the form in which we have them and with the exception of a very few, readily identifiable passages, was assumed to have been complete by a date no later than the eighth century BC.

That assumption survived, at least as the opinion of the great majority of Homeric scholars, through the 1960s, 1970s and much of the 1980s. For the archaeologists and indeed the historians, it meant that at least the playing-field remained level and the goal-posts fixed – or more accurately, the goal-post at the nearer end of the field. Wherever the features of material culture or social organisation reflected in the Homeric epics were to be looked for, at least we knew that they must have been in place by or before the end of the eighth century – apart, again, from a few identifiable exceptions. When, for example, Moses Finley in *The World of Odysseus* (Finley 1956) argued that a consistent and real picture of the society of the tenth and ninth centuries

BC was present in the poems, one might disagree with him, or criticise the fact that his conclusion did not work well for the elements of strictly material culture: what we had to admit was that, in principle, such a conclusion was compatible with the chronology of the poems' composition.

So too with the old, but then still quite fashionable, belief in substantial Mycenaean survivals in the material culture of the texts, which is inseparably associated with the first *Companion to Homer* (Wace and Stubbings 1962), in part because some of its contributions had been first written decades earlier. Improbable though their conclusions might seem to younger scholars, they could not be rejected in principle or out of hand, when the eighth century BC was known to have witnessed Mycenaean revivals of other kinds. Even when Adalberto Giovannini startled Homeric scholarship with his book arguing that the *Catalogue of Ships* in *Iliad* 2 was not, after all, a major textual survival from the Late Bronze Age and a support for the belief in other kinds of Mycenaean survival, but instead represented a *later* addition to the established text, essentially portraying the Archaic Greek world of, probably, the seventh century BC (Giovannini 1969), a possible reaction was to say that, even if he was right, then the *Catalogue* need only be moved across to make an addition (though admittedly a very substantial one) to what I have called the 'very few, readily identifiable passages' which had been late insertions into an otherwise finalised eighth-century BC text.

The first crack in this consensus appeared in a new movement to reconsider that one great constant, the date of the substantive completion of the texts of the poems as we have them. One leading scholar after another joined the wave, in finding new reasons for thinking that this had happened significantly later than everyone had assumed, not within the eighth century BC but some way down in the seventh. There were several planks to the new platform: or better, several planks to the old platform which had first to be pulled away, so that it would collapse. Perhaps the first of these to go, following the new editions by Martin West of the *Theogony* and the *Works and Days* (West 1966; 1978), was the comfortable belief that the texts of Hesiod's poems showed him to have been composing at a time when the Homeric epics were already circulating. Next to follow was a hitherto unquestioned, broader yet also more specifically-based belief, that there were cases of indebtedness to Homer in the work of the lyric and elegiac poets, some of whom could be assigned a date quite early in the seventh century BC. Here too, fresh scrutiny of Archilochos, Tyrtaios, Kallinos and others suggested that, once you gave up the preconception that they had anyway lived long after Homer, your certainty that they had paid occasional homage to his works might also begin to evaporate (see especially Fowler 1987). Against this growing tide, the contrary arguments of Richard Janko (1982), using linguistic evidence to form a relative chronology for the composition of the *Iliad*, *Odyssey*, Hesiod and the *Homeric Hymns* (they came out in that order) seem to have been rather swamped.

All of this was internally-directed scholarship, addressing literary and textual scholars with the arguments that counted most with them; and many such scholars duly reconsidered their former positions. But there were also more outward-looking contributions, from Hellenists who tried out this new conclusion on some of the external evidence: such as those of Walter Burkert with the special crux of Egyptian Thebes in *Iliad* 9 (Burkert 1978); Oliver Taplin with the visual arts (Taplin 1992: 33–35); Matthew Dickie with geography (Dickie 1995); or Hans van Wees with warfare (van Wees 1997).

As the 1980s moved into the 1990s, the claims grew stronger and more far-reaching: Dickie, for example, inclined to a date for the composition of the *Iliad* and *Odyssey* not in the first, but in the *second* half of the seventh century BC. An important advance on a different front came more recently still, with the book of Jonathan Burgess (Burgess 2001) arguing that the early versions of the Epic Cycle, dealing with episodes in the Trojan saga that fell before, between and after those narrated in the *Iliad* and *Odyssey*, must have had chronological priority over Homer. This had the great merit of offering, at long last, an answer to the puzzling question: why are so many of the first so-called 'Homeric' scenes in Greek art not strictly Homeric at all, since they instead portray the same prior and posterior stages in the Troy story?

One or two of the new contributions might still just be accommodated within the old assumption: thus, if Burkert (1978) was right that Achilles' brief reference in *Iliad* 9 to 'Egyptian Thebes of the Hundred Gates' only made sense after that city's brief revival under the 25th Ethiopian Dynasty between c. 715 and 663 BC, the easiest reaction was to add its three lines to the growing package of 'later insertions'. But you cannot do that with generalities like warfare or geography. What you can do is to contest the claims of this new movement, on the grounds that it consistently underrates the attainments of the eighth century BC in other directions; and I have tried this myself in the case of the visual arts (Snodgrass 1998: 40–66, 76–78).

The new trend does make a difference, however, to most attempts to find a material and social background for Homer. Because it admits impressive new developments in society, architecture and art from the seventh century BC as potential components of Homer's background, it further weakens the case for treating the Late Bronze Age as the only possible source for these 'impressive' material features of the poems (if indeed that cause still has any archaeological adherents). For exactly the same reason, it strengthens the hand of those who see the Homeric settings as primarily inspired by the situation in Homer's own lifetime. Its impact can be treated as marginal only perhaps by those who hold that the intervening Dark Age provided the main inspiration for the epics, or by those who find that Homer's background is an irredeemable composite of several different eras, as I still do (cf. Snodgrass 1974).

The recent move to down-date the completion of the Homeric texts, in more or less their present form, is however *not* my main theme in this contribution. I wish to distinguish this trend very clearly from another, even more recent movement, which at first glance looks very similar to it and has enlisted some of the same big names in its cause, but which is in fact more far-reaching and important.

This newer movement would revise, even perhaps contest, the whole notion of 'completion' of the Homeric epic texts. Instead, it posits a very long period of fluidity and variety in the versions of the poems, an era of continuous re-composition, which was brought to an end only in the sixth century BC by the action of 'freezing' these texts by committing them to writing. It thus brings another long phase of historical development into the potential frame of Homer's background; but it does much more than that. By arguing for at least the possibility of major changes in the versions of the epics that were in circulation, at a date very much later than had hitherto been supposed, it makes Homer into the 'moving target' of my title. It would appear to mean that, as archaeologists, we suddenly have a much freer hand in finding Homeric passages that might correspond with our material evidence, or material evidence that could provide a basis for the Homeric descriptions – though whether such a free hand is what we want is another question: a more cynical view would be that acceptance of this doctrine would make most such activity obsolete or a waste of time. I address the question more specifically below, but first let me sketch the history of this idea.

Once again, the names of Walter Burkert (1987) and Martin West (1988) appear either as early exponents, or at least as heralds of the new movement: for them, it was perhaps mainly an extension of their previous thoughts on the presence of relatively late features in the Homeric epics. But the real 'high priest' of this movement is Gregory Nagy, and its founding texts his writings of the 1990s. I was in the audience for Nagy's J.H. Gray Lectures at Cambridge in May 1993, when I first heard the doctrine expounded. He has since elaborated it in more than one book, but most valuable for our purposes is perhaps the succinct, 2-page outline that he appended at the end of a paper in what is primarily an archaeologist's book, *New Light on a Dark Age* (Nagy 1997: 206–207). I give here a summary of his summary.

There were 'Five ages of Homer', each showing progressively less flexibility and greater rigidity:

1. the most fluid period, with no written texts, extending from the second millennium to the later part of the eighth century BC
2. a more formative or 'pan-Hellenic' period, still with no written texts, from the later eighth to the mid-sixth century BC
3. a definitive period, centred on the Athens of the Peisistratids, with potential transcripts being taken down at any of several points from the mid-sixth to the later fourth century BC
4. a standardising period, perhaps with texts that were not mere transcripts, from the later fourth to the mid-second century BC
5. a most rigid period, with texts as 'scripture', from the mid-second century BC onward.

We shall not be concerned here with any stage later than the third, although the spectre of possible modification of the texts may still lurk even between the third and the fourth 'age'. The important feature for us is, of course, the continued absence of written texts down to the mid-sixth century and the fact that this second stage is still merely 'more formative', not definitive. As I listened in 1993, I remember thinking

'My Classicist colleagues will never buy this'; but how wrong I was. One component of the (often hostile) persona which archaeologists, including Aegean archaeologists, attribute to their Classicist colleagues is caution, to the point of timidity. In my experience, it is we archaeologists who often prove the more timid. In the event, the Nagy 'evolutionary model' of the Homeric texts has been embraced, not just by people in Cambridge but also by a wide spectrum of Classicists across the English-speaking world. Among younger scholars in the United States, we have the word of one of them that it 'has almost achieved the status of orthodoxy' (Reece 2005: 52). It may prove to have been only a fashion, but for the time being at least it is one that we must live with. What will this mean?

Let me first give an example of one branch of archaeology on which its effect is negative, perhaps to the point of being almost ruinous. This is the whole exercise of trying to match scenes in early Greek art with episodes of the *Iliad* and *Odyssey*, often extended into the further process of using such scenes as a *terminus* to date the circulation of the poems. If we cannot exclude the possibility that other versions of the poems, quite different in detail from those which we have, survived at least as late as the mid-sixth century BC before they were supplanted by the canonical version, then we lose all the ground rules for judging the pictures of the eighth, seventh and earlier sixth centuries. Any discrepancy from the *Iliad* or *Odyssey*'s version of a story can at once be explained away by saying that this different version was the one which was in circulation at the time.

Thus, perhaps, Menelaos at Troy, instead of being rather ignominiously driven back by Hektor away from the body of the fallen Trojan Euphorbos, as he is in *Iliad* 17, may in a previous version have successfully straddled and captured the dead man and his arms, as he seems to be doing on the 'Euphorbos Plate' of about 600 BC (Snodgrass 1998: 105, fig. 42). Or take the much more famous *Odyssey* scene from Book 9, where a world-wide folk-tale about the blinding of a murderous giant is adapted by Homer to the blinding of Polyphemos by Odysseus. In the version we have, the weapon for the blinding is a sharpened and heated-up tree-trunk, but faint traces still survive in the *Odyssey* text of a pre-Homeric version in which it was a metal spit. Why is it that most of the early pictures of the scene, around the middle of the seventh century BC (Snodgrass 1998: 91–93, figs. 36–37) show what is undoubtedly a spit? Instead of answering 'Because the artist did not yet know the Homeric version', we can now say 'Perhaps this *was* the Homeric version of the mid-seventh century BC', only later to be modified by the substitution of the tree-trunk in the version we have. Only in cases where there was a total congruency between the pictorial and the textual version could the old assumption of an early and canonical text still stand; but I myself have argued that there *are* virtually no such cases in the earliest phases of Greek art (Snodgrass 1998: 146–50 and *passim*).

I am speaking from bitter personal experience here, having published a book (Snodgrass 1998) which did not fully take on the 'evolutionary model' of the Homeric texts, then just becoming current. Perhaps I should have gone away and re-written the whole book; but the likelier outcome might have been not to publish the book at all, since one of its most basic assumptions was now under threat. True, a range of other conclusions could yet stand, among them the observation that something approaching 90% of the earliest legendary scenes are in any case debarred from being strictly illustrations of Homer, for the simple reason that they show stories that we know, not from the *Iliad* or *Odyssey*, but from the Trojan Epic Cycle or other epic poetry: here the findings of Jonathan Burgess's book on the antiquity of the Epic Cycle (Burgess 2001) are obviously important. But this whole activity is not one in which many people in this room are likely to be involved, and I leave it to return to the 'evolutionary model' itself.

Note how, by placing the important transition from the first to the second 'age' in the later eighth century BC, Nagy is implicitly rejecting one conclusion of the earlier movement, namely that a firm date for the consolidation of the texts must be set in the seventh century rather than the eighth. He is of course questioning the whole idea of such a consolidation, along with the appearance of written versions, as early as this; but merely by dating to the later eighth century BC a transition to a 'more formative' period and an advance to pan-Hellenic importance, he revives one basic element of the traditional account, namely that the later eighth century did indeed witness a significant moment of change in the formation of the Epics.

More generally, the importance of the 'evolutionary model' lies in the fact that its implications penetrate into so many corners, including archaeological corners of a kind very different from those of iconography. The model itself takes no account of such implications, and we must find our way for ourselves. But it will clearly be desirable, even necessary, for any future *Companion to Homer* or similar publication, either to renounce the 'evolutionary model' for Homeric transmission completely, or to include a lot more supporting material on the early and middle Archaic periods than did, say, the *Companion* of ten years ago (Morris and Powell 1997), or the more recent *Cambridge Companion* (Fowler 2004). Other than that, its effects on historical and archaeological enquiry look, at first glance, rather negative.

I have been discussing some of the implications for iconographical study. But much more important than that is the greatly increased uncertainty which will attend any attempts by archaeologists to find Homeric matches for the material culture: as indeed of Homerists to find archaeological matches. We – or rather the Homerists – may need to start by establishing some kinds of criteria of susceptibility to post-eighth-century BC change, perhaps along the lines of those advanced for the earlier stages of change by Sue Sherratt in her well-known *Antiquity* paper (Sherratt 1990). Thus, everyone agrees that the Homeric *similes* stand high in the list of passages likely to be inspired by recent experience. Until now, we have always taken 'recent' to mean 'eighth-century' and, as a matter of fact, I do not recall any simile which is too 'modern' to fit comfortably with that dating: they are mostly concerned with rather simple and unsophisticated activities, or with timeless natural phenomena. But on the other side, there is the passage which has been compared to a giant simile, the 131-line description of the Shield of Achilles in *Iliad* 18. Here there are at least two features, the developed nature of the society that is portrayed on the Shield and the artistic sophistication with which it is evidently executed, which have caused Homerists perplexity: in fact, it was among the features used, by the earlier of the two movements I have described, to argue for a date in the seventh rather than the eighth century BC for the completed *Iliad*. My own counter-arguments (Snodgrass 1998: 4), to the effect that, in judging the Shield as a work of art, the capacities of eighth-century artists were being under-rated, may now have been rendered obsolete: what if the whole description, composed in the world of the now developed *polis* around, say, 600 BC, had been inserted in place of a shorter, simpler account of the Shield? On the basis of the 'evolutionary model', it easily could have been.

Or to take another category that Sue Sherratt recognised as easily susceptible to change, the speeches. For example, perhaps the whole of Poseidon's rather absurd speech in *Iliad* 14, 364–77, where he orders the Greeks to carry out a mass-exchange of weapons, so that the best fighters end up with the biggest shields and the longest spears, was inserted by someone who had seen this tactic applied in equipping hoplite levies – though before rather than, as here, during the battle. And what about the alleged 'hoplite passages' themselves where, on top of hand-to-hand clashes of massed troops, we have the added feature that the troops are wearing some form of bronze panoply? Here, too, it would be easy to imagine a standard description of close-packed armies, as in *Iliad* 13, 339–40, being embellished, in the heyday of the hoplite phalanx, by adding two further lines (341–42) to give them 'bronze helmets, newly-burnished cuirasses and shining shields'. And so on. Note in passing that according to the 'evolutionary model', that very loose usage of the term 'Homeric' by the ancient Greeks who, down to the late fifth century BC, were in the habit of attaching to Homer any major epic poem other than those that were, equally loosely, attributed to Hesiod (for example, most or all of the Epic Cycle and the Homeric Hymns) may, though mistaken, have been not quite as foolish as we had always thought.

I have been looking at passages which have aroused the suspicion of being 'late' additions; but another, if unintended, effect of the 'evolutionary model' may be to thin out yet further the number of supposed Bronze Age recollections, when they are classified as such simply because of the impressive or luxurious material culture which they present. I am avoiding any reference to Troy and to the late Manfred Korfmann's interpretation of it, in case any Aegean prehistorian readers find my opinions too objectionable. But the *Catalogue of Ships* may once more arise here: instead of seeing it, with Giovannini (1969), as a consistent, probably seventh-century BC picture, we can remind ourselves that it contains one or two palpable, politically-inspired insertions which must be later still, extending into the sixth century at least; and can then search the rest of the 277 lines of the Achaean Catalogue (and indeed the 62 of the much shorter Trojan one) with a much closer scrutiny, on the look-out for other, equally late adjustments and additions, again made with ulterior motives, yet all the while carefully observing the rather rigid and formulaic language of the main *Catalogue*, however much older that was. It is worth noting here that the latest treatment of the subject (Visser 1997) stresses above all the element of potential *improvisation* present in the *Catalogue* entries, though Visser still stays with a terminal date of the eighth century BC for the operation of such ad hoc tinkering.

All this may seem a rather daunting exercise. But to shoot at moving targets, though very much harder than with stationary ones, is quite a different and also a more stimulating sport – and this particular target is an important one.

Bibliography

Burgess, J.

2001 *The Tradition of the Trojan War in Homer and the Epic Cycle.* Baltimore/London: Johns Hopkins University Press.

Burkert, W.

1976 Das hunderttorige Theben und die Datierung des *Ilias. Wiener Studien* 10: 5–21.

1987 The making of Homer in the sixth century B.C.: rhapsodes versus Stesichoros. In *Papers on the Amasis Painter and his World*: 43–63. Malibu: Getty Center for the History of Art/J. Paul Getty Museum.

Dickie, M. W.

1995 The geography of Homer's world. In Ø. Andersen and M. W. Dickie (eds.), *Homer's World: Fiction, Tradition, Reality*: 29–56. Bergen: Norwegian Institute at Athens.

Finley, M. I.

1956 *The World of Odysseus.* London: Chatto and Windus.

Fowler, R. L.

1987 *The Nature of Early Greek Lyric: Three Preliminary Studies.* Toronto: University of Toronto Press.

Fowler, R. (ed.)

2004 *The Cambridge Companion to Homer.* Cambridge: Cambridge University Press.

Giovannini, A.

1969 *Étude historique sur les origines du Catalogue des Vaisseaux.* Berne: Francke.

Janko, R.

1982 *Homer, Hesiod and the Hymns: Diachronic Development in Epic Diction.* Cambridge: Cambridge University Press.

Morris, I. and B. Powell (eds.)

1997 *A New Companion to Homer.* Leiden/New York/Köln: Brill.

Nagy, G.

1997 The Shield of Achilles: ends of the *Iliad* and beginnings of the polis. In S. Langdon (ed.), *New Light on a Dark Age: Exploring the Culture of Geometric Greece*: 194–207. Columbia, MO/London: University of Missouri Press.

Reece, S.

2005 Homer's *Iliad* and *Odyssey*: from oral performance to written text. In M. C. Amodio (ed.), *New Directions in Oral Theory*, 43–90. Tempe, AZ: Arizona Center for Medieval and Renaissance Studies.

Sherratt, E. S.

1990 'Reading the texts': archaeology and the Homeric question. *Antiquity* 64: 807–24.

Snodgrass, A. M.

1974 An historical Homeric society? *Journal of Hellenic Studies* 94: 114–25.

1998 *Homer and the Artists: Text and Picture in Early Greek Art.* Cambridge: Cambridge University Press.

Taplin, O.
1992 *Homeric Soundings: the Shaping of the Iliad*. Oxford: Clarendon Press.
van Wees, H.
1997 Homeric warfare. In Morris and Powell (eds.) 1997: 668–93.
Visser, E.
1997 *Homers Katalog der Schiffe*. Stuttgart/Leipzig: Teubner.
Wace, A. J. B. and F. H. Stubbings (eds.)
1962 *A Companion to Homer*. London: Macmillan.
West, M. L.
1988 The rise of the Greek epic. *Journal of Hellenic Studies* 108: 151–72.
West, M. L. (ed.)
1966 *Hesiod, the Theogony*. Oxford: Clarendon Press.
1978 *Hesiod, the Works and Days*. Oxford: Oxford University Press.

Chapter 2

The Will to Believe: Why Homer Cannot be 'True' in any Meaningful Sense

Oliver Dickinson[1]

The title of this paper might be thought to convey impatience, and I have to confess that there are times when, considering some of the arguments used in contributions to the ongoing debate about the historicity of the Trojan war, impatience is certainly what I feel. For the same or very similar arguments continue to be put forward, and the same assertions continue to be made, when they have been long ago countered or at least questioned. I acknowledge that my own contributions to the debate (Dickinson 1986; 1999; 2007; 2008; 2011) might be considered to be somewhat superficial, showing insufficiently wide reading. But I can lay claim to one advantage not available to many commentators on this topic, that my archaeological career and research interests have made me equally at home in the Late Bronze Age, including its final, Postpalatial phase, and the Early Iron Age, what used to be called the Dark Age, of Greece, and the writing of two general books (Dickinson 1994; 2006) has made me tolerably up to date on both periods.

It is this familiarity with both periods that emboldens me, for example, to contradict flatly the claim, strongly argued in Hope Simpson and Lazenby 1970 and embedded in recent discussions (e.g. Wood 1996: 113–21; Latacz 2004: 219–38), that the famous 'Catalogue of Ships', the list in *Iliad* 2 of the Greek contingents that took part in the Trojan War, is a good representation of the Mycenaean world at the time of the palaces, the period in which a historical Trojan War is normally set. I see this claim as the final fall-back position of those who want to argue that the Homeric tradition embodies real information about the Mycenaean world, even memories of historical events and individuals. It can be pointed out, and often has been, that in a whole range of features the Homeric picture is either wholly un-Mycenaean or heavily infected with post-Mycenaean features, and the defenders of what I would call the 'Mycenaean interpretation' will generally concede many of the points made. But the 'Catalogue of Ships' (henceforth simply 'the Catalogue') still seems to form the bedrock of their belief that more was handed down in the tradition than some references to obsolete types of object and social behaviour, and the memory that some sites that were insignificant by the eighth century BC were once very important.

I would assert that in every major region of the Mycenaean mainland, the picture presented by the 'Catalogue' is more or less *wrong*, if the criterion for inclusion of a site's name was its significance in the territory during the Mycenaean palace period – and what other criterion could there be? Sites are there which ought not to be there, and just as significantly, sites are not there which ought to be there. Take the Argolid, for example: apart from the totally implausible separation of the Argive plain and indeed the bulk of the Argolid from the control of Mycenae, as the realm of Diomedes, the list of sites in the Argolid lacks Midea (long identified with Palaiokastro near Dendra, the third great Mycenaean fortress of the Argolid with Mycenae and Tiryns) and Nauplia, where there is a major Mycenaean cemetery, while including places like Eiones and Mases whose supposed Mycenaean counterparts seem insignificant. In Messenia, as has been noted before, there is hardly any overlap between the sites listed in the Catalogue and the local administrative centres listed on the Linear B tablets from Pylos; moreover, Pylos is surely envisaged in *Odyssey* 3 as so close to the coast that Nestor and Telemachus can walk there in a short time, which would not be possible with Mycenaean Pylos. In Laconia, Menelaos's capital is consistently called Sparta (a case of smuggling Dorians in through the back door, in my belief), not Therapne, which was almost certainly the name of the biggest thirteenth century Mycenaean site in Laconia, that where the shrine of Helen and Menelaos was later sited, and is impeccably ancient-sounding, but is not to be found in the Catalogue at all (the situation is now further complicated by the recent discovery of a certainly palatial Laconian site, producing Linear B tablets, at Ayios Vasileios, which is south of Amyklai and so hardly likely to represent a Mycenaean Sparta). The major territorial divisions mostly bear their historical names, which may well be anachronistic; it certainly seems to be in Boeotia, where, also, we might expect Thebes and Orchomenos to be really prominent, if the 'Catalogue' reflects Mycenaean times – but they are not. Yet although interesting links can be made in the Catalogue with places that were important in Iron Age and Archaic times, this cannot be made a 'Geometric catalogue' either; it is a thorough mess (Dickinson 1999; 2011).

I chose to focus first on the 'Catalogue' because I believe it symbolises the nature of the epic tradition as a whole. In its account of social conditions and material culture, the epic tradition simply cannot be made to fit a single period; rather, it is a poetically created amalgam of features of different periods, that was probably developed over a considerable length of time before the Homeric poems were created in the form in which we have them. One of the most frustrating factors affecting discussion of this tradition is the failure of any pre-Homeric epic to survive, but at least it is incontrovertible that an epic tradition stretches back as far as Mycenaean times. Apart from the memory that Mycenae, Pylos and Troy were important places, which is only true of those times, there are some well-known references to objects and features that must derive from the Mycenaean period. Thus the helmet plated with boar's tusk, lent to Odysseus in *Iliad* 10, is an undoubtedly Mycenaean type. It can be traced back to the sixteenth century, but representations continue into the thirteenth (the date of various fresco representations, e.g. Demakopoulou 1988: 182 and fig. 149, and probably of a frequently illustrated ivory relief plaque from Mycenae Tomb 27, Demakopoulou 1988: 236 fig. 238), and actual plates can be found as late as twelfth and eleventh century contexts, but no later. But note that this helmet is represented in the *Iliad* as a quite exceptional item, whereas representations and finds are common enough in Mycenaean contexts that one might have expected a formula meaning 'wearing boar's tusk plated helmets' to be applied to the Achaeans as a whole, in the same way as the well-attested formula 'well-greaved'. Also note that the passage describing the helmet has been considered linguistically late (Janko 1992: 13), and the book in which it appears has often been thought an addition to the original poem.

If one could be sure that there was nothing like a body-covering shield in Early Iron Age times, then the references to shields of this type, especially the 'shield like a tower' that Ajax carries, could be considered to represent another Mycenaean memory, and often have been. I feel uneasy about dismissing the possibility of Iron Age body-covering shields altogether; on the Lechaion aryballos (dated c. 690–680 BC in Snodgrass 1964: 60, pl. 15b), the 'Boeotian' shields wielded by those attacking the 'hoplite', noted by Snodgrass as 'of bigger size than usual', look body-covering, and their wielders do not wear greaves, like the early Mycenaean wielders of body-covering shields. But if the references are to the Mycenaean shield form, this was a type that, like the boar's tusk-plated helmet, is most often represented in early Mycenaean contexts, but it is known from representations as late as the early fourteenth century (e.g. Catling 1980: 29, fig. 51, from Tiryns, of likely Late Helladic IIIA1 date though from a Late Helladic IIIB context). But Ajax's shield, like other shields mentioned in the poems, can *also* be described as round, and bossed. Yet metal shield bosses were only just becoming popular at the end of the Bronze Age, so combining one with a Mycenaean shield of any type is surely anachronistic. This would not bother the poet, however, who is not attempting to give a factually accurate picture of a period, as a historical novelist might; he has inherited the word *omphaloessa*, usefully fitting the last two feet of a hexameter, and he will apply it to a shield when it suits his purpose.

Wider analysis of the weapons, armour, and tactics described in scenes of warfare reveals comparable mixtures of features of different periods, although again there is a bias to the end of the Bronze Age and the Early Iron Age. Thus, the fondness for throwing spears, a major feature, hardly dates earlier than the Postpalatial period, when notably short spearheads that would be appropriate to such weapons begin to be found quite frequently, and there is at least one twelfth-century representation (Catling 1980: 29, fig. 50, from Tiryns) which probably shows two spears being carried, and not in a hunting context, as on a fresco from Tiryns (Hood 1978: 81, fig. 64). And of course there are the famous chariots, as seen on the Tiryns sherd just cited, undoubtedly used in Mycenaean times, probably for one of the two purposes for which chariots can be used in battle, to transport heavy-armed warriors quickly (as argued in Crouwel 1981). This is in fact how they are almost exclusively used in Homer, and this is surely most likely to be a Bronze Age memory. But the way they charge about the battlefield without apparently getting caught up in the mêlée is just one feature of the vivid but in fact totally unrealistic impression of warfare that is given in the epic, which switches from behaviour more appropriate to duels to battle between organised groups almost at will, and has to be imagined as continuing day after day into the tenth year, without any conclusion or even the death of any really leading heroes until then. The fact that the material of weapons, where cited, is almost exclusively bronze might well be considered something else handed down from Mycenaean times in the tradition; but archaeology shows that bronze-headed spears could continue in use until at least 1000 BC, and examples of bronze swords may have survived as long. Such survivals could have helped to preserve a memory that once, 'in the days of old', men fought only with bronze weapons: it need not have come down embedded in poetry actually deriving from the period of which this was true.

In general, the mixtures of old and new in the equipment and fighting methods attributed to Homeric warriors are handled with such apparent assurance as to suggest that they had become well established in epic tradition and vocabulary long before the Homeric poems were composed, and to me this does not suggest that they derive from poetry celebrating a historical war, composed at much the same time as the war itself.

Here we come back to 'the will to believe'. I see this as a conviction that the people of the epics and the world that they inhabit are so vividly portrayed that they *must* to some extent embody 'truth'. I have even, talking with a non-Aegean archaeologist, had the dear old 'no smoke without fire' argument produced, with regard to the historicity of the Trojan War. This of course invites a question immediately, by assuming that what we see in the Homeric tradition *can* be described as smoke; it may simply be mist. But can there be any justification for the view that, even if the material culture and account of the world are heavily infected by features of a later time, a real, historical war between a large coalition of forces drawn from many parts of Greece and an equally large coalition, centring on Troy, of western Anatolian and north Aegean peoples is being remembered? Two recent developments have strengthened this view, in the eyes of its upholders. The excavations of Manfred Korfmann have demonstrated that Troy was a considerably larger place than used to be thought, that there was a considerable settlement below the citadel that was once thought to be the whole of Troy, and that this was defended, though not by a stone wall (see recently Korfmann 2004). And it is now virtually certain that the territory in western Anatolia controlled by the state Ahhiyawa, which had considerable dealings with the Hittite empire in the fourteenth and thirteenth centuries BC, was precisely the region of south-western Anatolia which shows very strong evidence of 'Mycenaeanisation' (any other position is ruled out by the seemingly definitive distribution of western

Anatolian territories in Hawkins 1998), and where the most important centre, Miletus, on this interpretation the Millawanda of the Hittite texts, was effectively a Mycenaean town, to judge from its material culture. This indicates that Ahhiyawa must be part of the Mycenaean world.

Could the historical war have developed in the context of the well documented friction between the Hittite empire and Ahhiyawa (the texts are fully published in Beckman et al. 2011)? There are major problems, not least that Greek tradition retained no memory of the Hittites whatever. The historical fourteenth- and thirteenth-century BC Troy seems to have been a town in, if not the capital of, the state Wilusa, whose name is thought to be cognate with the alternative Homeric name for Troy, originally Wilios (Easton et al. 2002; Hawkins in Korfmann 2004). But this state was not independent, let alone the centre of a great alliance as it is presented as being in the *Iliad*; it was a dependent ally of the Hittites, apparently until the collapse of the Hittite empire. The Hittite collapse may well have post-dated that of the Mycenaean palace civilisation of Greece, after which an expedition like that mounted against Troy could hardly be conceivable. Furthermore, the Hittites and Ahhiyawa normally interacted in the region of Miletus and neighbouring territories; there is only one reference, in the notorious 'Piyamaradu letter', that indicates temporary hostility over Wilusa (Beckman et al. 2011: 115, 117, 121).

So it is hard to see that any genuine historical memories lie behind the tale of the Trojan War. But could the picture of life in Greece, at least, be appropriate to the Mycenaean age? Absolutely not, whether we are talking of the palace period of the fourteenth and thirteenth centuries BC, or the still Mycenaean Postpalatial period, which covers the twelfth and probably much of the eleventh centuries BC. A glaring difference is in the socially very important area of burial customs. The only custom ever referred to clearly in Homer involves cremation of the dead and burial in a receptacle under a mound, on which a marker may well be placed. This is not just a rite for heroes or an elite, but for everyone who merits a visible burial at all – so it is famously asked for by the ghost of Odysseus' luckless crewman Elpenor, and Achilles' horses can be described as standing in mourning for Patroclus, 'as a gravestone stands, set on the mound of a man or woman who has died' (*Iliad* 17.434–35; Hammond 1987: 286). There are a few Mycenaean cremations, most from the Postpalatial period, but inhumation is dominant. There are also cremations from Late Bronze Age Troy, but here as in Mycenaean Greece none resemble the Homeric form. In fact, cremation remains a minority rite even in the Early Iron Age, and where it involves a mound such mounds contain many burials (on Postpalatial and Early Iron Age cremation, see Dickinson 2006: 180–81, 186–89). The explanation for the dominance of this specific form in the poetic tradition is, I suspect, that this was the most flamboyant form of burial that could be imagined and the tradition applied it generally to everyone of the age of heroes. So the male burial in the structure at Lefkandi on Euboea, probably dating between 1000 and 950 BC, known as the 'Heroön', accompanied by a richly provided woman's burial and, in a separate pit, four horses, provides the closest analogy to the most elaborately described Homeric burial, that of Patroclus (Lemos 2002: 166–68; Dickinson 2006: 187–88, 190–91). But at present the Lefkandi 'Heroön' burial complex remains effectively unique in the Early Iron Age, though some of its features can be paralleled in other burials, and it can only be used to show that a burial of relative magnificence was possible then, a fact unknown to earlier generations of scholars, who assumed that any suggestion of magnificence must reflect Mycenaean times.

The dress of high-ranking women is another area where the picture is consistently post-Mycenaean. The poems make no clear references to typical Mycenaean finery, neither the elaborate dresses shown in the frescoes nor the rich range of beads represented in the archaeological material. Instead, dress basically consists of lengths of cloth, fastened with brooches; in *Odyssey* 18.292–94 a set of 12 of these, of gold, is given to Penelope by one of the suitors. These must be the fibulae, normally of bronze, that were only being introduced to Greece in the latest stages of the Mycenaean palace period and became typical later still (Dickinson 2006: 161–62, 164). Another of Penelope's presents, a pair of gold earrings (*Odyssey* 18.296–97), is striking, not only because the description fits Lefkandi examples of the late ninth century BC (Dickinson 2006: fig. 5.22:18), but also because I know of no examples of earrings from Greece dating between about 1400 and 900 BC. This is, then, surely a later Early Iron Age reference.

Other material references can be seen to suit the Early Iron Age and especially its later stages, such as the constant citations of bronze tripods and cauldrons as magnificent items, very appropriate for the ninth to seventh centuries BC. But there is one feature of material culture that could be argued to have a considerable Mycenaean element. For the picture of Odysseus' palace that can be built up from the *Odyssey* and the more vaguely described palaces of Menelaos, Nestor and Priam suggest buildings far more elaborate than any post-Mycenaean building known. Odysseus' is even two-storeyed, for Penelope's own room is clearly upstairs. But the trouble is, Odysseus' palace is not very like a Mycenaean palace either, as can be seen in Gray's reconstruction (in the figure attached to Gray 1955), which incorporates the un-Mycenaean fence or wall surrounding the building, but omits the *back* door out of the hall, beyond which lay the women's quarters (Eurykleia is described as bolting this in *Odyssey* 21 and unbolting it in 22; this cannot be the *front* door, for Odysseus and his supporters go in and out of this in Books 21–22 before Eurykleia's unlocking). Such a back door from the hall is totally unexampled in the 'megaron' complexes of Mycenaean palaces, but big Iron Age buildings can have a storeroom behind the great hall, and the hall can also have a side-door, a feature that plays a significant role in the battle with the suitors (two certain examples which have back room and side-door are the Lefkandi 'Heroön' and Unit IV-1 at Nichoria, Dickinson 2006: 108–09, figs. 4.8 and 4.9).

Further, no reference to a Homeric palace hints at a prominent feature of Mycenaean palaces' main rooms, their frescoes. In fact, no information about the decoration of the interior is given at all, apart from the weapons hanging on the walls in Odysseus' hall, referred to at the beginning of *Odyssey* 19. When Telemachos marvels at the wealth of Menelaos' palace, saying to his companion, 'The whole place gleams with bronze and gold, amber and silver and ivory' (*Odyssey* 4.72–73, Rieu 1991: 47), this is, I submit, like the frequent references to vessels of precious metal used to drink from and wash with, the magnificence of fairy tale, how heroes *ought* to live. But it has recently been argued that the elaborately described entrance to the palace of Alkinoös on Phaeacia may derive from travellers' tales about ninth-seventh-century BC Assyrian palaces (Cook 2004), and perhaps the general impression of wealth derives from the same source.

Another area of social custom, even more important than burial customs, is religion. As described in the poems, the practice of sacrifice seems closest to that of the later Greeks. A Homeric Greek, like a Classical one, most often slaughtered an animal at a temporary or permanent altar in the open air, and burned a portion on the altar, as described in most detail in *Odyssey* 3.430–63. There is increasing evidence that animal sacrifices were made in some ritual contexts in Mycenaean times, but whether this represented a common public practice with an established form like the Homeric and historical one remains very much open to question (Whittaker 2006–7), and the evidence for other forms of offering seems much more copious. As for the gods themselves, barely half of the Homeric pantheon can be identified in the Linear B texts: absentees who play a major role in Homer include Apollo (the single reference to *pa-ja-wo-ne* on Knossos tablet V 52 is hardly enough, when Paieon is a separate god in *Iliad* 5.401, 899–900), Athena (the identification of *a-ta-na-po-ti-ni-ja* on V 52 with Athena is much disputed), and Aphrodite. Those who are certainly found in Mycenaean sources are mingled with other figures, often of apparently equal or greater importance (e.g. Potnia), who are unknown or very obscure later. To me, Mycenaean religion looks very different from later Greek religion.

Despite the material references that clearly or plausibly belong to earlier periods and have been passed down through the poetic tradition, it has been argued by prominent scholars that the picture of society given does reflect a single period, that of the poet's own day. But is this society actually real? Can we draw conclusions about the society of Homer's day from the picture the poems present? Certainly, the behaviour of the characters often seems to be consistent with a certain set of values, but there are difficulties. For example, persons who act like monarchs, i.e. kings, are all over the place in the poems, but it is not clear to me that any real impression of how kings exercise their power was preserved in the tradition. There is an obvious tension between the notion of assemblies that take decisions and kings who may take advice, but give orders. More significant, to me, is the absence of royal officers apart from heralds; so when the king is absent, as in Ithaca, there seem to be no provisions for carrying on the machinery of administration (in Agamemnon's absence he leaves simply a bard to keep watch on his wife's behaviour, who is easily disposed of: *Odyssey* 3.267–68). This is, frankly, unbelievable in any real monarchy.

It is not surprising that kingship was not really understood, for despite the various stories suggesting the existence of kings in Early Iron Age times, not to mention the reality of the two royal lines in Sparta, archaeology has been remarkably unhelpful in offering us any evidence that might seem to represent such kings, with the sole exception of the male burial in the Lefkandi Heroön. If there was ever a monarchy at Lefkandi, then surely he was a monarch. But both before and especially after the date of this burial, we are presented with a scatter of rich burials in different cemeteries, and even in the Toumba cemetery associated with the Heroön there are far too many rich burials to represent simply a line of kings. The situation is similar at any site where we find a lot of burial evidence: material that could represent a spectrum of more or less aristocratic families, yes – but no monarchs.

So kings appear in Homer because they are in the tradition, and the audience knew that they should be there, as it knew that once upon a time weapons were made solely of bronze, that chariots were used in warfare, and so on. But the audience of an epic does not expect a fully realistic and consistent portrayal of a society. If I may quote from the first paper that I wrote on this topic:

> No epic is a realistic presentation of a society or age; it is a fantasy, but a fantasy in which, because neither composer nor audience can imagine or sympathize with a wholly alien world, reality keeps breaking through. (Dickinson 1986: 24).

Epic poetry focuses on heroic individuals and their deeds, typically placing them in a setting that has a strong flavour of the supernatural, so that the fabulous element should be considered an integral part of the story, not simply something 'bolted on' for effect. Its heroes move in a world of dreamlike splendour, handling items of precious materials of all kinds casually; but the tradition will not concern itself with such mundane matters as the trade by which such luxuries, and the more practically necessary metals, iron and bronze, must normally have been acquired (it is naïve in the extreme to suppose that this could be done purely by raiding).

Also, epics share basic story-telling devices with folktale, and this will affect all references to social arrangements. Thus, it is surely a requirement of the plot, not a reflection of any real type of society, that Telemachos should be presented in the *Odyssey* as being without effective support. His isolated position would be virtually impossible in a kin-based society like that of Greece throughout the historical period. He does not even have tenants and dependents at his command, as a major land owner surely would have done. But it is *artistically* necessary that Telemachos should be presented in this way, and the poet's vivid narrative blinds us to the implausibilities. I suspect the problem here is that the poet is trying to create an epic about Odysseus that made use of a very bare folktale, that might have begun something like this: 'Once there was a king who was away at the wars so long that everyone thought he was dead, and all the young noblemen wanted to marry his wife, who was very beautiful. But she wanted to wait for her husband. She had only one son, but he was not of full age and not able to protect her ...' Such a focus on a few central individuals, ignoring the social context in which they would have acted, is typical of folktale, covering up inconvenient questions like, what about the nobleman of Same who married Odysseus' sister (*Odyssey* 15.362–67)? Why did not he or his family try to help? But he too might have been an invention of the poet, useful at the point where the reference is made, but not intended to be a major figure in the story.

Ian Morris once commented 'the epic ... was a poetic creation, what *some* eighth-century Greeks thought the heroic world *ought* to have been like' (Morris 1997: 558, emphasis in original), and to me this makes good sense. It is certainly possible to identify some patterns of behaviour that are consistently depicted in the poems, but it seems risky in the extreme to assume that they give a reliable depiction of a historical society or period, while any historical element in the account of events is likely to have been so distorted as to be unrecognisable. So, I submit, they are neither historically nor socially 'true'.

Acknowledgements

I would like to thank Sue Sherratt and John Bennet for inviting me to speak at the Round Table, and John especially for his help with preparing PowerPoint illustrations for me to use.

Note

1. Author's note: In response to the editors' invitation to update the paper I have incorporated references to some significant recent discoveries and have made various changes to the language, but I have left the traces of the original somewhat informal delivery untouched, and have not added very many references. More are offered in my papers listed here.

Bibliography

Beckman, G. M., T. R. Bryce and E. H. Cline (eds.)
2011 *The Ahhiyawa Texts* (Writings from the Ancient World 28). Atlanta: Society of Biblical Literature.
Catling, H. W.
1980 Archaeology in Greece, 1979–80. *Archaeological Reports* 26: 1–53.
Cook, E.
2004 Near Eastern sources for the palace of Alkinoos. *American Journal of Archaeology* 108: 43–77.
Crouwel, J.
1981 *Chariots and Other Means of Land Transport in Bronze Age Greece.* Amsterdam: Allard Pierson.
Demakopoulou, K. (ed.)
1988 *The Mycenaean world. Five Centuries of Early Greek Culture, 1600–1100 B.C.* Athens: Greek Ministry of Culture.
Dickinson, O.
1986 Homer, the poet of the Dark Age. *Greece and Rome* 33: 20–37.
1994 *The Aegean Bronze Age.* Cambridge: Cambridge University Press.
1999 The Catalogue of Ships and all that. In P. P. Betancourt, V. Karageorghis, R. Laffineur and W.-D. Niemeier (eds.), *MELETEMATA. Studies in Aegean Archaeology presented to Malcolm H. Wiener as he Enters his 65th Year* (Aegaeum 20): 207–10. Liège: Université de Liège, Histoire de l'art et archéologie de la Grèce antique.

2006 *The Aegean from Bronze Age to Iron Age. Continuity and Change between the Twelfth and Eighth Centuries BC*. London: Routledge.
2007 Aspects of Homeric geography. In S. Morris and R. Laffineur (eds.), *EPOS. Reconsidering Greek epic and Aegean Bronze Age Archaeology* (Aegaeum 28): 233–38. Liège: Université de Liège.
2008 Was there really a Trojan War? In C. Gallou, M. Georgiadis and G. Muskett (eds.), *DIOSKOUROI. Studies Presented to Bill Cavanagh and Chris Mee for their Contribution to Aegean Archaeology*: 189–97. Oxford: Archaeopress.
2011 Catalogue of Ships. In M. Finkelberg (ed.), *The Homer Encyclopaedia:* 150–55. Chichester: Wiley-Blackwell.

Easton, D. F., J. D. Hawkins, A. G. Sherratt and E. S. Sherratt
2002 Troy in recent perspective. *Anatolian Studies* 52: 75–109.

Finley, M.
1977 *The World of Odysseus* (second edition). London: Chatto & Windus.

Gray, D. H. F.
1955 Houses in the Odyssey. *The Classical Quarterly* New Series 5: 1–12.

Gurney, O. R.
1990 *The Hittites* (fourth edition). Harmondsworth: Penguin.

Hammond, M. (translation)
1987 *Homer: The Iliad*. Harmondsworth: Penguin.

Hawkins, J. D.
1998 Tarkasnawa king of Mira, 'Tarkondemos', Boğazköy sealings and Karabel. *Anatolian Studies* 48: 1–31.

Hood, S.
1978 *The Arts in Prehistoric Greece*. Harmondsworth: Penguin.

Hope Simpson, R.
2003 The Dodecanese and the Ahhiyawa question. *Annual of the British School at Athens* 98: 205–37.

Hope Simpson, R. and J. F. Lazenby
1970 *The Catalogue of Ships in Homer's Iliad*. Oxford: Clarendon Press.

Janko, R.
1992 *The Iliad: a Commentary IV. Books 13–16*. Cambridge: Cambridge University Press.

Korfmann, M.
2004 Was there a Trojan War? *Archaeology* 57: 36–41.

Latacz, J.
2004 *Troy and Homer: towards a Solution of an Old Mystery*. Oxford: Oxford University Press.

Lemos, I. S.
2002 *The Protogeometric Aegean. The Archaeology of the late Eleventh and Tenth centuries BC*. Oxford: Oxford University Press.

Morris, I.
1997 Homer and the Iron Age. In I. Morris and B. Powell (eds.), *A New Companion to Homer:* 534–39. Leiden: Brill.

Rieu, E. V. (translation)
1991 *Homer: The Odyssey* (revised by C. H. Rieu). Harmondsworth: Penguin.

Snodgrass, A. M.
1964 *Early Greek Armour and Weapons*. Edinburgh: Edinburgh University Press.

Whittaker, H.
2006–7 Burnt animal sacrifice in Mycenaean cult. A review of the evidence. *Opuscula Atheniensia* 31–32: 183–90.

Wood, M.
1996 *In Search of the Trojan War* (third edition). Harmondsworth: Penguin.

Chapter 3

Dream and Reality in the Work of Heinrich Schliemann and Manfred Korfmann

Johannes Haubold

Our understanding of the relationship between archaeology and Homer is fundamentally shaped by the work of the late Manfred Korfmann. Korfmann electrified the general public and polarised scholarly opinion in equal measure, especially in his native Germany. He started digging at Hisarlık in 1988, and exhibited his findings before a wider public in 2001/02.[1] There have been heated debates about his achievements ever since. Was he right to identify ancient Troy with the Hittite principality of Wilusa?[2] Is the Bronze Age settlement at Hisarlık best described as a 'centre of commerce', or do such claims amount to 'misleading the public', as one prominent critic of Korfmann has put it?[3] Was there ever a large and densely populated lower city around the citadel at Hisarlık?[4] If so, what difference would that make to readers of Homer? Yet it would be a mistake to assume that the challenge Korfmann's work represents can be met with the help of archaeological scholarship alone; hence the present contribution to this volume.

The nature of Korfmann's work and the response it has had were deeply informed by the cultural and political climate of post-unification Germany. When the Berlin Wall fell in 1989, after decades of occupation and intellectual stagnation on both sides of the Iron Curtain, the newly unified German state experienced a powerful demand for fresh mythologies and institutional reform. The meaning and purpose of classical learning, the nature of academic scholarship, and the university as an institution all came under intense scrutiny. Who should produce scholarship and for whom? Was the state monopoly on scholarship a good thing? Did classical learning, which had for decades been an ideological battleground between the two German states, need to be updated and modified? Even before the partition of 1945/49, classical *Bildung* (at once 'character formation', 'education' and 'learning') had played a crucial role in debates about what it meant to be German; and Homer had been at the heart of classical *Bildung* ever since the days of Goethe and F. A. Wolf. In the context of the first

German unification of 1871, Schliemann's excavations at Troy played an important, if complex, part in forging a collective German identity.[5] After the second unification of 1990 Korfmann's excavations at Troy very quickly took on an iconic status of their own, suggesting a new role for classical learning in the context of a more open and more culturally diverse German society (Haubold 2002: 567–71). My intention here is not to unpick the tangle between culture, politics and academic scholarship that informed Korfmann's work and its reception among the German public and German academics. Rather, I wish to draw attention to a conceptual issue that arises from the controversies surrounding Manfred Korfmann's work, an issue that goes to the very heart of Homeric archaeology wherever it is currently practised. We may put it in the form of a question: what type of 'reality' do archaeologists claim to uncover when they work in and around Homer's Troy?

Contested areas of scholarship have a way of generating their own characteristic blind spots: amidst the constant clashes of opinion, the questions of what exactly is at issue, and how progress can be made, are all too easily lost. In the case of Homeric archaeology, the problem is further aggravated by the fact that poetry meets history at Hisarlık in a way that tends to encourage unhealthy polarisations (Kolb 2004: 577). Already Homer claimed to tell things as they really were, and already Stesichorus knew that he was lying.[6] The 'truth about Troy' has been on the agenda ever since: Homeric archaeology with its particular claim to setting the record straight is in many ways a variation on an old theme. However, there are more specific issues to be understood about Homeric archaeology as a discipline and its peculiar relationship with the Homeric text. Occasional comparisons between Korfmann and Schliemann, the most recent excavator at Hisarlık and the first, suggest that the history of the discipline has in some ways come full circle.[7] Korfmann and his collaborators were of course careful to distance themselves from Schliemann: unlike him they did not hope to discover gold, and they always emphasised their credentials as professional academics (e.g. Jansen 2001). Moreover, Korfmann's excavation reports tend to be praised for their accuracy even by some of his most trenchant critics: to call him a latter-day Schliemann is at one level little more than empty polemic. Yet, at another level, there are clear connections between Schliemann and Korfmann. One such connection, I argue, may be found precisely in the way in which they both framed and defined Homeric archaeology as a discipline that is essentially concerned with unearthing 'reality'.

Quite apart from recent debates about the persuasiveness of Manfred Korfmann's work, 'reality' has become a key issue in current archaeology. Museums and their audiences are getting ever more interested in the possibilities of virtual reality, and there has been a steady stream of work on what it might mean to reconstruct the past with the help of computer simulation (e.g. Reilly 1990; Barceló, Forte and Sanders 2000). The issue itself is of course much older than computer software. In the field of Homeric archaeology, 'myth' and 'reality' have been contested ever since Schliemann claimed to have excavated Troy. This chapter revisits some of the pertinent issues in Schliemann's own work before turning to that of Manfred Korfmann and the new Troy debate. Both Heinrich Schliemann and Manfred Korfmann were prolific writers as well as excavators, and for the purposes of the present argument I shall concentrate on their publications rather than their excavations (for Schliemann's publications, see Cobet 1997, with further bibliography; for Korfmann's, see the literature cited in Latacz et al. 2001; Korfmann 2002; 2004; 2006). In fact, I shall concentrate on Schliemann's and Korfmann's popular works rather than letters, diaries, notes or archaeological reports (for Schliemann's excavation diaries, see Easton 2002; Korfmann's excavation reports are available in Cohen and Korfmann 1991–2005). The reason for this is that I see the issue of 'reality' primarily as a matter of how the archaeologist frames his or her work for an interested public. What I am trying to understand, then, is not what Schliemann and Korfmann really believed, but what they said they believed to an audience that included experts and non-experts alike. In order to keep the discussion within manageable proportions, I focus on two books in particular, which can with some right be seen to contain the sum of their authors' work: Schliemann's *Ilios* (1880; 1881) and Korfmann's *Troia - Traum und Wirklichkeit* (Latacz et al. 2001), the catalogue for the 2001–2 exhibition with the same title, for which Korfmann had overall responsibility. He also contributed the introduction and several chapters to the catalogue, although he was only one among several editors.

Heinrich Schliemann: Bourgeois Dream and Archaeological Reality

Let us then start with Heinrich Schliemann and his claim to have recovered the reality behind the Homeric poems. As David Traill has shown in meticulous detail, Schliemann routinely lied about his life (Traill 1993; 1995). Of particular interest here is the fact that he did *not* have a childhood dream about excavating Troy; at least not in the way he describes it in the opening pages of his book *Ilios* (Schliemann 1881: 1–67). Schliemann there explains how already as a child he dreamed of digging at Troy, and how despite many obstacles he finally fulfilled his dream. The truth of the matter appears to have been rather more prosaic. As Justus Cobet points out, Schliemann does not mention any plans of excavating Troy until well into his St Petersburg years. It is only in his much later autobiography that such plans are backdated to the childhood in Ankershagen:

> Schliemann's childhood dream of Troy is a biographical construct of the 45-year-old man who had come to prominence with his discovery of the 'Great Tower of Ilium' and the 'Treasure of Priam.' (Cobet 1997: 22)

Why did Schliemann lie about his life, especially when this made him appear naïve in the eyes of professional scholars? *Pace* Wilamowitz, the answer is not that Schliemann was in fact naïve.[8] Rather, he constructed a highly public narrative framework within which the 'reality' of his archaeological work could appear in a specific light and take on a specific meaning. As has often been pointed out, Schliemann's autobiography is in effect a carefully constructed myth of the bourgeois hero.[9] Jørgen Mejer has shown the extent to which Schliemann resembles Peer Gynt, the everyman of Ibsen's play (written in 1867, three years before Schliemann started digging at Troy) (Mejer 1990; cf. Cobet 1997: 45). In a similar vein, Harold Hammer-Schenk traces Schliemann's self-stylisation as bourgeois hero in the tradition of Goethe's Werther (Hammer-Schenk 1992; cf. Schindler 1989, who discusses the literary background to Schliemann's biographical writings). It is no coincidence that the young Schliemann, like the young Werther, reads Homer: in the class and culture wars of the nineteenth century, Homeric poetry had long been powerful ammunition. Who was Homer? To whom did he belong? These were questions that mattered because they hinted at the much larger issue of who controlled the defining myths of the time (for the politics of appropriating Homer see Porter 2002: 65–68, who points out that Schliemann's excavations represent only one act of appropriation among many).

At the heart of Schliemann's self-dramatisation stands a strategic split between dream and reality. Dreams are elusive. We cannot control them, and as long as they remain mere dreams, they tend to instil a sense of loss.[10] Loss and exclusion are in fact among the most important themes in Schliemann's account of his life in *Ilios*. He is denied a good upbringing, a classical education, and must renounce the love of his early years. This is how Schliemann describes the news that his childhood sweetheart Minna Meincke has married someone else:

> Why then should fate be so cruel as to tear her from me when, after having for sixteen long years striven to reach her, I seemed at last to have succeeded in attaining her? It had indeed happened to Minna and me as it often happens to us in our sleep, when we dream that we are pursuing somebody and can never catch him, because as often as we reach him he escapes us again. (Schliemann 1881: 14)

The image that Schliemann employs to describe his dream-like pursuit of Minna is in fact Homeric (*Iliad* 22.199–201). However, the underlying sentiment is firmly in the tradition of the nineteenth-century German *Bildungsroman*, where the issue of heterosexual longing and its successful or unsuccessful resolution in marriage comes to represent most poignantly the main character's social aspirations (Minden 1997: 1–2, who discusses the crisis brought on by early disappointment in Goethe's influential novel *Wilhelm Meisters Lehrjahre* of 1795–6). In the opening pages of *Ilios*, Schliemann strategically intertwines the issue of a happy ending in marriage with his interest in Troy:

> It was agreed between us [i.e. Minna Meincke and Heinrich Schliemann] that as soon as we were grown up we would marry, and then at once set to work to explore all the mysteries of Ankershagen; excavating the golden cradle, the silver basin, the vast treasures hidden by Henning, then Henning's sepulchre and lastly Troy. (Schliemann 1881: 5)

To marry Minna is to excavate Troy. When Schliemann fails to secure the hand of his beloved, the pursuit of Troy takes on heightened significance as a way of recovering his lost bourgeois paradise.

The author himself answers the question as to why fate should have been so cruel as to rob him of Minna: she was socially better placed, and his lowly circumstances meant that he had to wait before proposing to her. By the time he felt himself to be acceptable to her, she had already married. Schliemann's sense of disappointment and social exclusion also plays itself out in his struggle to acquire a classical education. He describes the sad career of a man trapped by the limitations of his existence:

> He was the son of a protestant clergyman in Roebel (Mecklenburg), and had almost completed his studies at the grammar school of Neu Ruppin, when he was expelled on account of his bad conduct. Not knowing what to do with him, his father apprenticed him to the farmer Langermann in the village of Dambeck; and, as even there his conduct was not exemplary, he again apprenticed him for two years to the miller Dettmann at Güstrow. Dissatisfied with his lot, the young man gave himself up to drink, which, however, had not made him forget his Homer; for on the evening that he entered the shop he recited to us about a hundred lines of the poet, observing the rhythmic cadence of the verses. Although I did not understand a syllable, the melodious sound of the words made a deep impression upon me, and I wept bitter tears over my unhappy fate. Three times over did I get him to repeat to me those divine verses, rewarding his trouble with three glasses of whiskey, which I bought with the few pence that made up my whole fortune. From that moment I never ceased to pray God that by His grace I might yet have the happiness of learning Greek. (Schliemann 1881: 7)

It does not take much to see that this man is an alter ego of Schliemann himself: both are children of protestant preachers, and both struggle in life after failing to complete their classical education. Notice the symbolic charge Homer is made to bear: the 'divine poet' hints at a promised land of bourgeois empowerment that is close enough to tantalise but ultimately remains unattainable to the man in the story. The poor miller tragically lacks manners and responds to social exclusion by descending into alcoholism. Schliemann, by contrast, will break the spell, and with the help of God – in a true act of grace – open up classical *Bildung* to himself and his social peers.

The decisive moment of grace in Schliemann's carefully constructed account of his tribulations comes when a fire at the port city of Memel threatens to destroy all his possessions. This is how he describes the event:

> I was for some minutes speechless; it seemed to me like a dream and incredible that I alone should have escaped unhurt from the universal ruin. But so it was. (Schliemann 1881: 14)

The dream of a better life had for the first time become reality; and it had done so in a way that singled out Schliemann as a child of destiny. Shortly after, Schliemann reports his first visit to the classical lands. We may once again note the language of dream and reality:

> At last I was able to realize the dream of my life, and to visit at my leisure the scene of those events which had always had such intense interest for me, and the country of the heroes whose adventures had delighted and comforted my childhood. (Schliemann 1881: 18)

In due course, the realisation of his dream takes Schliemann to Hisarlık and ultimately results in the reality that he claims to have unearthed there:

> May this research with the pickaxe and the spade prove more and more that the events described in the divine Homeric poems are not mythic tales, but that they are based on real facts; and, in proving this, may it augment the universal love for the noble study of the beautiful Greek classics, and particularly of Homer, that brilliant sun of all literature! (Schliemann 1881: 672)

Archaeological 'reality', at the end of Schliemann's *Ilios*, is cast as the realisation of bourgeois longing for access and empowerment. Schliemann's research with pickaxe and spade is expressly meant to open out the classics to *everybody*. This process is in many ways a paradoxical affair. On the one hand, Schliemann takes aim at the self-enlightened arrogance of those who dismiss the Homeric texts as 'mere myth', surely a barbed reference to the methodological advances of professional Homerists. On the other hand, Schliemann takes up precisely the rhetoric of fact with which an increasingly professional cast of scholars was threatening to fence off the classical world from bourgeois sensitivities. In an egregious act of equivocation, 'reality' becomes both the weapon and the goal in his quest.

By the time Schliemann started excavating at Hisarlık, classics as a discipline had been very largely professionalised, especially in Schliemann's native Germany, where this process coincided with increasing levels of state funding and state control (some aspects of this process are discussed in Most 2002). Outsiders and newcomers were not suffered lightly, witness Wilamowitz' disdainful caricature of Schliemann as someone who feeds archaeological pseudo-reality to the masses like fodder to the pigs (see note 8: Wilamowitz 1906: 59). Schliemann challenged the dominant model of knowledge production and dissemination: he held no university position; his allegiance to the German state was precarious; and most important of all, he emphasised that ownership of the classical past belonged to the economically vibrant bourgeoisie rather than to state-sponsored professionals.

Manfred Korfmann: Dream and Reality after the Cold War

From Schliemann's heroics in the late nineteenth century we take a giant leap to the excavations by Manfred Korfmann. Korfmann appears to have had an instinctive sympathy for the young Schliemann, though their life and work were in many ways very different: 'All these developments shaped the personality of Heinrich Schliemann, though he could not yet fully participate in them as part of his school education.' (Korfmann 2001a: 16, my translation; for Korfmann's life and work, see Jansen 2006). After initial excavations in Beşik Bay, Korfmann started digging at Hisarlık in 1988, where he continued work until his death in 2005. As I have pointed out already, Korfmann was a tenured professional academic whose scholarly credentials are not usually called into doubt (with some exceptions, most notably Frank Kolb who has called Korfmann's approach 'ahistorical': Kolb in Schweizer

2002: 14, 70). And yet, his work raises some issues that can be usefully compared to those already discussed.

Korfmann himself repeatedly claimed that he had excavated the 'real' Troy as opposed to the dream of generations of Philhellenes. As he explains in the introduction to the exhibition catalogue of *Troia - Traum und Wirklichkeit*, archaeology is the science that produces historical reality:

> Without doubt there existed from the beginning fantastic ideas (sc. about Troy) which had no basis in reality:
>
> 1. in the world of Homer, the late eighth century BC, where for example gods intervened directly in the fighting around Troy,
> 2. in Greco-Roman antiquity and
> 3. in the Middle Ages and the Early Modern Period, when the myth of Troy was increasingly embellished. And it is fascinating to look under the heading of 'dream' at the founding period of the nineteenth century, that is, at Heinrich Schliemann and the first internationally significant results of archaeological excavations.
>
> Then we turn to:
>
> 4. the reality of the results of modern, systematic excavation
> 5. without, however, neglecting the ideas, dreams and scholarly views about Troy in modern Western culture. (Korfmann 2001a: 4, my translation)[11]

Korfmann here presents modern archaeology as the sole guarantee of historical reality (*Wirklichkeit*) amidst a host of other disciplines. Schliemann's work is subsumed under the category of dream but serves as a bridge to modern, methodical excavation. Already in this brief résumé, Korfmann hints that for him too 'reality' is a charged term. Like Schliemann before him, Korfmann polarises dream (or myth) and reality in such a way as to make the archaeologist appear properly in charge of the latter. This time, the polarisation is not achieved autobiographically but historically. That is to say, it is not Korfmann himself who was dreaming and then discovered reality. Now it is the whole world who has made, historically, that transition:

> These are the beginnings of a scholarly approach ... The advent of print made publishing scholarly findings relatively cheap. As a result of this explosion of knowledge, an ultimately irrational fascination [sc. with Troy] lost ground to the question of what was credible and what was not. (Korfmann 2001a: 15, my translation)[12]

The underlying rhetoric of Korfmann's introduction as a whole is this: after so many centuries of irrational mythmaking, Korfmann and his team recover what Troy really was: a city on the intersection of Europe and Asia, a much fought-over centre of commerce. As with Schliemann, reality and myth serve as a mutually defining pair of opposites that paradoxically function best when taken together:

> In chapter four you find a detailed description of the reality of Troy which fascinates us archaeologists no less than the myth. (Korfmann 2001a: 9)[13]

Note how reality becomes fascinating in association with myth; and how myth in turn gains definition by being juxtaposed with reality. Importantly, this system of contrasting but interlocking notions is embedded in a specific public context: the end of the Cold War, German reunification, and the enlargement of the EU. To take the latter first, the exhibition catalogue of 'Troia – Traum und Wirklichkeit' contains a string of high-profile addresses which leave no doubt about the fact that Korfmann's excavations were perceived to further the cause of Turkey as a European nation (Latacz et al. 2001: *Grußwort* 1–8). More importantly for a German audience, Korfmann's Troy (a.k.a. Wilusa) soon became a founding myth of post-unification German society. Wilusa as Korfmann described it was old, but new; a place of classical *Bildung* yet economically successful, European yet Anatolian – in short, it was an Archimedean point from which one could shake the world. The excavations themselves were presented as hands-on, open-minded and up-to-date. They stood for a new type of *Bildung* that no longer dreamed of a marble Greece but re-discovered the realities of life in the post-modern world (Haubold 2002: 567–71).

Korfmann's 'reality' helped his German audiences rethink their identity as a newly constituted nation (for Korfmann's work in the context of the German citizenship debate, see Haubold 2002: 569–70; in 2003, Korfmann himself acquired Turkish as well as German citizenship and displayed this dual identity in his chosen second name Osman). At a more practical level, Korfmann could be seen as blazing a trail in ongoing debates about academic reform. After decades of stagnation and underfunding during the post-war years, successive German governments had been attempting to reform the universities by making them more independent of state patronage and demanding that they subscribe to a broadly Anglo-American model of competitive excellence. Korfmann was of course himself employed by Tübingen University, but he also relied on unusually large private donations. In this context it is significant that he was able to attract an audience of some 850,000 people with his Troy exhibition, as well as sparking endless rows among German academics and the German media about whether or not his public office as an academic was compatible with his popular appeal and large reserves of private funding (for the large private funds supporting Korfmann's excavations, see Haubold 2002: 568, n. 25). In practice, disagreement centred on the question of whether Korfmann's exhibition represented the 'reality' at Troy or whether he had merely added more by way of dream and fantasy. Thus, Korfmann's main critic, Frank Kolb, notoriously called the model of Troy VI which was presented at the Troy exhibition 'a dream, not a reconstruction' – a dream designed, moreover, to please private investors in the excavations (Kolb in Schweizer 2002: 13 – 'Traum nicht Rekonstruktion'). Troy was an ancient centre of commerce, and the modern market economy funded this discovery.

My purpose here is not to rehearse the disagreement, much less to settle it one way or the other. What interests me is the way in which archaeological 'reality' becomes a battleground between competing disciplines and competing ways of conceptualising – and funding – scholarly work at a critical moment in German history (see Kienlin and Schweitzer 2001/2002, who discuss the role of competing academic disciplines in the disagreement). For the ancient historian Kolb, the 'reality' at Troy is an abstract notion of what is or is not the case. This notion of reality presents itself as utterly insensitive to the demands of interested members of the public (and potential donors) (Kolb in Schweizer 2002: 39). Indeed, what is real, for Kolb, can *ipso facto* not be interesting or relevant to us today, for partial interests produce only partial truths. The institutional context to this view is a state-sponsored academia whose task it has been, since the days of Schliemann and Wilamowitz, to produce timeless, objective and non-partisan *Wissen* ('knowledge') (Haubold 2002: 571–74). By contrast, Manfred Korfmann often emphasised the social and cultural relevance of the reality which archaeology uncovers. Homer himself becomes a proto-archaeologist who saw the ruins of Bronze Age Troy, and on that basis formed an image of the city and its environs (Korfmann 2001b: 69–71, 75–76; 2001c: 347; 2004: 16–17). Thus, for Korfmann, archaeological reality mattered primarily in so far as it spoke to the imagination of an interested observer. In their recent book entitled *Troy as it Really Looked* (*Troia wie es wirklich aussah*), Birgit Brandau, Hartmut Schickert and Korfmann's colleague in Hisarlık, Peter Jablonka, emphasise even more strongly the idea that the reality of Troy is *always* relative to the interests of an audience (Brandau, Schickert and Jablonka 2004). It is worth noting the equivocating title: 'Troy as it really looked'; reality is here construed as a matter of appearance.

As we have seen, the expectations of German audiences were indeed crucial to Korfmann's enterprise. Indeed, he appears to have been aware of the wider political and historical circumstances of his excavations to a remarkable degree. In a telling section of the catalogue for his Troy exhibition he writes about the work of Heinrich Schliemann:

> Other powers had acquired colonies all over the world. The museums of Brussels, Madrid, Lisbon, Paris and London were filled with loot, if I may use this much-debated term here. The world had been conquered and the most valued possessions of the colonised – or suppressed – populations had been carried off to the (European) capitals. The Germans had largely missed the boat, and Michel with his night cap was ridiculed (i.e. as an embodiment of German slovenliness). Only in the field which fascinated people because of its connection with Greek myth – I am referring to the Trojan finds and the Pergamon altar – had Germany shown herself worthy of the expectations that weighed on the 'people of poets and thinkers'. The then curator of the British Museum, Charles Newton, praised Berlin on visiting its museums: 'Now you really do have a capital city here in Berlin.' (Korfmann 2001a: 19, my translation)[14]

In many ways, this is precisely what Korfmann often insisted he was not going to do: the new excavations were not going to force respect through conquest, and Korfmann always insisted that his finds were to stay in Turkey. But he also promised some of the catching up that was necessary for a new state to find itself, although the terms of that project had changed. The point was no longer to colonise the past in a way familiar from the nineteenth century. Korfmann did not style himself or his collaborators as nineteenth-century bourgeois heroes. But he did draw on a functionally similar mythology of 'dream and reality', in a bid to galvanise and empower his audiences.

Once again, archaeology promised to open access to the paradise of *Bildung* and hence the realisation of collective social and political aspirations. Perhaps *the* most telling gesture in this context is the setting up of a 'national park of peace' around the new excavations. As Korfmann explains:

> The archaeological finds from Troy should ultimately be returned to their place of origin. [...] The historic National Park of Peace at the Dardanelles ought to have more than just a political dimension; and it ought to comprise not just peace with the local nature. At Troy, as a place which has come to symbolize 'War' and where Western culture and hence world culture have strong roots, one can and should make symbolic gestures. In intellectual matters too we should aim to live together in peace and think about new ways forward. (Korfmann 2001a: 23, my translation)[15]

'Nie wieder Krieg!' ('Never again a war!') had been one of the most potent slogans of the two traumatised post-war Germanies, a motto that goes back to the famous poster by Käthe Kollwitz of 1924 (discussed in Kearns 1976: 177; Withers 1981: 76–7). Again, it is not so easy to disentangle dream and fact, reality and aspiration.

Conclusion

Both Heinrich Schliemann and Manfred Korfmann defined archaeology as a science of 'the real', understood primarily as the realisation of earlier dreams. Both of them were active at crucial moments in history, Schliemann during the first period of German unification, Korfmann during the second. Schliemann cast archaeological reality as the realisation of *petit bourgeois* yearnings. Thanks to him, everybody would henceforth be able to make their home in the secular paradise of the divine Homer. Manfred Korfmann unearthed an archaeological reality that fulfilled the dreams of late twentieth-century Germans for a new and better society; and for a new role for Germany on the world stage. Troy as the city of war turned into a symbol of peace – and an international, intercultural, centre of trade.

At first glance, the argument of this chapter may seem more relevant to the student of German history and culture than to the Homeric archaeologist. However, it seems to me that there are lessons to be learned here for Homeric Archaeology too. My point is not simply that thinking about the history of a discipline should always be part of what that discipline does. At a more specific level, understanding the work of Schliemann and Korfmann, and their views on what counts as 'real' and why, puts us in a better position to understand what is at stake when we make connections of our own between the poems of Homer and the archaeology of Hisarlık and other sites. Such connections may be more or less persuasive, but they are never innocent. Indeed, to suggest that we might make them so by developing new and better methodologies seems to me to be mystification on a scale that dwarfs even the most serious methodological errors of which one might accuse Schliemann or Korfmann (see Ulf 2003, for a useful discussion of the methodological pitfalls involved in tracking the 'realities' behind Homeric poetry). As things stand, the archaeological playing field around Hisarlık (or Mycenae, or Ithaca) is not level and will not be level as long as the Homeric poems are read and rewritten at anything like the current level of intensity (e.g., Graziosi and Greenwood 2007; Hall 2008). Reality warps around Homer, which means that Homeric Archaeology will for some time longer have to live with such disturbingly 'unscientific' factors as loss and recovery, redemption and realisation.

Notes

1. For the exhibition in Stuttgart, Braunschweig and Bonn (all cities of the former FRG), see Haubold 2002: 566.
2. In favour of this identification: e.g. Easton, Hawkins, Sherratt and Sherratt 2002: 94–101; Latacz 2004: 75–92. Others remain sceptical: e.g. Hertel and Kolb 2003: 74; Heinhold-Krahmer 2003; 2004; Kolb 2004.
3. For Troy as a centre of commerce see Korfmann 2001d. For the claim that Korfmann was 'misleading the public' see Kolb in Schweizer 2002: 17.
4. In favour: Easton, Hawkins, Sherratt and Sherratt 2002: 77–94; Latacz 2004: 22–37. Against: Hertel and Kolb 2003: 77–86; cf. Kolb 2004.
5. The work of Schliemann has been much discussed in the wake of Calder 1972. See e.g. Calder and Traill 1986; Calder and Cobet 1990; Cobet and Patzek 1992; Gamer-Wallert 1992; Herrmann 1992; Traill 1993; 1995; Boedeker 1997; Cobet 1997; Zintzen 1998; 2001.
6. For Homer's claims to report what really happened see Graziosi and Haubold 2005: 45–47. For Stesichorus see Stesichorus fragment 192 (Davies 1991).
7. Korfmann himself regarded Schliemann as his intellectual ancestor; cf. Korfmann 2001a: 19, my translation: 'He was a pioneer of my subject, that is to say, of prehistoric and early historic archaeology. We owe him a great deal, more than many people today would like to, or feel able to, admit.' For a critical view of Korfmann's debt to Schliemann see Cobet and Gehrke 2002.
8. Wilamowitz' notorious assessment of Schliemann is deliberately distorting. Cf. Wilamowitz 1906: 59, my translation: 'One generation ago, Heinrich Schliemann began rummaging through the ground of the Greek city of Ilion, unencumbered by any linguistic or historical scholarship, driven on by the naïve belief that anything that is in Homer must be real [...] It was only fair that the world should applaud his discoveries; and at least excusable that the masses who cannot grasp historical scholarship should take the real treasures as proof of the reality of the Homeric accounts. [...] One does not get excited about this sort of thing; but one does not take it seriously either.'
9. The 1869 version of Schliemann's autobiography is discussed in Goldmann 1990. For the autobiographical letter to his sisters Wilhelmine and Doris of 1842 see Schindler 1990. Here I focus on the version of Schliemann's autobiography printed in Schliemann 1880 and 1881 (citations are from the 1881 New York edn).
10. Goldmann (1989) offers a psychoanalytical reading of Schliemann's autobiography in its 1869 version. He argues that Schliemann projected 'infantile sexual phantasies' (p. 203) onto his relationship with Homeric Greece. Here I am more interested in the social and cultural implications of his writings than in what they tell us about Schliemann's psyche.
11. 'Ohne Zweifel gab es von Anfang an ins Unwirkliche greifende Fantasievorstellungen

    1. in der Welt Homers, dem ausgehenden 8. Jh. v. Chr., wo beispielsweise die Götter konkret am Kampfgeschehen um Troia teilnahmen,
    2. auch im Zeitalter der griechischen und der römischen Antike und
    3. in der Epoche des Mittelalters und der Frühen Neuzeit, als der Troiamythos mehr und mehr ausgeschmückt wurde. Und es ist spannend, sich unter dem Blickwinkel "Traum" mit der

Gründerzeit des 19. Jh. n. Chr. zu beschäftigen, d.h. mit Heinrich Schliemann und den ersten international beachteten Ausgrabungsergebnissen der Archäologie.

Danach geht es

4. um die Wirklichkeit der Ergebnisse moderner, methodischer Ausgrabungen
5. werden jedoch die Vorstellungen, Träume und ebenso wissenschaftlichen Aspekte von Troia in der modernen westlichen Kultur nicht außer Acht gelassen.'

12. 'Damit beginnt die Wissenschaftlichkeit ... Durch den Buchdruck können die Erkenntnisse nun vergleichsweise billig publiziert werden. Eine Konsequenz dieser Wissensexplosion ist, dass die im Irrationalen wurzelnde Faszination zurückgeht und die Frage *nach der Glaubwürdigkeit* in den Vordergrund tritt.'
13. Korfmann 2001a: 9, my translation: 'Im vierten Kapitel finden Sie die Realität Troias ausführlich dargestellt, die uns Archäologen nicht weniger fasziniert als der Mythos.'
14. 'Andere Großmächte hatten sich Kolonien auf der ganzen Erde verschafft. Die Museen in Brüssel, Madrid, Lissabon, Paris und London waren gefüllt mit Beutestücken, um einen viel zitierten Ausdruck bewusst zu benutzen. Man hatte sich der Welt bemächtigt und das Wertvollste der Kolonisierten oder Unterdrückten in die Hauptstädte geholt. Die Deutschen hatten diesen Trend der Einverleibung von Kolonien weitgehend verschlafen, und der Michel mit seiner Mütze wurde karikiert. Nur auf dem Gebiet, das durch den Mythos der Griechen faszinierte – bei den Troiafunden und beim Pergamonaltar –, hatte man sich aus damaliger Sicht würdig gezeigt und den Erwartungen an das "Volk der Dichter und Denker" entsprochen. So lobte auch der Kurator des British Museums, Charles Newton, anlässlich eines Besuchs der Berliner Museen: "Nun haben Sie hier wirklich in Berlin eine Hauptstadt."' (Korfmann 2001a: 19)
15. 'In Troia, einem Ort der als gleichbedeutend mit "Krieg" verstanden wird und in dem sich starke Wurzeln der abendländischen Kultur und damit der Weltkultur befinden, könnten und sollten Zeichen gesetzt werden. Denn auch auf geistigem Gebiet sollten ein friedliches Miteinander angestrebt und neue Wege angedacht und begangen werden.' (Korfmann 2001a: 23)

Bibliography

Barceló, J. A, M. Forte and D. H. Sanders (eds.)
2000 *Virtual Reality in Archaeology* (BAR International Series 843). Oxford: British Archaeological Reports.

Boedeker, D. (ed.)
1997 *The World of Troy: Homer, Schliemann, and the Treasures of Priam*. Washington, DC: Society for the Preservation of the Greek Heritage.

Brandau, B., H. Schickert and P. Jablonka
2004 *Troia wie es wirklich aussah*. Munich and Zurich: Piper.

Calder, W. M. III
1972 Schliemann on Schliemann: a study in the use of sources. *Greek, Roman and Byzantine Studies* 13: 335–53.

Calder, W. M. III and J. Cobet (eds.)
1990 *Heinrich Schliemann nach hundert Jahren*. Frankfurt: Vittorio Klostermann.

Calder, W. M. III and D. A. Traill
1986 *Myth, Scandal and History: the Heinrich Schliemann Controversy and a First Edition of the Mycenaean Diary*. Detroit: Wayne State University Press.

Cobet, J.
1997 *Heinrich Schliemann: Archäologe und Abenteurer*. Munich: C. H. Beck.

Cobet, J. and H.-J. Gehrke
2002 Warum um Troia immer wieder streiten? *Geschichte in Wissenschaft und Unterricht* 53: 290–325.
Cobet, J. and B. Patzek (eds.)
1992 *Archäologie und historische Erinnerung: Nach 100 Jahren Heinrich Schliemann*. Essen: Klartext.
Cohen, G. M. and M. Korfmann (eds.)
1991–2005 *Studia Troica* 1–15. Mainz: Philipp von Zabern.
Davies, M. (ed.)
1991 *Poetarum Melicorum Graecorum Fragmenta, vol. 1*. Oxford: Clarendon Press.
Easton, D. F.
2002 *Schliemann's Excavations at Troia 1870–1873*. Mainz: Philipp von Zabern.
Easton, D. F., J. D. Hawkins, A. G. Sherratt and E. S. Sherratt
2002 Troy in recent perspective. *Anatolian Studies* 52: 75–109.
Goldmann, S.
1990 Die homerische Welt als Symbol verschütteter Kindheit. In W. M. Calder III and J. Cobet (eds.): 191–205.
Graziosi, B. and E. Greenwood (eds.)
2007 *Homer in the Twentieth Century: Between World Literature and the Western Canon*. Oxford: Oxford University Press.
Graziosi, B. and J. Haubold
2005 *Homer: the Resonance of Epic*. London: Duckworth.
Hall, E.
2008 *The Return of Odysseus: a Cultural History of Homer's Odyssey*. London: I.B. Tauris.
Hammer-Schenk, H.
1992 "Dem Heros". Anmerkungen zu Heinrich Schliemanns Grabmahl in Athen. In J. Cobet and B. Patzek (eds.): 31–50.
Haubold, J.
2002 Wars of *Wissenschaft*: the new quest for Troy. *International Journal of the Classical Tradition* 8: 564–79.
Heinhold-Krahmer, S.
2003 Zur Gleichsetzung der Namen Ilias-Wiluša und Troia-Taruiša. In C. Ulf (ed.), *Der neue Streit um Troia: Eine Bilanz*: 146–68.
Munich: C.H. Beck
2004 Ist die Identität von Ilios mit Wilusa endgültig erwiesen? *Studi micenei ed egeo-anatolici* 46: 29–57.
Herrmann, J. (ed.)
1992 *Heinrich Schliemann: Grundlagen und Ergebnisse moderner Archäologie 100 Jahre nach Schliemanns Tod*. Berlin: Akademie Verlag.
Hertel, D. and F. Kolb
2003 Troy in clearer perspective. *Anatolian Studies* 53: 71–88.
Jansen, H. G.
2001 Die neuen internationalen Grabungen. Auswirkungen in Wissenschaft und Öffentlichkeit. In J. Latacz *et al.* (eds.): 338–42.
Jansen, H. G. (ed.)
2006 *Der letzte Ring: Epilog zur "Mauerschau". In Erinnerung an Manfred Osman Korfmann*. Remshalden: B. A. Greiner.
Kearns, M.
1976 *Käthe Kollwitz: Woman and Artist*. New York: The Feminist Press.
Kienlin, T. L. and B. Schweitzer
2001/2002 Das Troia-Symposium in Tübingen. Eine Diskussion um Geschichte und Archäologie. *Hephaistos* 19/20: 7–38.

Kolb, F.
2004 Troy VI: a trading center and commercial city? *American Journal of Archaeology* 108: 577–613.
Korfmann, M.
2001a Troia – Traum und Wirklichkeit. Eine Einführung in das Thema. In J. Latacz *et al.* (eds.): 4–23.
2001b Wilusa/(W)Ilios ca. 1200 v.Chr. – Ilion ca. 700 v.Chr. Fundberichte aus der Archäologie. In J. Latacz *et al.* (eds.): 64–76.
2001c Der prähistorische Siedlungshügel Hisarlik. Die “zehn Städte Troias” – von unten nach oben. In J. Latacz *et al.* (eds.): 347–54.
2001d Troia als Drehscheibe des Handels im 2. und 3. vorchristlichen Jahrtausend. Erkenntnisse zur Troianischen Hochkultur und zur maritimen Troia-Kultur. In J. Latacz *et al.* (eds.): 355–72.
2002 Troia II (Archäologie). In *Der neue Pauly* XII 1: 857–62. Stuttgart: J. B. Metzler.
2004 Troia in light of new research, trans J. Clough. Keynote lecture at Dies academicus Universität Trier Nov. 2003. Offprint from German original in *Reden an der Universität.* Trier 2/2004: 1–70. http://www.uni-tuebingen.de/troia/eng/trier_eng.pdf [last accessed 23/2/15].
Korfmann, M. (ed.)
2006 *Troia. Archäologie eines Siedlungshügels und seiner Landschaft.* Mainz: Philipp von Zabern.
Latacz, J.
2004 *Troy and Homer: Towards a Solution of an Old Mystery* (trans.). Oxford: Oxford University Press.
Latacz, J. et al. (eds.)
2001 *Troia. Traum und Wirklichkeit. Begleitband zur Auststellung “Troia - Traum und Wirklichkeit”.* Stuttgart: Konrad Theiss Verlag.
Mejer, J.
1990 Henrik Ibsen’s Peer Gynt and Heinrich Schliemann: fact and fiction. In W. M. Calder III and J. Cobet (eds.): 296–308.
Minden, M.
1997 *The German Bildungsroman: Incest and Inheritance.* Cambridge, New York and Melbourne: Cambridge University Press.
Most, G. W. (ed.)
2002 *Disciplining Classics - Altertumswissenschaft als Beruf.* Göttingen: Vandenhoeck & Ruprecht.
Porter, J.
2002 Homer: the very idea. *Arion* 10: 57–86.
Reilly, P.
1990 Towards a virtual archaeology. In K. Lockyear and S. Rahtz (eds.), *Computer Applications in Archaeology* (BAR International Series 565): 133–39. Oxford: British Archaeological Reports.
Schindler, W.
1990 Dichtung und Wahrheit. Schliemanns Selbstbiographie im Kontext. In W. M. Calder III and J. Cobet (eds.): 152–69.
Schliemann, H.
1869 *Ithaka, der Peloponnes und Troia.* Leipzig: Gieseke und Devrient.
1880 *Ilios: The City and the Country of the Trojans.* London: John Murray.
1881 *Ilios: The City and the Country of the Trojans.* New York: Harper.
Schweizer, C. (ed.)
2002 *Traum oder Wirklichkeit? Troia. Die Dokumentation eines Wissenschaftlerstreits.* Tübingen: Schwäbisches Tagblatt.
Traill, D. A.
1993 *Excavating Schliemann: Collected Papers on Schliemann.* Atlanta, GA: Scholars Press.
1995 *Schliemann of Troy: Treasure and Deceit.* New York: St. Martin’s Press.

Ulf, C.

2003 'Vorurteile' – Die Grundlage für die historische Auswertung der homerischen Epen. In H.-J. Behr, G. Biegel and H. Castritius (eds.), *Troia – Traum und Wirklichkeit. Ein Mythos in Geschichte und Rezeption*: 58–67. Braunschweig: Braunschweigisches Landesmuseum.

Wilamowitz-Moellendorff, U. von

1906 Über die ionische Wanderung. In *Sitzungsberichte der Königlich Preußischen Akademie der Wissenschaften*: 59–79. Berlin: Verlag der Königlichen Akademie der Wissenschaften.

Withers, J.

1981 No more war: an art essay. *Feminist Studies* 7: 76–88.

Zintzen, C.

1998 Von Pompeji nach Troja: Archäologie, Literatur und Öffentlichkeit im 19. Jahrhundert. Vienna: WUV Universitätsverlag.

2001 'Ich taufe sie mit den Namen Troia und Ilium ...'. Heinrich Schliemann, Grenzgänger zwischen Fakten und Fiktionen. In J. Latacz et al. (eds.): 430–39.

Chapter 4

Homeric Epic and Contexts of Bardic Creation

Susan Sherratt

Introduction: Homer's Bards

In this paper, the word 'bard' (with its adjective 'bardic') is used as a convenient translation of the Greek word *aoidos* (ἀοιδός) – a word which is both traditionally identified with Homer himself (e.g., *Homeric Hymn to Delian Apollo* 166–73) and which appears several times in the Homeric epics (e.g. *Iliad* 24.720; *Odyssey* 8.43, 479; 17.385, 518). It comes from the verb *a(w)eido* (ἀ(Ϝ)ειδω), 'I sing', and is sometimes translated as 'singer'; but the rather more archaic English alternatives of 'bard' or 'minstrel' in their original or historical senses probably actually provide the closest translations, particularly as regards the social function of the *aoidos*. Apart from these, Albert Lord's soubriquet for Homer himself – 'the singer of tales' (Lord 1960) – probably offers the most transparent description of the actual practical activities of the Homeric aoidos.

In the Iliad and the Odyssey the word aoidos (along with its related verb and its end-product the *aoidē* (ἀοιδή), the 'song' or 'tale', is applied to a number of different people and in a number of different contexts. By far the best known *aoidoi*, however, are Phemios and Demodokos in the *Odyssey*, the singers associated respectively with Odysseus' court in Ithaca and with Alkinoos' court on Phaeacia, the rather strange island set at the far end of the sea where everything seems perfect, and the gateway through which Odysseus is able to conclude his adventures and return finally to Ithaca. Although I think in the Homeric epics as a whole we have a potentially very complex series of contradictory images of *aoidoi*, and of their social contexts and perceived roles (e.g. Maas and Snyder 1989: 5-6), I shall concentrate for the moment on these two. This is because they seem to me to bring out particularly nicely some of the more important contrasts which we may be able to trace in the archaeological record.

In the *Odyssey* we have relatively coherent pictures of these two bards. Demodokos, who is blind (*Odyssey* 8.64), was identified in some later Greek literature with Homer himself (see Thucydides 3.104; and cf. *Homeric Hymn to Delian Apollo* cited above). Both he and Phemios are professional *aoidoi*, official bards attached to the courts or households of Alkinoos and Odysseus respectively. In the course of the *Odyssey* both sing tales about the Trojan war, though in Demodokos' case these are only part of a wider repertoire which includes such things as the relationship of the gods Aphrodite and Hephaistos. There, however, the similarity seems to end. In Phemios' case his tales are sung at the Ithacan court near the beginning of the *Odyssey* (1.153–55, 325–27). Ten years after the end of the Trojan war, Odysseus' family are still waiting faithfully for his return. His wife Penelope is besieged by a number of suitors who have made themselves at home in his palace and are trying to persuade her to marry one of them, so that he can take control of Odysseus' kingdom. The song that Phemios sings in this context tells of the 'events' which are part of the general setting of the *Odyssey* – that is, the homecoming of the Greek heroes from Troy. However, it is quite clear, from the upsetting effects of his song on Penelope in *Odyssey* 1.336–44 and from his later terror of Odysseus' anger in 22.330–49, that his song is deliberately angled to further the ambitions of his current patrons, the suitors. We are not specifically told that he actually sings of the death of Odysseus (which the epic's audiences know to be untrue), but there is a strong implication that he does (*Odyssey* 1.350–55). We are, however, quite explicitly told that it is the suitors who coerce him into singing for them (*Odyssey* 1.154; 22.351–53). The implication of this is that Phemios' art is seen by them (and later by the vengeful Odysseus) as a potentially very effective instrument of political manipulation for partisan purposes: in other words, the furthering of the suitors' ambitions to take over Odysseus' kingdom.[1]

Demodokos, on the other hand, when he sings of Troy (*Odyssey* 8.73–82), is praised for singing his tale 'correctly', *kata kosmon* (κατὰ κόσμον), literally what is accepted as true by the world in general (*Odyssey* 8.489). Moreover, it is a tale which not only his immediate listeners (including Odysseus) recognise as true, but one which the epic's audience, through the medium of Odysseus, also know to be 'true'. Another contrast is that, while Phemios' clearly manipulative bardic activity takes place in the real but unstable setting of the crisis-torn Ithacan court, Demodokos' takes place in the well-ordered, established Scherian community, and in the ideal, perfect palace of its ruler.

It is worth looking more closely at the names of these two aoidoi. *Redende Namen* ('meaningful names') have rather fallen out of fashion in Homeric studies (although see Higbie 1995; Kahane 2005: 197), but these names – and the contrast between them – seem altogether too apt to ignore. Phemios is clearly connected with the verb *phēmi* (φημί) ('I declare', 'make known', 'speak'), someone who says or states something (Latacz 1996: 30); and we might perhaps translate him as something like the 'statement maker', with the sense that he has the ability to persuade people that something is true simply because he says so. His patronymic is Terpiades (*Odyssey* 22.330), roughly translatable as 'son of pleasure', and it seems likely that his song gives some pleasure to the suitors, if not to Penelope. Later on, Odysseus calls him *polyphēmos* (πολύφημος) (*Odyssey* 22.376), 'many-voiced', or perhaps in this context 'versatile' or 'all things to all men'.

On the other hand, a plausible translation for Demodokos (from *dēmos* (δῆμος), 'the people', and *dokos* (*δόκος* = *δόκη*, meaning 'opinion' or 'belief') might be 'popular consensus' – 'what is believed or agreed by people in general'. We are explicitly told that he was honoured by the population of Alkinoos' kingdom (λαοῖσι τετιμένον: *Odyssey* 8.472) and regarded as a hero (8.483).

Before leaving Homer and turning more explicitly to the archaeological record, there are just a couple more things to which I should like to draw attention. First of all, in *Iliad* 9 (186–89), Achilles acts as his own *aoidos*, accompanying himself on his beautifully decorated lyre with its silver bridge or crossbar (actually a spoil of war) to sing tales of the glory or fame of heroes (the *klea andron* [κλέα ἀνδρῶν] – which is about as good a definition of heroic song as you can get). The other thing is that, in the *Odyssey*, the action-man hero Odysseus also acts as his own storyteller, though in his case as a teller rather than singer of tales. And while the story he tells in Alkinoos' well-ordered and ideally established kingdom is the *true*, but fantastic, story of his wanderings (*Odyssey* 9–12), the ones he tells in the real but unstable setting of Ithaca (*Odyssey* 13.254–86; 14.191-359; 19.165–307) are highly plausible and eminently realistic *lies*. It seems to me that, just taking the contrasting receptions accorded to Phemios and Demodokos, together with the contrasting story-telling behaviour of Odysseus in Ithaca and Phaeacia, we have a potentially very interesting distinction between different perceptions of the role of *aoidoi* in particular, and of epic composition and performance in general, which we may just possibly find reflected in some way – however obliquely – in the archaeological record.

Modes of Heroic Creation and their Contexts

Archaeologically datable elements of material culture contained within the epics seem to produce some interesting patterns, in that they appear to cluster in certain chronological periods more than others. As Oliver Dickinson (1986; also, this volume) argued long ago, the great majority of these can be seen to fall within the approximate limits of the twelfth and early eighth centuries BC. Nevertheless, there are a few elements that are difficult to place any earlier than the later eighth century, and an irreducible minimum of others for which the material correlations are best provided by a much earlier period – in most cases preceding the Mycenaean palatial period of the later fourteenth and thirteenth centuries BC (Dickinson 1986: 28–30; Sherratt 1990: 810–12). This is a curious pattern, which needs some explanation. What it implies is that the prehistory of bardic activity that ultimately fed into the epics was a complex one, determined less by straightforward passage of time than by different modes of creation and use of heroic song in different social or political contexts. That some periods seem to have contributed more material cultural elements than others suggests that these may have been periods in which a great deal of bardic creation was actively focussed on contemporary image and lifestyle and possibly aimed at defining and projecting the ideals and deeds of contemporary or near-contemporary individuals or small groups with social or political aspirations within their particular communities – what might be called a 'statement' mode. These may have been interspersed by periods in which 'possession' of a commonly agreed past, inherited by a community as a whole, may have been more important, and in which the main concern of bards and their patrons was to preserve the general themes and forms – and already antique settings – of inherited bardic creations (Sherratt 1990: 817–21).

Both of these modes arguably have fairly widespread correlates in the archaeological record, but it is perhaps above all in imagery, and especially representational art, that this sort of contrast between individual or group 'statement' grounded in the present and 'possession' of a shared inherited past can most easily be detected. Before turning to imagery in the Greek archaeological record, let me try to illustrate what I mean with some examples drawn from a study by Bill Rolston (1991) of the changing political role of street murals in Loyalist areas of Belfast during the course of the twentieth century. A favourite theme of the street murals to be found in Loyalist areas, particularly from the establishment of partition in 1922 onwards, was a stylised portrayal of William of Orange (King Billy) on a white horse crossing the Boyne in 1690 (Rolston 1991: 20–29): an icon of the far distant past and a symbol of enormous historical significance to the Loyalist community as a whole (Fig. 4.1). If one were to look closely at some of these images I have no doubt that one could probably find some small detail which was strictly anachronistic, but the overall impression is certainly archaic, firmly set in the late seventeenth century. In the period between the 1920s and the end of

Fig. 4.1: Mural of William of Orange crossing the River Boyne in 1692, Lindsay Street, Belfast 1984 (Rolston 1991: opp. p. 32). Courtesy of Bill Rolston.

the 1960s, it was an image with which, on the whole – and precisely because of its chronological distance – the entire Protestant–Loyalist community could identify to a greater or lesser extent, even though, for many, it was an essentially passive symbol of the shared long-term inheritance of a British Protestant Ulster rather than a focus of contemporary ideological activity.

Following the start of the troubles in the late 1960s, images of King Billy in the Loyalist areas began gradually to be supplemented and supplanted by new images (Rolston 1991: 31–32): among them, the foundation of Carson's Ulster Volunteer Force at the time of Asquith's Home Rule Bill in 1912 (Fig. 4.2), and the legitimate and wholly patriotic part the UVF, as the 36th Ulster Division, played in the battles of the Western Front in the First World War (Rolston 1991: 44–45). Such images were often juxtaposed to the paramilitary image and activities of the UVF's murky 'reincarnation' in the late 1960s; and the juxtaposition of these contemporary and near-contemporary images – one strictly contemporary, the other set within the three generations or so which bound historical memory – served the purpose, by association, of legitimising the contemporary UVF and its activities (Rolston 1991: 45). At the same time, these were images with which only a section of the Loyalist community as a whole could identify unambiguously – above all, those who were members or supporters of the activities and ideology of the contemporary paramilitary organisations. A contrast that

Fig. 4.2: Mural of the Motorised Division, Ulster Volunteer Force, 1912. Shankill Road, Belfast 1987 (Rolston 1991: 44). Courtesy of Bill Rolston.

is perhaps worth noting between these images and the William of Orange ones of the 1960s and earlier is that, while the latter were of an identifiable individual and referred to a specific narrative (that of the victory at the Boyne), the contemporary UVF ones were overwhelmingly generic in character. On the whole, they did not represent identifiable individuals or specific, identifiable events or stories: only anonymous gun-toting paramilitaries (Fig. 4.3), stylised encounters with Republican paramilitaries, or emblematic weapons (Rolston 1991: 31, 40–43). Particularly prominent was the representation of contemporary paramilitary weaponry. Indeed, the ability to produce accurate representations of such things as AK-47 assault rifles and rocket-launchers was an acknowledged source of pride among the young – predominantly male – mural artists, in both Loyalist and Republican areas (Rolston 1991: 48–49, 94).

Similar sorts of alternation between generic representations and representations of more specific narrative can, I think, also be seen in Greece in the period between the early Late Bronze Age and the early seventh century BC. The anonymous scenes of chariots, or hunting and fighting which characterise the personal and often portable art of the Shaft Grave period, or the anonymous battle and funerary scenes found on pots associated with individual graves in the eighth century cemeteries at Athens (Ahlberg 1971a; 1971b), can be contrasted, on the one hand, with aspects of the more public art of the frescoes which adorned the Mycenaean palaces in the thirteenth century (to which I shall return below), or, on the other, with some of the scenes

Fig. 4.3: Mural of armed loyalists, Severn Street, Belfast 1987 (Rolston 1991: 42). Courtesy of Bill Rolston.

found on seventh century BC pots – like the scenes of the blinding of the Cyclops on pots from Eleusis, Argos and the central Mediterranean, or the Trojan horse on a relief pithos from Mykonos (Snodgrass 1998: 88–92, figs. 34–37) – which I suspect would be easily recognisable as telling specific stories, even if the stories themselves were unfamiliar. Insofar as it is possible to tell, this kind of alternation seems to form some distinct chronological patterns. What appear to be generic scenes predominate in the early Mycenaean period, in the period immediately following the collapse of the Mycenaean palaces, and again in the period immediately preceding or surrounding the rise of the historical city-states (*poleis*) in the eighth century BC. Art of a specific narrative nature, on the other hand, seems more immediately recognisable in some of the Mycenaean palace frescoes (Davis and Bennet 1999), and again in the early Archaic period of the seventh century BC.

Archaeological Images of Bards

With this in mind, let us turn to the question of archaeological images of bards. What do we know from archaeology of *aoidoi* and their contexts in the centuries before 700 BC? The answer is not a great deal – but just enough to know that they existed, and possibly in just the sorts of contrasting contexts and roles in which we see them in the *Odyssey*. In the absence of other identifying attributes, as it were, we are thrown back on lyres, as associated with Phemios, Demodokos, Odysseus and others in the epics (mainly the *phorminx* [φόρμιγξ], e.g. *Iliad* 1.603; 9.186, 194; 18.569; 24.63; *Odyssey* 8.67, 99, 105, 254, 261, 537; 17.262, 270; 21.406, 430; 22.332, 340; 23.133, 144; and less often the *kitharis* [κίθαρις], e.g. *Odyssey* 1.153, 159; 8.248; *Iliad* 3.54; 13.731), to give us a clue to these aoidoi.[2]

It is not entirely clear, least of all in Homer, what the difference, if any, between a *kitharis* and a *phorminx* consists in (cf. Maas and Snyder 1989: 4–5). In the epics, at least, they seem to be interchangeable, since, although Phemios takes up a κίθαρις in *Odyssey* 1.153, what he does with it in the following lines is 'play the *phorminx*' (*Odyssey* 1.155: ἦ τοι φορμίζων ἀνεβάλλετο καλὸν ἀείδειν ['and playing his lyre, he struck up a fine song']); while, conversely, the youth who 'was playing the *kitharis*' (κιθάριζε) on the shield of Achilles was doing so with a *phorminx* (*Iliad* 18.569-70). The distinction is equally unclear in later Greek literature, where the *kitharis* usually appears in the form *kithara* (κιθάρα). *Phorminx* and *kithara* still often seem interchangeable: according to Strabo (13.2.4), Terpander was the first to use a *phorminx* with seven instead of four strings, while according to Plutarch (*Instituta Laconica* 17) it was the *kithara* to which Terpander was the first to add an extra string; the instrument of Apollo can be a *phorminx*, as it is in the *Iliad* (*Homeric Hymn to Delian Apollo* 179; Pindar, *Pythian* 1; Euripides *Ion* 144; Aristophanes, *Birds* 209; *Thesmophoriazusae* 312; Athenaeus, *Deipnosophistae* I 40; cf. *Iliad* 1.603), or it can be a *kithara* (Euripides, *Iphigeneia in Tauris* 1234; Apollodorus, *Bibliotheca* I 4; Plutarch, *Sulla* 12); and Orpheus plays an interchangeable *phorminx* and *kithara* within the space of a few lines in Apollonius

Rhodius, *Argonautica* (512, 540). This has not stopped modern scholars applying these respective terms to ancient representations of different types of lyres, however, and characterising the resulting descriptions as applicable in turn to these two terms (e.g. Younger 1998, 18–28; though cf. Younger 2007, 71–72; Bundrick 2005, 18–21, 25–26). Nevertheless, it seems reasonably clear from the generality of fifth century or later references that the *phorminx*, which figures most frequently in Homer, Hesiod, the Homeric Hymns and literary epic, is regarded primarily as an antique instrument (cf. Pindar, *Isthmian* 2, 1–2). It appears chiefly in references or allusions to Homer or the Homeric Hymns (e.g. Pausanias 9.29; Pseudo-Plutarch, *De Musica* 1145e; Athenaeus, *Deipnosophistae* XIV 24), in association with gods (especially Apollo) and mythical figures (e.g. Pindar, *Pythian* 1, 1–2; Euripides, *Ion* 164; *Helen* 172; Aristophanes, *Birds* 219; *Thesmophoriazusae* 327; Theocritus, *Idylls* VII, 101) and in metaphorical aphorisms (Aristotle, *Rhetoric* III 11; Demetrius of Phaleron, *De Elocutione* II 85). As in Homer and the Homeric Hymns, it is associated with singing, including the singing of praises and sacred song, and with dancing (Bacchylides, *Epinicians* XIV, 13–14; Pindar, *Isthmian* 2, 2-3; *Nemean* 4, 4, 44–45; *Pythian* 1, 1–3; Euripides, *Ion* 164–65; Aristophanes, *Birds* 219; Theocritus, *Idylls* VII 100–01; *Anthologia Graeca* VII 612; cf. *Odyssey* 8.73–74). Also as in Homer, where the phrase φόρμιγγα λιγεῖαν occurs seven times in the *Odyssey* as a 'formulaic' line-ending, it is conventionally described as 'clear-toned' (λιγεῖα: *Odyssey* 8.67) or variations thereon, and as 'hollow' (γλαφυρή: *Odyssey* 8.257), which presumably refers to a hollow sound-box. As for other characteristics of the Homeric *phorminx*, all it is possible to glean from the epics is that it is strung, with each string (χορδή) stretched around a peg (κόλλοψ) (*Odyssey* 21.406–07), and that it has a bridge or cross-bar (ζυγόν) (*Iliad* 9.186–87; cf. Maas and Snyder 1989: 6). We do not know, for instance, how many strings it may be supposed to have had, or whether these were plucked with the fingers or with a plectrum, or both (a plectrum is mentioned in connection with a *phorminx* in the *Homeric Hymn to Apollo* and is depicted in some Aegean Late Bronze Age representations [Younger 1998: pls. 11, 24:1], though no plectrum is mentioned in either the *Iliad* or *Odyssey*). We are thus thrown back on representations of lyres or remains of actual lyres in the archaeological record for information about the instruments which Homeric *aoidoi* and their pre-Homeric predecessors might be supposed to have used.

Lyres are instruments which are now all but obsolete, at least in modern western musical traditions. They were, in effect, small harps, the main difference being that the strings (all of the same length) passed over a bridge of some form rather than entering the body of the instrument directly and were often plucked with the aid of a plectrum (Scholes 1970: 585 *s.v.* lyre (1)). They had a long history in the ancient Near East as well as in Greek lands, being represented, for instance, in the hands of an Asiatic in the 12th Dynasty tomb of Khnumhotpe at Beni Hasan in Egypt (Evans 1928: 837, fig. 554). In the Aegean, where J.G. Younger (1998) has collected all known Bronze Age examples and others (e.g. Wegner 1968; Maas and Snyder 1989) have collected examples of Early Iron Age date down to c. 700 BC, remains of actual lyres are very rare indeed. Representations of them are more common, but I shall ignore those with no very helpful context for elucidating early bardic practices, such as the often rather ambiguous lyre or harp signs or representations found on Middle Minoan seals (Evans 1928: 834, figs. 550–51; Younger 1998: 76–78, pls. 23–24), or those representations which seem to be associated primarily with dancing or mixed ensembles (Younger 1998: 66–68 no. 29, 75 no. 54, 78–79 no. 66, pls. 1, 10–12, 18–19, 25:1). Among the very few actual lyres known is an ivory one – possibly one of two, together with a probable plectrum – from the Menidhi tholos in Attica (Younger 1998: 61–62, pls. 5–6, 9). Though these remains are often dated to the thirteenth century, they may well be earlier. The tholos itself was probably first constructed in the late fifteenth or early fourteenth century BC (Galanakis 2008: 238–39), and though the only pottery found in it seems to have been later, fragments of gold leaf (including gold rosettes) and silver vessels also remained - almost certainly belonging to an earlier burial or burials, quite probably of mid-fourteenth century date (I. Galanakis, pers. comm.). If the lyre or lyres (which were found in a very fragmentary state) do belong to such an earlier burial (and fragments of another ivory lyre from Chamber Tomb 81 at Mycenae, possibly of fifteenth century BC date [Kontorli-Papadopoulou 1987: 153; cf. Younger 1998: 61 no. 1, pls. 3–4, 7] might give some support to this), then it was a pretty impressive one. At any rate, only someone of a fairly exalted status (possibly with a lineal connection to the original inmates) is likely to have been buried in the tholos. We may therefore here have something in the nature of an aristocratic lyre-player, reminding us of a passage in *Iliad* 13 (730–31) where Poulydamas, a Trojan noble, compares lyre-playing with the other possible accomplishments of a hero, including skill in warfare; and reminding us too, perhaps, of Achilles himself singing of the *klea andron* accompanied by his prized silver-ornamented lyre.

In the palatial period of the thirteenth century we have the very well-known character of a lyre-player on a fresco, sitting on the wall of the main megaron in the palace at Pylos (Lang 1969: 79–81 nos. 43–44 H6, pls. 27–28, 125–26, col. pl. A; cf. Younger 1998: 69 no. 31, pl. 13). After Mabel Lang's reconstruction suggested that he was flanked by groups of men seated at tables, she suggested that he should be called the 'Bard at the Banquet' (Lang 1969: 194–95, pl. 125) (Fig. 4.4). His long enveloping robe may be some kind of a professional or even priestly dress; at any rate, it seems unlikely that he could do anything very much more active than sit and play a lyre while wearing it. He is perched on top of what looks like a high rock while his head bumps against the clouds. This, and the large bird (or, less likely perhaps, griffin: see Younger 1998: 69) just in front of him, suggests that there is some sort of divine presence or inspiration mixed up in all this. At this point, we might just remember that Demodokos is described as '*theios*' (θεῖος, 'divine' or 'divinely inspired' [*Odyssey* 8.43]) – an adjective which is *not* applied to Phemios, whose main boast is that he is *autodidaktos* (αὐτοδίδακτος, 'self-taught' [*Odyssey* 22.347]), which seems rather at odds with his claim in the same line that a god has implanted songs of every sort in his mind.

Moving away from the inner sanctum of the main megaron at Pylos, we find some particularly interesting frescoes, which, as has often been suggested (e.g. Davis and

Fig. 4.4: Reconstructed scene of the 'Bard at the Banquet' from the main megaron at Pylos. After Wright 2004: fig. 13, drawn by K.E. Leaman after McCallum 1987: pl. 10, based on reconstruction drawing by Piet de Jong (Lang 1969: pl. 125).

Bennet 1999), may have a bearing on part at least of what the 'Bard at the Banquet' might have sung about. These are the frescoes found in Hall 64, which acts as the main entrance to the southwestern complex of the Palace, and was in a more publicly visible position. They include the well-known scene of a battle between warriors in boar's tusk helmets and men dressed in animal skins (Lang 1969: 71 no. 22 H 64, pls. 16, 117, col. pls. A, M), which (as reconstructed by Piet de Jong: Lang 1969: col. pl. M; here Fig. 4.5) seems to have some sort of fairly vivid narrative emphasis, to be telling some particular story, possibly even with the hint of a non-contemporary setting

Fig. 4.5: Reconstruction by Piet de Jong of battle scene in Hall 64 at Pylos (Lang 1969: col. pl. M). Courtesy of The Department of Classics, University of Cincinnati and American School of Classical Studies at Athens, Pylos Archive, Piet de Jong Collection of Watercolors. Photo Jennifer F. Stephens and Arthur E. Stephens.

(Shelmerdine 1996: 474–77). These warriors with boar's tusk helmets, for instance, were painted at a time when bronze body armour is recorded on the Pylos Linear B tablets, but for some reason they are shown semi-naked, just like the warriors on early Mycenaean representations. Is this therefore a representation – in a fairly visible area of the palace – of some event or story which was important in the 'history' of the Pylos palace rulers, and which was consciously set in some notion of the past (cf. Bennet 2007: 15–17)? And might we suggest, for instance, that the 'Bard at the Banquet' could, among other things, have sung about just such stories? Signs of the deliberate incorporation of 'history' into the fabric of palaces, as it were, appear even more unambiguously at Mycenae, where Circle A of the Shaft Graves, which had fallen out of use by the early fifteenth century BC, was refurbished sometime around 1300 BC and included inside the newly redesigned citadel walls right by the monumental Lion Gate (see also Panagiotopoulos, this volume).

The next image is a fragmentary one, on a fragment of a collar-necked jar from Tiryns which probably dates from the twelfth century BC, immediately following the collapse of the palaces (Fig. 4.6: Slenczka 1974: 69 no. 159, 166, fig. 24:7, pl. 9:1d; Maas and Snyder 1989: 18 fig. 3b). Although I would not want to put too much stress on the details of what is after all a fairly rough and ready type of representation, it is perhaps worth pointing out that, unlike the 'Bard at the Banquet's' lyre, which seems to have had five strings (cf. Younger 1998: 69, pl. 13), or other Aegean representations of lyres which seem frequently to have had seven strings (Maas and Snyder 1989: 2–3, 7; Younger 1998: 20), this one has only 3 strings – a type of lyre (with only three or four strings) which, it has been suggested, may have been particularly suitable for providing relatively simple accompaniments to the tonal accentuation of sung or chanted hexameter verse (Deubner 1929; West 1981; cf. Franklin 2004: 247). Although nothing more remains of this particular representation, we can, I think, put this lyre player in a more general context by considering the types of representational scenes frequently found on contemporary twelfth-century BC pottery: a renewed interest (at least compared with fourteenth- and thirteenth-century scenes) in military representation of an apparently generic nature, with new types of up-to-date equipment, including new forms of sword, shields and helmets (Popham and Sackett 1968: figs. 38–44; Buchholz and Karageorghis 1973: nos. 999–1001, 1025, 1071; Crouwel 1981: 140–41; cf. Sherratt 1990: 816). The frescoes associated with the palaces have gone, and instead representational art is again found almost exclusively on more portable personal types of objects.

Fig. 4.6: Sherd from shoulder of collar-necked jar from Tiryns, showing part of lyre player (Slenczka 1974: pl. 9:1d). Negative: D-DAI-ATH 1971/767, photographer: Tsimas. Courtesy of the German Archaeological Institute.

My next representation (Fig. 4.7) seems to encapsulate quite neatly both the Tiryns lyre player and the sort of contemporary representational context in which he is found. It is not actually from Greece, but from eleventh century Cyprus (Iacovou 1988: 26 no. 29, fig. 70:29; Maas and Snyder 1989: 19, fig. 4; Karageorghis 2006: 78–79). I would not want to draw any conclusions about this representation necessarily having anything to do with Greek epic, but what is possibly more important is that, for various reasons, social conditions in Cyprus in the mid-eleventh century BC were possibly comparable in several significant ways to those in post-palatial Greece.

Fig. 4.7: Armed lyre player on Proto-White-Painted kalathos from tomb at Palaepaphos-Xerolimni, Cyprus. From Karageorghis 2006: fig. 64b.

This lyre-player is very visibly armed with contemporary weaponry, and he strides out purposefully. What he clearly appears to do is combine both warrior and *aoidos* in one image. What he suggests, in fact, is a close association between the image of the contemporary warrior hero himself, and the means of actively defining and propagating that image through song.

Finally, we have a series of Late Geometric images of lyres (cf., e.g. Maas and Snyder 1989: 20–23, figs. 6–7a, 8–13). These include one on a Late Geometric jug from Athens (Fig. 4.8; NM 17497: Wegner 1968: 73 no. 45, pl. II:a; Hahland 1954: 179 no. 8; Karouzou 1954: 9–10, pl. 12), dating to somewhere around the end of the eighth century BC. A seated figure playing a four-stringed lyre sits opposite another seated figure. The figure opposite the lyre-player also has a footstool, a sign of exalted status. Between them, and behind the lyre-player, are some pedestalled objects, which could be cauldrons for purificatory washing, or possibly braziers. Each of the figures on either side of the lyre-player holds a couple of enigmatic objects, which have variously been interpreted as sprinklers or as rattles or clappers for waking – or keeping at bay – the spirits of the dead (Cook 1946: 101; Hahland 1954: 187–92; Boardman 1966: 5). This scene belongs to a series of related scenes on jugs which some have interpreted as depictions of ceremonies – perhaps commemorative feasts – related to ancestor cult

Fig. 4.8: Late Geometric jug (Athens, National Museum 17497). From Wegner 1968: pl. II:a.

(Cook 1946; Hahland 1954; Karouzou 1954: 10; Wegner 1968: 38–40; McNally 1969: 462–64). On some, what appears to be a table is shown between the figures, and on several of them shields are shown hanging on the wall, some show helmeted figures and some are combined with scenes of warriors (Hahland 1954:178 nos. 1–4, 179 nos. 6–7, pls. VII–XI, XIII–XVII), suggesting some sort of military or warrior reference, but one which is implicitly in the past rather than the active present. Problematic though its interpretation is, I suggest that with this and other similar scenes we are perhaps back again with something a bit closer to the professional 'bard at the banquet' that we saw on the walls of the Pylos megaron, rather than the active warrior *aoidos* we met in eleventh-century BC Cyprus. The one is concerned with self-definition and active propagation of a contemporary image; the other, perhaps, with the commemoration of inherited 'history' as an integral part of an emerging religious and social fabric.

I propose to end there, because it brings us back full circle to where we started, with Phemios the active 'statement maker' or divisive propagandist, and Demodokos the purveyor of 'popular consensus' or generally accepted 'true' histories. These, I suggest, embody two modes of creation and transmission of what we might call heroic or pre-epic song, which tended to dominate alternately over a long period, and together contributed to the generation and maintenance of long-lived oral traditions which formed part of the 'prehistory' which fed into Homeric epic: phases of active generation and reinterpretation of inherited songs based on 'statement' grounded in the ideals and lifestyles of the present or near-present, and particularly aimed at the definition and image projection of individuals and small groups with social or political aspirations; and, on the other hand, phases in which 'possession' of a commonly agreed, inherited past are more important to societies as a whole. It is these alternating modes of active generation and more passive maintenance which, I think, account for the odd chronological pattern of material cultural references in the Homeric epics, dominated by the last phase of active generation based on contemporary 'statement' (the 'Dark Age' Homer of Finley [1956] and Dickinson [1986]), but with relics of much earlier phases of active generation of heroic song (the early Mycenaean period) left fossilised in the structure, for instance in the language of some traditional formulae or as structural elements of certain traditional story patterns.

It is my belief that the Homeric epics of around 700 BC, or, at least, the phase of development or 'crystallisation' they embarked on around then (see Nagy 1996: 42; 2003: 2; and cf. Snodgrass, this volume), were quite deliberately and consciously designed to encourage a notion of collective Greek identity. In several aspects they are deliberately inclusive in nature, and they appear in several ways to be concerned with reconciling historical tensions (Nagy 1979; cf. Sherratt 1990: 820). And it is in this sense that they need both Phemios and Demodokos. Phemios is there as an acknowledgement of how 'history' is created and manipulated in the real world, particularly at times of crisis or social and political disintegration or fluidity. With all its imperfections, this is part of the Greek past (particularly the near-contemporary past), and can be understood and forgiven, just as Odysseus forgives Phemios in *Odyssey* 22.371–77. Demodokos, on the other hand, represents the acceptance of this imperfectly created past within a growing sense of the linear progression of history, and its transformation into an ideal of a universally acknowledged 'history' that can be possessed by everyone, and that is 'true' precisely because everyone accepts it. It seems to me no coincidence that it was with Demodokos rather than Phemios that the Greeks themselves identified Homer, traditionally one of the last and greatest of the *aoidoi* (Kirk 1962: 312–14) and at the head of a line of rhapsodes whose ideal purpose was to ensure that a commonly possessed 'history' was henceforth preserved and transmitted to future generations.

Acknowledgements

I am extremely grateful to Emeritus Professor Bill Rolston, University of Ulster, for very kindly supplying the photographs for Figs. 4.1–4.3, and for his permission to reproduce them here; to Dr Natalia Vogeikoff-Brogan of the American School of Classical Studies in Athens for supplying Fig. 4.5, and to her and Carol Hershenson of the Department of Classics, University of Cincinnati, for permission to reproduce it; to Dr Joachim Heiden of the Deutsches Archäologisches Institut, Abteilung Athen, for the photograph for Fig. 4.6 and permission to reproduce it here, and to Dr Ulrich Thaler, also of the DAI for his help in obtaining it.

Notes

1. Another possible illustration of the manipulative political/partisan power of the court *aoidos* lies in the mention of the (unnamed) *aoidos* whom Agamemnon left to protect Clytemnestra when he went to Troy, particularly since Aegisthus felt it necessary in pursuit of his purpose of seducing her, not just to sideline or even kill him, but to maroon him on a deserted island, thus removing him as far from audiences at Mycenae (and elsewhere) as he possibly could. Aegisthus was so relieved that he then gave thanks to the gods for the unexpected success of his mission (*Odyssey* 3.267–75).
2. The word λύρα (*lyra*), which first appears in the *Homeric Hymn to Hermes* 423, does not occur in Homer. For a possible hint of its presence in the form ru-ra-ta-e (λυραστής [dual]? – 'lyre-players'?) on one of the Linear B tablets from Thebes, see Aravantinos, Godart and Sacconi 2001: 176–78; Killen 2001: 443.

Bibliography

Ahlberg, G.
1971a *Fighting on Land and Sea in Greek Geometric Art*. Stockholm: Skrifter utgivna av Svenska Institutet i Athen. ser. 4°. no. 16.
1971b *Prothesis and Ekphora in Greek Geometric Art* (Studies in Mediterranean Archaeology 32). Göteborg: Paul Åströms Förlag.
Aravantinos, V. L., L. Godart and A. Sacconi
2001 *Thèbes. Fouilles de la Cadmée 1: Les tablettes en linéaire B de la Odos Pelopidou. Edition et commentaire*. Pisa: Istituti editoriali e poligrafici internazionali.
Bennet, J.
2007 Representations of power in Mycenaean Pylos: script, orality, iconograpy. In F. Lang, C. Reinholdt and J. Weilhartner (eds.), *ΣΤΕΦΑΝΟΣ ΑΡΙΣΤΕΙΟΣ. Archäologische Forschungen zwischen Nil und Istros. Festschrift für Stefan Hiller zum 65. Geburtstag*: 11–22. Wien: Phoibos Verlag.
Boardman, J.
1966 Attic Geometric vase scenes, old and new. *Journal of Hellenic Studies* 86: 1–5.
Buchholz, H.-G. and V. Karageorghis
1973 *Prehistoric Greece and Cyprus*. London: Phaidon.
Bundrick, S. D.
2005 *Music and Image in Classical Athens*. Cambridge: Cambridge University Press.
Cook, J. M.
1946 A Geometric graveyard scene. *Bulletin de Correspondance Hellénique* 70: 97–101.
Crouwel, J. H.
1981 *Chariots and other means of land transport in Bronze Age Greece*. Amsterdam: Allard Pierson Series 3.
Davis, J. L. and J. Bennet
1999 Making Mycenaeans: warfare, territorial expansion, and representations of the other in the Pylian kingdom. In R. Laffineur (ed.), *Polemos. Le contexte guerrier en Égée à l'âge du bronze. Actes de la 7e Rencontre égéenne internationale, Université de Liège, 14–17 avril 1998* (Aegaeum 19): 105–20. Liège: Université de Liège, Histoire de l'art et archéologie de la Grèce antique.
Deubner, L.
1929 Die viersaitige Leier. *Athenische Mitteilungen* 54: 194–200.
Dickinson, O.
1986 Homer, the poet of the Dark Age. *Greece & Rome* 33: 20–37.

Evans, A. J.
1928 *The Palace of Minos at Knossos, vol. 2.* London: MacMillan.
Finley, M. I.
1956 *The World of Odysseus.* London: Chatto & Windus.
Franklin, J. C.
2004 Structural sympathies in ancient Greek and South-Slavic heroic song. In E. Hickmann and R. Eichmann (eds.), *Musikarchäologische Quellengruppen: Bodenurkunden, mündliche Überlieferung, Aufzeichnung. Vorträge des 3. Symposiums der Internationalen Studiengruppe Musikarchäologie im Kloster Michaelstein, 9. –16. Juni 2002* (Orient-Archäologie 15): 241–51. Rahden: M. Leidorf.
Galanakis, I.
2008 *A study of Late Bronze Age Tholos Tombs in the Aegean, 1700–1200 BC.* Unpublished DPhil thesis, Keble College, Oxford.
Hahland, W.
1954 Neue Denkmäler des attischen Heroen- und Totenkultes. In W. Müller (ed.), *Festschrift für Friedrich Zucker zum 70. Geburtstage*: 177–94. Berlin: Akademie-Verlag.
Higbie, C.
1995 *Heroes' Names, Homeric Identities.* New York/London: Garland.
Iacovou, M.
1988 *The Pictorial Pottery of Eleventh Century B.C. Cyprus* (Studies in Mediterranean Archaeology 78). Göteborg: Paul Åströms Förlag.
Kahane, A.
2005 *Diachronic Dialogues: Authority and Continuity in Homer and the Homeric Tradition.* Lanham, MD: Lexington Books.
Karageorghis, V.
2006 *Aspects of Everyday Life in Ancient Cyprus: Iconographic Representations.* Nicosia: A.G. Leventis Foundation.
Karouzou, S.
1954 *Corpus Vasorum Antiquorum. Grèce. Athènes, Musée National, Fasc. 2.* Paris: Librairie ancienne Honoré Champion.
Killen, J. T.
2001 Religion at Pylos: the evidence of the Fn tablets. In R. Laffineur and R. Hägg (eds.), *POTNIA. Deities and Religion in the Aegean Bronze Age* (Aegaeum 22): 435–43. Liège and Austin: Université de Liège and University of Texas.
Kirk, G. S.
1962 *The Songs of Homer.* Cambridge: Cambridge University Press.
Kontorli-Papadopoulou, L.
1987 Some aspects concerning local peculiarities of the Mycenaean chamber tombs. In R. Laffineur (ed.), *Thanatos. Les coutûmes funéraires en Égée à l'âge du Bronze* (Aegaeum 1): 14–60. Liège: Université de l'Etat à Liège, Histoire de l'art et archéologie de la Grèce antique.
Lang, M. L.
1969 *The Palace of Nestor at Pylos in Western Messenia. Vol. 2. The Frescoes.* Princeton: Princeton University Press.
Latacz, J.
1996 *Homer, his Art and his World* (translated from the original German by J. P. Holoka). Ann Arbor: University of Michigan Press.
Lord, A. B.
1960 *The Singer of Tales* (Harvard Studies in Comparative Literature 24). Cambridge, MA: Harvard University Press.
Maas, M. and J. M. Snyder
1989 *Stringed Instruments of Ancient Greece.* New Haven: Yale University Press.

McCallum, L. R.
1987 *Decorative Program in the Mycenaean Palace of Pylos: the Megaron Frescoes*. PhD Dissertation, University of Pennsylvania.
McNally, S.
1969 An Attic Geometric vase in the collection of Mt. Holyoke College. *American Journal of Archaeology* 73: 459–64.
Nagy, G.
1979 *The Best of the Achaeans: Concepts of the Hero in Archaic Greek Poetry*. Baltimore: John Hopkins University Press.
1996 *Homeric Questions*. Austin: University of Texas Press.
2003 *Homeric Responses*. Austin: University of Texas Press.
Popham, M. R. and L. H. Sackett
1968 *Excavations at Lefkandi, Euboea 1964–66*. London: Thames & Hudson.
Rolston, B.
1991 *Politics and Painting: Murals and Conflict in Northern Ireland*. Rutherford, NJ: Fairleigh Dickinson University Press.
Scholes, P. A.
1970 *The Oxford Companion to Music* (10th edition, revised and edited by J. O. Ward). London: Oxford University Press.
Shelmerdine, C. W.
1996 From Mycenae to Homer: the next generation. In E. de Miro, L. Godart and A. Sacconi (eds.), *Atti e Memorie del Secondo Congresso Internazionale di Micenologia*: 467–78. Rome: Gruppo editoriale internazionale.
Sherratt, E. S.
1990 'Reading the texts': archaeology and the Homeric question. *Antiquity* 84: 807–24.
Slenczka, E.
1974 *Tiryns: Forschungen und Berichte 7. Figürlich bemalte mykenische Keramik aus Tiryns*. Mainz am Rhein: von Zabern.
Snodgrass, A. M.
1998 *Homer and the Artists: Text and Picture in Early Greek Art*. Cambridge: Cambridge University Press.
Wegner, M.
1968 *Archaeologia Homerica: die Denkmäler und das frühgriechische Epos, Kapitel U: Musik und Tanz*. Göttingen: Vandenhoeck & Ruprecht.
West, M. L.
1981 The singing of Homer and the modes of early Greek music. *Journal of Hellenic Studies* 101: 113–29.
Wright, J. C.
2004 A survey of evidence for feasting in Mycenaean society. *Hesperia* 73: 133–78.
Younger, J. G.
1998 *Music in the Aegean Bronze Age* (Studies in Mediterranean Archaeology and Literature, Pocket-book 144). Jonsered: Paul Åström.
2007 The Aegean bard: evidence for sound and song. In S. Morris and R. Laffineur (eds.), *EPOS. Reconsidering Greek Epic and Aegean Bronze Age Archaeology* (Aegaeum 28): 71–78. Liège/Austin: Université de Liège/University of Texas at Austin.

Chapter 5

Remembering and Forgetting Nestor: Pylian Pasts Pluperfect?

Jack L. Davis and Kathleen M. Lynch, with a contribution by Susanne Hofstra

> *What [the Cyclopean walls of the Argolid] indicate is the handiwork of the great constructing race or races, made up of several elements, who migrated into Greece, and elsewhere on the Mediterranean, from the south and east, and who exhibit an usual, though perhaps not an invariable connection with the Poseidon-worship, a worship, with which the Cyclopean name is, through the Odyssey, perceptibly associated, and which is one of the main keys, as I have long been persuaded, wherewith in time to unlock, for Hellenic and Homeric regions, the secrets of antiquity* (Gladstone 1878: viii).

Mycenaean Remembrances and Homeric Resonances

Philologists, archaeologists, and amateurs alike, since the beginnings of our discipline, have supposed the existence of intertwined relationships between the material remains of prehistory, Homer, and the epic tradition. Gladstone imagined that the *Odyssey* was key to unlocking the significance of the Argolid's Cyclopean walls. More recently Korfmann asserted that he regarded 'Homer as a "contemporary witness", that is, as reporting on what was the condition of Ilios in about 700 B.C.E.' (Korfmann 2000: 32; also 2001: 39–40). How earlier prehistoric 'sanctuaries, tombs, and habitation sites structured the landscape in certain parts of Greece' (Antonaccio 1994: 80) during the Iron Age is also a theme that has, in the past two decades, generated an enormous bibliography.

Waterhouse saw the fame of Dark Age cult practice in the Polis Cave of Ithaca (supposing its origins in Mycenaean times) as a determinant of Odysseus's central role in Homeric epic (Waterhouse 1996: 312–13; cf. Malkin 1998: 117), and imagined that those who left dedications in the cave were expressing a wish 'to emulate not merely a general heroic concept but also quintessential episodes in the lives of the heroes emulated'.

Homeric associations of monuments at Mycenae, particularly tombs, were postulated already in Antiquity and were then again drawn in modern times (e.g. see Gell [1810: 30–44], at the start of the nineteenth century, or by Venetian travelers and surveyors, more than a century before [e.g. Malliaris 1997: 45; Lavery and French 2003: 1–2]). In antiquity cults were established in its prehistoric ruins. A monumental temple of Athena was constructed in the seventh century on the acropolis, following worship in Geometric times (Klein 1997). There were historical cults of Perseus and Enyalios, and dedications made to Agamemnon at the Agamemnoneion by the fourth century (French 2003: 26, 58, F4:16; Antonaccio 1994: 92; also Antonaccio 1995: 147–51 for doubts about earlier activity in honour of Agamemnon).

Similar associations have been explored elsewhere. The Archaic sanctuary of Menelaos and Helen at Therapne lies adjacent to a Mycenaean mansion, presumed by some to have been the place identified with the palace of the Homeric king (e.g. Catling 2009: 456); but this idea has now largely been abandoned since the discovery of the palace at Ayios Vasilios. However, prehistoric remains recently found under the altar do raise the possibility that a cult was established there in the Late Bronze Age (in opposition to Antonaccio's scepticism [1995: 155–66], now see Whitley et al. 2006: 37).

The situation is ambiguous in the case of the Acropolis of Athens and for Tiryns. The two limestone column bases within the foundations of the Archaic 'Old Athena' temple on the Acropolis do not seem to derive from the porch of a Mycenaean megaron; at least one is not *in situ* and both are later in date than the Mycenaean period (Iakovides 1962: 62–64; 2006: 65–68; Nylander 1962; Hurwit 1985: 237). Little else, if anything, can be assigned to a Bronze Age palace (Iakovides 1983: 87; 2006: 190–96).

At Tiryns Archaic monumental remains are documented (Schwandner 1988: 269–88) and Archaic inscriptions attest to cults of Athena, Herakles, and Zeus (Verdelis, Jameson and Papachristodoulou 1975). And it was long believed that the megaron of the Bronze Age palace served as a prototype for the cella of a post-Bronze Age Hera temple (Building 'T') built over it (Iakovides 1983: 19; Mylonas 1966: 48–49), remains that Frickenhaus (1912) dated to the seventh century. Blegen (1921: 130–34) argued, to the contrary, that Building 'T' belonged to the latest Mycenaean period, while recent excavations (Maran 2000; 2001; 2006) have shown that he was correct. Building 'T' was a twelfth century BC construction, perhaps a meeting hall of the elite, no longer a megaron serving a full range of palatial functions.

It is perhaps surprising that, until recently, Pylos was one of the few major Mycenaean and Homeric centres not to have figured significantly in discussions of religious continuity or the ritual reuse of Bronze Age sites. Antonaccio (1994: 92) only briefly mentions evidence for activities post-1200 BC, the 'extent and purposes' of which she considers to be unclear. But, since her last publication (Antonaccio 1995: 100–01), it has been announced that, in the historical period, three successive temples were built at this former palatial site, and even that parts of a mould for a large-scale bronze cult statue have been identified.

Such hypotheses were developed in the course of the preparation of an actual state plan of the architectural remains at the Palace of Nestor by members of a team organised and directed by Frederick Cooper of the University of Minnesota (among the preliminary publications of that project, see particularly Griebel and Nelson 1993; Brenningmeyer

2000; Verfenstein 2000; Jackson and Ross 2000; Nelson 2001) and have been presented most fully in Todd Brenningmeyer's PhD thesis (2003). Evidence for historical cult has been adduced principally from three parts of the site: in Court 88, between the Main Building and the Southwestern Building; in the northwest around the so-called 'Circular Building' 87; and in the southeast, in the area of Court 42 and Court 47 (Fig. 5.1).

Brenningmeyer's dissertation expands and elaborates several arguments developed in an earlier MA thesis submitted to the University of Minnesota by Charles Griebel (1993). Griebel had argued that a Dark Age village was built over the ruins of Palace of Nestor, one that consisted of five architectural units, which, in part, employed walls of the Bronze Age structure. The hypothesis of later cultic activities at Pylos was not an entirely new idea: Coulson (1986: 68–69) suggested that the presence of Dark Age pottery was probably related to 'some ritual or sacrifice connected with hero worship'. Schachermeyr (1980: 235) had already attributed the existence of certain Late Helladic IIIC groups of vases in the remains of the palace to a *Ruinenkult*.

The idea that Pylos enjoyed a significant afterlife has been cited in recent synthetic studies (e.g. Eder 1998: 147). There are, in our view, serious reasons to be cautious in accepting the proposition that an historical cult was established in the ruins of the Palace of Nestor. Unlike Mycenae, Tiryns, and Athens, there is no ancient written

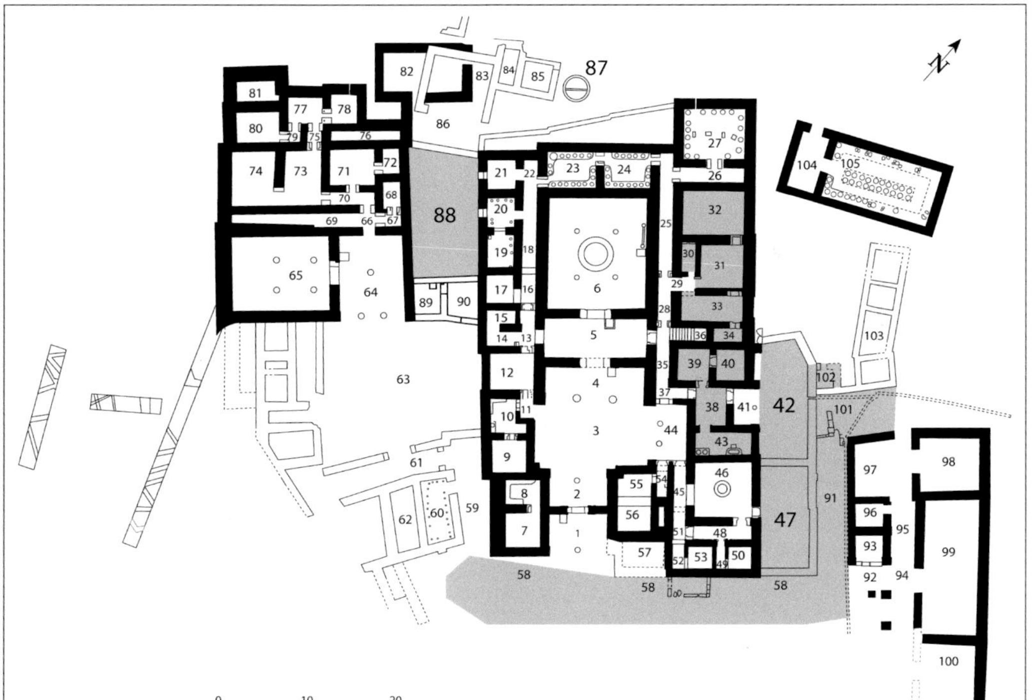

Fig. 5.1: The Palace of Nestor and location of principal groups of post-Bronze Age pottery. R. J. Robertson after M. E. Nelson, with permission.

testimony suggesting that the 'correct' location of Pylos was known to Greeks of historical times. To the contrary, already in pre-Roman times, the Palace of Nestor was consistently identified with the citadel of Paleonavarino on the bay of modern Pylos (McDonald 1942), and never with a location on the Englianos Ridge (see further discussion below).

We are thus dependent on material remains alone to test the hypotheses of the Minnesota team. So is there, in fact, convincing evidence that Messenians of Classical antiquity associated Homeric or other epic traditions with the ruins on the Englianos Ridge that we now call the Palace of Nestor, the Bronze Age name of which we know was Pylos? Although post-Bronze Age remains were noted by Blegen and Rawson elsewhere in and around the ruins of the palace (e.g. Griebel and Nelson 2008) and have recently been found in still other locations nearby, we focus here on a re-examination of the three locations, and the finds from which Brenningmeyer rested his case.

Post-Bronze Age Stratigraphy at the Palace of Nestor

Blegen and Rawson wrote in reference to the palace that:

> ... it is clear that the entire complex of buildings was in use and fully occupied until the end ... the furniture, equipment, and other contents not carried by the plunderers, remained in various states of damage and disintegration, buried in the ruins under the debris of walls, floor, and roof. This was the end of human occupation at the site (Blegen and Rawson1966: 424).

Still, Blegen and Rawson obviously did not mean this statement to be taken literally, since, in their published reports, they frequently described the discovery of 'Geometric' pottery.

Because of such indications of a continuing post-Bronze Age human presence at the site, doubts have long been expressed about the date and character of the destruction of the palace itself.

Mervyn Popham (1991) suggested a date in early Late Helladic IIIB for the destruction, with a reoccupation in advanced IIIC or the early Iron Age, propositions which, have, however, been refuted by Penelope Mountjoy (1997) and, more recently, by Salvatore Vitale (2006: 190–91). Vitale accepts Mountjoy's observations that there are transitional and early IIIC features in the pottery from the final destruction of the palace, which he assigns to his Late Helladic IIIC, Phase 1 – a conclusion that seems warranted by the stratigraphy.

As already noted, it has been argued that the site enjoyed a cultic aftermath after the final destruction. In the earth used by Blegen and Rawson for backfilling parts of the archaeological site, Cooper's University of Minnesota team found unstratified finds that they believe attest to a tradition of historical cult practice. These discoveries provided the impetus for Griebel and Nelson's and Brenningmeyer's studies.

The pottery from this earth is presumed to have been discarded by Blegen and Rawson (Jackson and Ross 2000), and thus represents finds they did not wish to retain in the Hora Museum. Jackson and Ross mention 'Dark Age (Nichoria periods I–III), Archaic, Classical, Hellenistic, and occasional Roman wares that have parallels with both local pottery and pottery from Laconia and elsewhere in the Peloponnese.' Brenningmeyer (2003) has claimed that roof tiles from the backfill belong to three separate roofing systems for temples: one, Corinthian of the late seventh century; a second, Laconian of the sixth century; and a third, of the fourth century. Several terracotta fragments are said to derive from simas and akroteria associated with these temples. Iron objects from Court 42 supposedly were dedicatory spits. In addition, the 'Circular Building' 87 is interpreted as a temple altar, and walls to the west of it as temple foundations (Rooms 83, 84, and 85) (Fig. 5.1).

We do not intend here to critique Brenningmeyer's PhD thesis in detail prior to its revision and full publication, but it seems worth noting that his attempt to determine the original find-spots of the roof tiles from the backfill has not been entirely successful and arguments that they derive from three successive roofs of temples are not convincing thus far. For example, while it is true that Rosemary Hope recorded a few fragments of possible Corinthian tiles in Court 88 (Brenningmeyer 2003: 29, 75–80), the artefacts to which she referred seem to be fragments of a terracotta chimney (Elizabeth Blegen also found the same in this court), a Mycenaean-type drain, and a pithos.[1] More significantly, the total weight of the 'Corinthian' tiles recovered by the Minnesota team was only ca. 55 kg., perhaps the equivalent of only two complete tiles.

Among the pottery we ourselves have examined in the Museum of Hora, the fourth century is not represented (see Appendix I). And Brenningmeyer's restoration of temples on foundations excavated by Blegen's team to the west of the 'Circular Structure' (Brenningmeyer 2003: 25) depends on the unlikely assumption that, among the finds recovered there, George Papathanasopoulos, an experienced excavator, as well as Blegen and Rawson, mistakenly identified tiles as pithos sherds.

Brenningmeyer's arguments based on tile finds thus do not seem compelling. The Cincinnati team did not find masses of tiles, such as might have derived from the collapse of temple roofs. And there may be other explanations for the presence of small quantities of tiles at the site. Fragments of Corinthian and Laconian tiles have been found to be widely distributed in most landscapes of southern Greece that have been targets of intensive survey. Might a few have been used at the Palace of Nestor for secondary purposes? Can the possibility even be excluded that Archaic or Classical tiles were brought to the site much later than the time of their production – for example, for use in the small building that in Medieval times was built over the gateway of the early Mycenaean fortification wall (Blegen et al. 1973: 6; Davis and Stocker 2013)?

What was the character of artefacts other than tile retained by the Cincinnati team from excavations in the areas of Court 88, Court 42 and Court 47, and the 'Circular Building' 87 (Fig. 5.1)? What can be said about their association with architectural remains? Does their nature attest to cultic activities?

Court 88 is a large rectangular space, everywhere paved in the final phase of the palace, with a thick plaster floor, on top of which was set a small structure, consisting of Rooms 89 and 90. The excavation of this area was complicated, and was accomplished over a number of years in no really systematic manner (Fig. 5.2). A half-dozen archaeologists

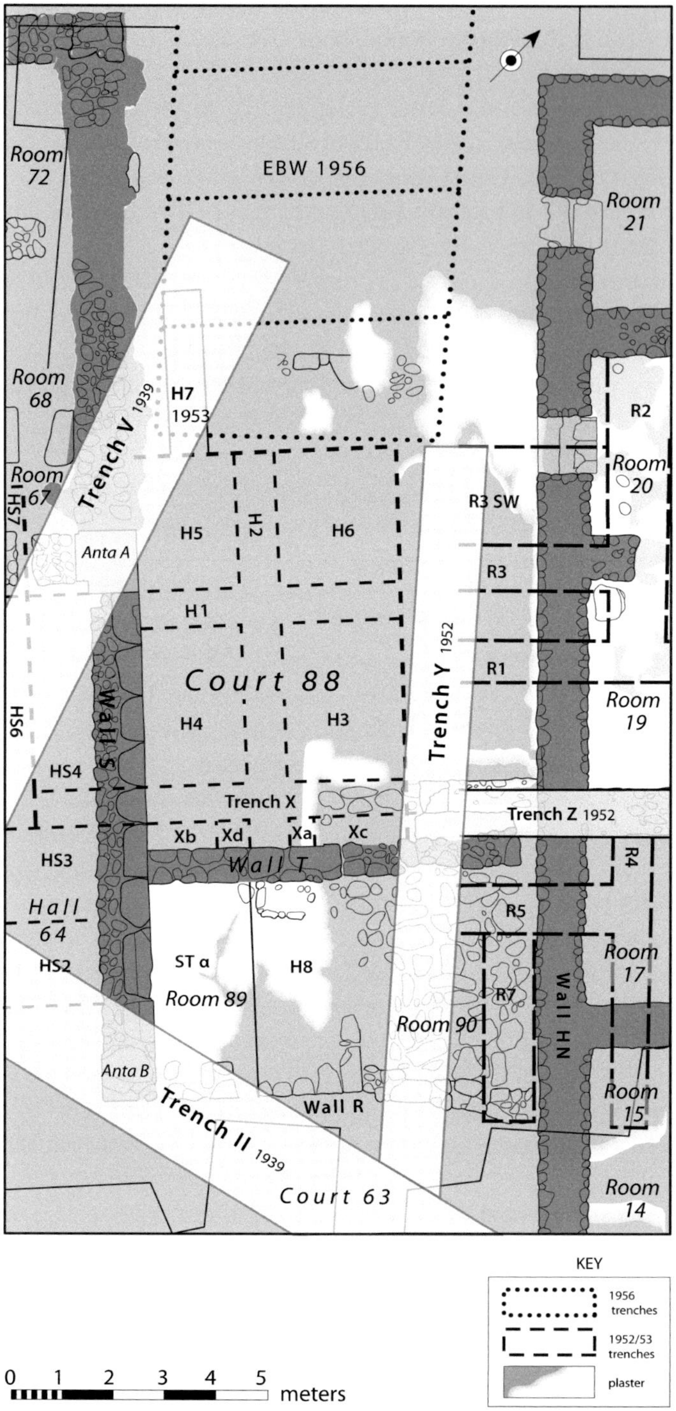

Fig. 5.2: Court 88 with excavation trenches. R. J. Robertson and J. L. Davis.

were involved: George Mylonas in 1952; Rosemary Hope, William A. McDonald, and Marion Rawson in 1953; Robert Buck in 1954; and, finally, Elizabeth Blegen in 1956.

Because each researcher employed his or her own idiosyncratic approach to excavation, the quality of information recorded is remarkably varied, as is the quantity of pottery retained in the storerooms of the Museum of Hora. Nonetheless, from notes made prior to the discard of any ceramics, it is clear that most excavators were careful to save a representative sample of what was recovered. Groups of pottery from the parts of Court 88 excavated by Rosemary Hope and by Elizabeth Blegen are particularly large and diverse. Hope kept approximately 75 sherds and these may constitute nearly all the post-Bronze Age pottery that she found.

It was argued by Blegen and Rawson that Rooms 89 and 90 were, in the seventh century BC, inserted between the Main Building and the Southwestern Building as an oil-pressing facility. Michael Nelson and Charles Griebel have more recently suggested that the structure was a house of the Dark Ages (Griebel and Nelson 1993; Nelson and Griebel 2008), part of Griebel's Dark Age village. Griebel (1993: 12–17) fully discusses the architectural history of these two rooms, and their relationship to each other and to the stucco floor of the court.

The finds from Mylonas's explorations of Rooms 89 and 90 do not clearly date their walls to the Dark Ages. From his Trench Y, which included part of Room 90, comes a large fragment of a deep bowl of Late Helladic IIIB, while all finds from his Trench STa, entirely within Room 89, date to the final phase of the Mycenaean palace. The walls of Rooms 89 and 90 contain ashlar blocks, apparently reused from outer walls of the palace, but this fact alone cannot support a Dark Age date. Ashlar blocks were being recycled, and had, in fact, ceased to be cut anew, already by the time when the final palace was built in Late Helladic IIIB (Nelson 2001: 187–216, esp. 179–87). But it is clear that Rooms 89 and 90 are later than the stucco floor of the court, which must date to the final period of the palace.

There is no question that a certain amount of post-Bronze Age pottery was discovered in Court 88, and it is clear from Mrs Blegen's descriptions that she found it down to the level of the floor of the court. (See Griebel [1993: 12–13] on this point [contra Blegen and Rawson 1966: 294]: he argues that the court was cleared of debris from the final destruction of the palace before being occupied in the Dark Ages.) What is surprising, however, is the variety of periods represented among the retained sherds. They are not all 'Geometric', even if Blegen and Rawson employed this term to refer to material as late as the seventh century. Although sherds retained by Hope may all date to Coulson's Dark Age III phase at Nichoria (i.e., the end of the ninth to the mid-eighth century BC; see Coulson 1983: 96–109), some of Elizabeth Blegen's finds are as late as the sixth century BC. Nevertheless, no characteristics of the pottery point to cultic activities (see Appendix 1).

Court 42 and its vicinity is a second principal location where a significant quantity of post-Bronze Age pottery was found, and, most significantly for Brenningmeyer, the 'iron spits' already mentioned. Post-Bronze Age pottery was recognized in Courts 47, 58, and 101, most often in levels near the surface (Blegen and Rawson 1966: 203–08, 227–30, 326–29). In Room 39, Blegen and Rawson described a 'very black layer with stones' that marked the northwestern limit of an 'intrusive deposit of Late Geometric times' (Blegen and Rawson 1966: 175). They imagined that the dark earth resulted from olive oil seeping into the ground from the oil-pressing facility, although mentioned in connection with Court 88 (for other suggestions, see Antonaccio 1995: 101).

In Room 40, this black earth continued deeper and was thought responsible for the pitting, and sometimes total erosion, of the surface of the ashlar limestone blocks that formed the outer wall of the palace (Blegen and Rawson 1966: 177). Blegen and Rawson speak of 'a good deal of Geometric ware for the most part coated with black or brownish glaze' in the black layer, which pottery they date to the end of the seventh century (1966: 177–78). In Court 42, the black layer reached the stucco floor of the Mycenaean room, and it was possible to reconstruct in whole or in part four nearly complete Dark Age pots from within its matrix (Blegen and Rawson 1966: 184).

These parts of the palace were explored in 1955 and 1956 by Marion Rawson, whose methods and practices were more rigorous than those of most other excavators. (For trench and architectural plans, see Rawson's field notebooks: 1955: 13, 110 and 1956: 13.) We can thus be even more certain than elsewhere that retained finds are representative: even thumbnail-sized body sherds are preserved and labelled with their precise excavation unit. While, as in Court 88, some of the sherds, like the restored vessels published by Blegen and Rawson, date to Coulson's Dark Age III (the finds deriving from a relatively few large smashed vessels), other periods include Early Geometric, Late Geometric, Archaic, Classical, and even Middle Hellenistic. It is thus far from certain that the extensive (Nelson and Griebel 2008: 98 and 99, fig. 48) black stratum described by Blegen and Rawson in the area of Court 42 and Court 47 was exclusively associated with Dark Age artefacts. As for Court 88, nothing in the character of the assemblage from these rooms is indicative of cultic activities, and the supposedly dedicatory 'iron spits' from Court 42 are more likely nails (see Appendix 2).

Finally we turn to 'Circular Structure' 87. Just as there is no evidence that historical tiles were found in this part of the site, Blegen and Rawson reported no post-Bronze Age pottery in association with Structure 87 or nearby. Nor did George Papathanasopoulos, the excavator, mention historical-period ceramics in his 1958 notebook where he described groups of context-pottery (Papathanasopoulos 1958: 88–99). To the contrary, he believed that a stratum over the 'Circular Structure' represented debris from the destruction of the palace. Blegen's own comments on June 17th, 1958, are instructive: 'The whole thing looks to me as if it belongs to a late phase – the latest [sc. of the palace]' (Blegen 1958: 80).

The Palace of Nestor Acropolis in Its Local Context

There is a pressing need to insert the acropolis where the Palace of Nestor stood into the overall picture of human settlement on the Englianos ridge. Only in this way is it possible to grasp the significance of the exiguous post-Bronze Age remains on and around the ruins of the palace itself. There are published finds from the 'Lower Town' recovered in trenches excavated by Rawson in 1960 on the Anastasopoulos property (not indicated on Fig. 5.1: Blegen and Rawson 1966: 21, fig. 347:982; 1973: 62). In 2006 and 2007, we re-examined pottery from these trenches. Mixed with Bronze Age was a small amount of Dark Age pottery; all diagnostic fragments came from drinking vessels, probably cups. It was in the 'Lower Town' that Coulson believed that a larger Dark Age community would be found if one had existed (Coulson 1986: 68–69).

On the basis of fieldwork sponsored by the Pylos Regional Archaeological Project, it is now clear that, after the Bronze Age, there was little activity in many places on the ridge, but far from obvious that the ruins of the palace were a focus for it (Fig. 5.3). Small quantities of Geometric (and Archaic) pottery were widely distributed over the area of the 'Lower Town'. More recently, excavations in 2012–2013 in the former upper parking lot of the archaeological site, in association with the construction of new touristic facilities, uncovered additional Dark Age finds there.

This picture of Dark Age activity at and around the archaeological site is echoed by finds from nearby cemeteries: e.g. the Kokkevis tholos, dated by Coulson to 975–850, his Dark Age II (Coulson 1986: 48-51) and pottery from the Volimidia chamber tombs, for the most part dated to the Late Geometric period (Coulson 1988: 73–74; see also Antonaccio 1995: 94–100).

Clearly a small number of people lived in the ruins of the palace and nearby after its final destruction. How dense and continuous that settlement was remains unclear. We have found no evidence for the practice of cult among finds retained by Blegen and Rawson. Did they miss evidence for post-Bronze Age ritual? Did they deliberately ignore it? Did they hide evidence from us? Rawson's meticulous records speak to the contrary. In addition, the subject of religious continuity had interested Blegen since he published Korakou as a graduate student. Would he have avoided addressing it at Pylos?

Finally, there are other reasons to doubt that a cult with Homeric resonances was established in the ruins of the Palace of Nestor, since it does not seem obvious that in antiquity the Englianos Ridge was tied to the epic tradition in the imagination of Messenians. Nor is there evidence elsewhere in Messenia for the establishment of cult places in the remains of Mycenaean settlements (although it is true that shrines of Geometric and Archaic date are in general rare in Messenia [see Brückner, Engel and Kiderlen 2006, 191, n. 8; also Davis 2008: 277–78]). For example, a temple uncovered recently on the grounds of the 'Costanavarino' resort near Pylos, although near a Mycenaean settlement at Romanou, is not obviously associated with it (Rambach 2012).

Hollows in the debris of the Palace of Nestor, former courts in particular, were doubtless used for shelter until the walls that defined them collapsed totally. But it was not cult in their ruins that was responsible for the tradition reported by Strabo that a Palaipylos lay under Mt Aigaleon. As Marinatos (1952: 496; 1955: 162–63) long

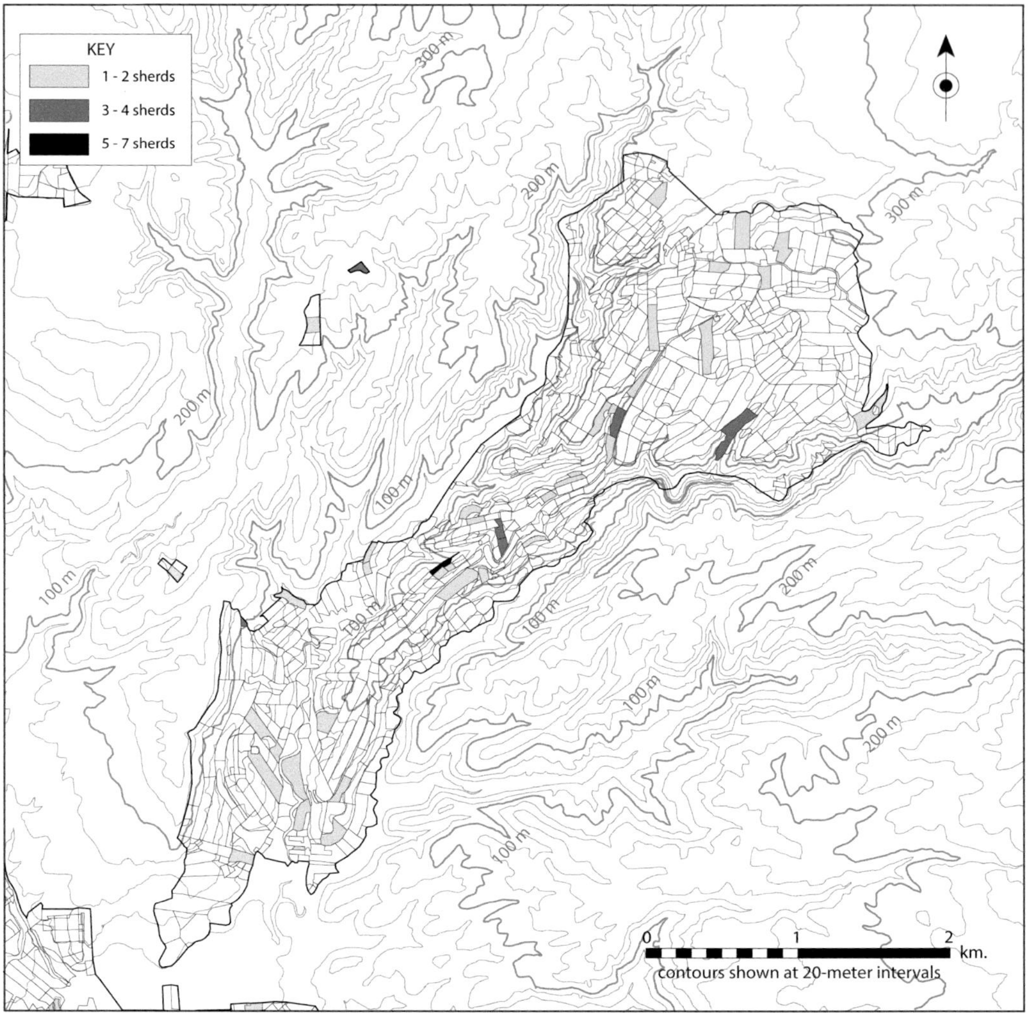

Fig. 5.3: Post-Bronze Age pottery on the Englianos ridge. Data from Pylos Regional Archaeological Project. R. J. Robertson and S. F .S. Heath.

ago suggested, it was probably the discovery of tombs at Volimidia in later historical times that lay behind that tradition. Mycenaean tombs in Messenia commonly did remain a focus for cult (Alcock 1991: 460–62, and with references to earlier studies by Korres; Alcock 2008; Hatzi-Spiliotopoulou 2001: 293–97).

But when historical Messenians sought the home of King Nestor, would not Palaionavarino, a lofty acropolis like that of Agamemnon at Mycenae, have seemed a more suitable location for it than the Englianos Ridge? A location near the sea might easily be deduced from descriptions in Book 3 of the *Odyssey*. It was at coastal

Koryphasion, of course, that Pausanias (4.36) located Pylos, King Nestor's house and grave, and that of Thrasymedes, his son. Mylonopoulos (2003: 421) has suggested, moreover, that connections between a cult of Poseidon and Nestor, as expressed in the *Odyssey*, had evolved at a time when Pylian associations were displaced to Koryphasion.

In conclusion, evidence from the excavations of the Palace of Nestor at Pylos and from historical records does not support the hypothesis that there were historical period temples or hero cults on the Englianos Ridge. Instead, a review of archaeological finds, primarily ceramics, indicates that small-scale activities did occur within the ruins of the palace in historical times. How frequent and continuous these were, we may never know.

Appendix 1: The Post-Bronze Age Pottery

In the Museum of Hora in 2006 and 2007 most retained post-Bronze Age pottery from Blegen's excavations at the Palace of Nestor was reviewed. Finds were distributed in a subset of rooms of the palace (Fig. 5.1). There follows a general characterisation of the chronological and formal range of the ceramics. As already noted, we are confident that excavators retained at least representative, potentially diagnostic fragments, and in some trenches all fragments, recognising them as post-palatial and of potential significance for documenting the later history of the site. It is likely, however, that post-Bronze Age undecorated fine wares and coarse wares were culled, as they are nearly absent among the sherds that now remain. True 'minimum number of vessels' counts are thus impossible to determine; all non-joining fragments are here considered to represent separate vases.

Relative Chronology of the Post-Bronze Age Pottery

Of 126 fragments examined, 86 dated to the Iron Age, or to Coulson's 'Dark Age' (DA) generally, 11 to the Geometric period (plus two dated sometime in the Geometric or Archaic period), 15 to the Archaic period, four sometime in the Archaic or Classical period, three sometime in the Classical or Hellenistic period, one certainly to the Hellenistic period, and one each to the Roman and Early Modern periods; two fragments could not be closely dated. Even if one adds to these the six Dark Age vessels discussed in Blegen and Rawson (1966: 64, 185, fig. 347), in sum the overall picture reveals severely diminished activity during the immediate post-Bronze Age period, activity which lessens further by the early Archaic period. The scale of decline after the Bronze Age is illustrated well by comparing the 132 mainly fragmentary examples of post-Bronze Age pots with the 2,146 whole pots Blegen counted in a single pantry, Room 21, of the Mycenaean Palace of Nestor. Only one area preserved pottery of the Classical to Hellenistic periods, Court 58, and only five pieces at that.

If there had been an Iron Age, Archaic, or Classical temple on the site of the Palace of Nestor, one would expect much larger concentrations of pottery from these post-Bronze Age periods.

A Conspectus of the 'Dark Age' Pottery

Although the majority of post-Bronze Age pottery belongs to 'Dark Age' types described by Coulson for Nichoria (Coulson 1983; 1986), we do not expect the development of Dark Age ceramic styles at Pylos to be identical with those at Nichoria, nor do we assume Coulson's absolute dates should be applied; however, the sequence described by Coulson provides a framework for discussing most of the Pylos finds of this period.[2]

The most common Dark Age shape from Pylos is a drinking vessel. Most base fragments from the Palace are flat, with a slightly concave underside, and are bevelled to the body. This base form is associated with cups rather than skyphoi, which have a conical foot (Coulson 1983: 79 (DA II), 80; see, for example, Blegen and Rawson 1966: 185 no. 615, 616 fig. 347). Cup bodies are low and squat, and can have everted or straight rims, but the former are much more common at Pylos. The numerous preserved everted rim fragments, therefore, most likely represent cups. Decoration consists of brown to black slip applied and preserved unevenly, often better preserved on the exterior; the underside is usually reserved except for some run-over from the body slip. That Pylos features more cups than skyphoi for the Dark Age period contrasts with the situation at Nichoria, where the skyphos predominates (Coulson 1983: 79).

A few conical bases must, however, be from skyphoi like the well-preserved example from Court 42 (Blegen and Rawson 1966: 347 no. 617, fig. 347). No other horizontal skyphos handles are preserved, but some of the everted rims could belong to skyphoi.

The Dark Age cups at Pylos seem characteristic of Coulson's DA II and DA III periods. Although Coulson could recognise a suite of characteristics that distinguished DA II from DA III at Nichoria,[3] at Pylos only changes in rims and bases reflect chronological developments, while small fragments can only be assigned to the 'Dark Age' in general. DA III cups and skyphoi have thinner walls and sharper, more articulated rims and bases. These forms of rims and bases continue from DA II, but are more refined in DA III than their heavier predecessors. There does not seem to be a significant difference in the distribution of DA II and DA III pottery within the ruins of the palace, suggesting that activities during those two periods (ca. 975–850 BC and 800–750 BC, respectively) were focused in the same locations. Coulson examined five post-Bronze Age vases from the Palace of Nestor, all of which he dated to his DA III period, noting that they '... belong rather to the second half of the Eighth Century B.C.' (Coulson 1986: 67–69, fig. 20, pl. 15:a–f).

It is difficult to differentiate amphorae from oinochoae on the basis of rim, handle, and body sherd fragments; however, rare closed forms are clearly distinguishable from the numerous small, open forms. Of the 86 Dark Age fragments, only five are from closed vessels. In contrast, 14 of the 28 Geometric and Archaic fragments are from closed vessels, a far greater proportion than for those of the Dark Age types. Nor were the Dark Age closed vessels found in contexts with the most Dark Age drinking vessels, except for Court 42. There is evidence for only one krater: a pedestal foot of DA III in Court 42 (Blegen and Rawson 1966: 185 no. 618, fig. 347; Coulson 1986: 67–68 no. 363, fig. 20, pl. 15). Therefore, the ceramic evidence does not attest to the use of communal drinking for social definition, a practice documented elsewhere in Iron Age Greece, for example by the Protogeometric drinking set in the Toumba building at Lefkandi (Catling and Lemos 1990: 3–5) or Dark Age pottery in Unit IV at Nichoria (Coulson 1983).

Coulson thought that the presence of Dark Age pottery in Court 42 and the megaron of the palace may have resulted from its use in a ritual, even in 'hero worship' (Coulson 1986: 68). He associated the black soil of these rooms (discussed above) with ritual burning; however, none of the fragments from Court 42 themselves preserved signs of burning. Thus, it is unlikely that the pottery was placed on an altar or pyre. The extensive deposition of the black earth at the palace and the absence from it of votives and burnt animal bones argue against it being a product of ritual activity.

After the Dark Ages

The ceramic remains do not reflect continuous presence at Pylos from the late Iron Age through the Archaic and Classical periods. Instead, a dramatic drop-off in the Archaic period suggests an even less frequent use of the ruins, perhaps by occasional, even seasonal, occupants, rather than full-time squatters. Closed shapes are more common in these periods than in the Dark Age, but there are far fewer drinking vessels. Nothing in the forms themselves or their decoration (mainly black-glazed) suggests that they represent anything but ordinary, domestic fine ware. The scant quantity as well as the average to poor quality of the pottery speaks against any ritual activity at the site or the establishment of a hero cult in the ruins of the palace. Ceramics are inexpensive offerings, and thus they abound in Archaic sanctuaries (e.g. Pemberton 1989 [Demeter and Kore Sanctuary at Corinth]).

Classical and Hellenistic fragments occurred infrequently, but, with the exception of Court 58, are found in areas of the palace with Dark Age pottery. The area of Court 58, outside the palace proper, preserved the highest concentration of Archaic to Hellenistic pottery (seven fragments), but only a single Geometric fragment (there was no Dark Age pottery). This is the only area of the palace with any signs of Hellenistic activity, but the small number of fragments suggests only temporary or opportunistic use of the space. Nothing about the Classical and Hellenistic fragments is indicative of a 'votive' use. However, the fabric of several of the fragments from Court 58 appears to be tinged gray from burning; only one of the other post-Bronze Age fragments from the palace appeared discoloured from fire. This burning may be result of much later – even modern – activities that occurred in the area of this former court.

Finally, there is only one fragment that might be Roman, a coarseware fragment, possibly of a cooking jar (from Court 42).

The ceramic evidence from the area of the Palace of Nestor in the post-Bronze Age period paints a bleak picture. Activity continued only in certain restricted areas. These few pockets are likely to have been in sheltered corners where still-standing Bronze Age architecture afforded protection (cf. McDonald and Coulson 1983: 322 for a similar scenario during this time at Nichoria).[4] 'Occupants' did not have ceramic sets, but made do with multi-functional cups. There is no evidence for continuity in the socio-political institutions of the Bronze Age palace in the immediate post-Bronze Age period. Towards the end of the Iron Age, activity nearly ceased. The small amount of Archaic and later pottery has no connection whatsoever with ritual or even informal veneration (contrast Morgan and Whitelaw 1991, who review evidence for Iron Age cults in the Argolid, many in association with Mycenaean remains; and Aslan 2011 on evidence for Iron Age ritual at Troy).

The ceramic remains preserve no trace of votive activity: no miniatures, special-use vessels, or dedications exist among the scant fragments. No votive figurines or miniature sculptures are preserved in post-Bronze Age contexts either. Instead, the post-Bronze Age pottery comprises a subset of an ordinary 'domestic assemblage' – a 'subset' because only the fineware components seem to have been recognised and retained by the excavators. If we had the full picture, it would likely include the range of fine- and coarseware pottery found at contemporary Nichoria (Coulson 1983), but in smaller quantities. Even when 'domestic' objects are dedicated in sanctuaries, their status as votives can be recognised by the density of offerings (Pemberton 1989), since sanctuary personnel tidied up pottery dedications from time to time and buried them in refuse deposits. There is no trace of similar behaviour at the Palace of Nestor, and thus no reason to imagine that the palace ruins were regarded as a sacred site in historical times.

Appendix 2: Iron Artefacts from the Site of the Palace

Thirty-two iron artefacts from the Palace of Nestor were examined in 1997 and 1998. Most had been mentioned by Blegen and Rawson in their publication of the palatial buildings and their surroundings (1966), but not all were there described in detail, particularly those from the South Slope of the acropolis. The objects include tools (4 examples); fasteners (24); and small formless fragments (4). None is so distinctive in form or style that it can be dated on the basis of style alone.

Among the fasteners, large nails or spikes (l. 5–10 cm.) are common, most of which were recovered from the South Slope of the acropolis. It is likely, as Blegen and Rawson believed, that the majority, if not all, of these, resulted from Byzantine or even post-Byzantine activities. An axe (CM 4094) found on the Southwest Slope of the acropolis and a knife (CM 4211) found at a high elevation in a trench dug by William Kittredge on the North Slope of the acropolis are probably also later in date. Those found in an excellent state of preservation on the South Slope and in the Southwestern area (CM4094, 4113, 4118, 4122, 4136, 4151) were considered by Blegen and Rawson (1966: 285) to be modern.

Large nails and spikes like those from the South Slope trenches were essential for tying together wooden beams, particularly in door frames and roofs (Shaw and Shaw 2000: 373–86, esp. 381 'Type 2 nail', and table 5.5), and their basic form remained constant over a long period of time. At Nichoria a number of large iron nails and spikes were found in Byzantine and post-Byzantine levels (Rosser 1983: pls. 12-14 to 12-17, figs. 12-21 to 12-25; Aschenbrenner, Hope Simpson and Rosser 1983: 430, figs. 14.3–4). Examples much like those from the Palace of Nestor are preserved in early modern buildings in the area of the palace.

It is extremely unlikely that any of the iron artefacts from Englianos date to the Dark Ages, given what we know about the history of iron use in Greek construction. Tools such as axes and knives were among the earliest iron objects produced in Greece in the Late Bronze Age–Early Iron Age transition (Kübler 1943: 41–42, pl. 38, inv. M49; Snodgrass 1962: 408–10), but, on the Greek mainland, fasteners, such as nails or spikes, were introduced only in the late Archaic period and did not come into regular use until Classical times (see Robinson 1941: 323–28 nos. 1486–1540; Raubitschek 1998: 131, 134–35; compare Shaw and Shaw 2000: 384, for Crete).

Many of the iron objects were, however, found in locations where historical ceramics of pre-modern date were identified. A small cluster of five iron objects (CM3987a, 3987b, 4051, 4051, 4052) was associated with the 'stratum of black earth with small stones' in Court 42 that has been argued to be of Dark Age date, as was an iron nail or spike (CM4024) and an iron nail (CM4003) from Court 58. It is possible that other iron objects (CM3985, 4009, 4014, 4021) from the nearby areas 91, 95 101 and 102 were found in black earth.

Blegen and Rawson's attribution of those objects from Court 42 to the 'Geometric period ... perhaps to the seventh or sixth century', rested entirely on the presumption that they were contemporary with the three complete ceramic vessels in Court 42 (Blegen and Rawson 1966: 184). It is now clear, however, from re-examination of the retained pottery from Court 42 that there was activity in this part of the site as late as Hellenistic times. The size of three iron shafts from Court 42 (CM3987a, 3987b, and 4052) falls, in fact, within the size range of iron spikes found in Archaic and Classical contexts elsewhere (Raubitschek 1998: 140 nos. 504 [l. 23 cm], 505 [16.2 cm], 506 [12.2 cm] and pls. 77–78; Robinson 1941: pl. 94 nos. 1439–82 [max. 19 cm]).

It is, furthermore, likely that the iron shafts in Court 42 found their way to the site at a time when iron was fairly ubiquitous. Although Popham (1991: 317) identified them as iron spits of a type found elsewhere in Greece, Crete, and Ionia in sanctuaries, spits as early as the eleventh–ninth centuries (the date of the three complete pots in Court 42) are rare in the Aegean and seem then only to have been used by members of the elite in lavish feasts of the types described in Homeric epic (e.g. Sherratt 2004: 312–13 and notes 35–39). The earliest iron spit from the Greek mainland comes from a rich grave at Lefkandi, dated to Sub-Protogeometric II (ca. 875–850), but it is not until the eighth century BC that these objects are found in more modest graves and in votive deposits from sanctuaries. They remain uncommon until the sixth century, when they were bundled together as votives (e.g. Simon 1986: 346–52), and only in the Classical period are they regularly found in domestic contexts (e.g. Kostoglou 2003).

In general, an absence of any other rich post-Bronze Age finds associated with the iron finds in Court 42 or elsewhere does not support the proposition that the iron artefacts from the palace were components of votive deposits. Their presence thus provides no basis for concluding that the site was a focus for post-Bronze Age cult. It is, moreover, worth emphasising that the number of iron objects found in Blegen and Rawson's excavations is small compared to quantities typically recovered in excavations of post-Bronze Age sanctuaries: a total of 32 objects compared to 75 from the Greek sanctuary at Kommos (Shaw and Shaw 2000: 373–86) or 137 inventoried nails alone from Isthmia (Raubitschek 1998: 178–81, Appendices 2–4, 6). If the finds from Pylos were associated with ritual use of the site it would also be surprising that the range of bronze objects, typically deposited in large numbers in Greek sanctuaries as votives, is entirely unrepresented.

Acknowledgements

The examination of the post-Bronze Age finds from the Palace of Nestor in 2006 and 2007, on which this study is based, has been a fully collaborative enterprise between Davis and Lynch. The summary of ceramics presented in Appendix 1 is entirely the work of Lynch; the report on iron objects in Appendix 2, of Susanne Hofstra. In the execution of this project we enjoyed the support and collaboration of Sharon Stocker in the field. We are particularly grateful to Xeni Arapogianni, Director of Prehistoric and Classical Antiquities in Kalamata, for facilitating our research. We also thank Michael Nelson and Todd Brenningmeyer for making their unpublished research available to us, and for commenting on earlier drafts of this article.

Notes

1. Hope (1953: 27) mentioned these ceramics, noting 'many pieces of roof tiles (in Basket #5), suspiciously (plan, p. 20) like Corinthian'. Blegen and Rawson later rejected her hypothesis, but retained the finds, which are now labelled: 'Section H8. Heavy tiles. –0.20 to –0.50. RH, p. 27. June 22, 1953'.
2. The term 'Dark Age' is retained here to recall Coulson's study and to distinguish regional Messenian Iron Age pottery from that of a more pan-Hellenic Geometric tradition. 'Geometric', therefore, is applied here to pottery decorated with linear and pattern designs in keeping with styles typically called Early, Middle, and Late Geometric. For a similar distinction at Nichoria, but limited to the Late Geometric period, see Coulson 1983: 109–10.
3. In Coulson's study, differences in decorative treatment and fabric characterise the difference between DA II and DA III. It seems clear that the Pylos Dark Age pottery is coming from a

different production site. Fabric changes do not coincide with formal changes associated with the periods, and almost all drinking cups are plainly decorated.

4. We thank Shannon LaFayette for discussing with us the state of the palace after the conflagration, the subject of her thesis, *The Destruction and Afterlife of the Palace of Nestor at Pylos: The Making of a Forgotten Landmark*, (PhD dissertation, University of Cincinnati, 2011), in which she builds on the ideas presented here.

Bibliography

Alcock, S. E.

1991 Tomb cult and the post-Classical polis. *American Journal of Archaeology* 95: 447–67.

2008 Tomb cult in postliberation Messenia. In J.L. Davis (ed.), *Sandy Pylos: An Archaeological History from Nestor to Navarino* (2nd ed.): 199–204. Princeton: American School of Classical Studies at Athens.

Antonaccio, C.

1994 Placing the past: the Bronze Age in the cultic topography of early Greece. In S.E. Alcock (ed.), *Placing the Gods: Sanctuaries and Sacred Space in Ancient Greece*: 79–104. Oxford: Clarendon Press.

1995 *An Archaeology of Ancestors: Tomb Cult and Hero Cult in Early Greece*. Lanham: Rowman & Littlefield.

Ashenbrenner, S. E., R. Hope Simpson, and J. Rosser.

1983 The site and environs. In W. A. McDonald, W. D. E. Coulson and J. Rosser (eds.), *Excavations at Nichoria in Southwest Greece* III: *The Dark Age and Byzantine Occupation*: 427–34. Minneapolis: University of Minnesota Press.

Aslan, C. C.

2011 A place of burning: hero or ancestor cult at Troy. *Hesperia* 80: 381–429.

Blegen, C. W.

1921 *Korakou: A Prehistoric Settlement Near Corinth*. Boston and New York: American School of Classical Studies at Athens.

1958 Palace of Nestor Excavations. Field Notebook 1958.

Blegen, C. W. and M. Rawson

1966 *The Palace of Nestor at Pylos* I: *The Buildings and Their Contents*. Princeton: Princeton University Press.

Blegen, C. W., M. Rawson, Lord W. Taylour and W. P. Donovan

1973 *The Palace of Nestor at Pylos* III: *Acropolis and Lower Town: Tholoi, Grave Circle, and Chamber Tombs;* Discoveries *Outside the Citadel*. Princeton: Princeton University Press.

Brenningmeyer, T.

2000 Post-Bronze Age architecture at the Palace of Nestor. *American Journal of Archaeology* 104: 329.

2003 *Post Bronze Age Architecture at Ano Englianos: Architectural Commemoration of a Bronze Age Site (Greece)*. PhD dissertation, University of Minnesota.

Brückner, H., M. Engel and M. Kiderlen

2006 Geoarchäologische Studie über das Poseidon-Heiligtum von Akovitika in Messenien. *Archäologischer Anzeiger* 2006: 189–202.

Catling, H.

1977 Excavations at the Menelaion, Sparta, 1973–76. *Archaeological Reports* 23: 24–42.

2009 *Sparta: Menelaion I: The Bronze Age*. London: British School at Athens.

Catling, R. W. V. and I. S. Lemos

1990 Part I: The pottery. In M. R. Popham, P. G. Calligas and L. H. Sackett (eds.), *Lefkandi II: The Protogeometric Building at Toumba*. London: British School of Archaeology at Athens.

Coulson, W. D. E.
1983 The pottery. In W. A. McDonald, W. D. E. Coulson and J. Rosser (eds.), *Excavations at Nichoria in Southwest Greece III: The Dark Age and Byzantine Occupation*: 61–259. Minneapolis: University of Minnesota Press.
1986 *The Dark Age Pottery of Messenia*. Göteborg: Paul Åströms Förlag.
1988 Geometric pottery from Volimidia. *American Journal of Archaeology* 92: 53–74.
Davis, J. L.
2008 From Pausanias to the present. In J. L. Davis (ed.), *Sandy Pylos: An Archaeological History from Nestor to Navarino* (2nd ed.): 273–91. Princeton: American School of Classical Studies at Athens.
Davis, J. L. and S. R. Stocker
2013 The Medieval deposit from the Northeast Gateway at the Palace of Nestor. *Hesperia* 82: 673–731.
Eder, B.
1998 *Argolis, Lakonien, Messenien: vom Ende der mykenischen Palastzeit bis zur Einwanderung der Dorier.* Vienna: Verlag der Österreichischen Akademie der Wissenschaften.
French, E.
2003 Chronological commentary. *Archaeological Atlas of Mycenae*: 26–27. Athens: Archaeological Society.
Frickenhaus, A.
1912 *Tiryns* I: *Die Hera von Tiryns*: 1–126. Athens: Eleutheroudakis and Barth.
Gell, W.
1810 *The Itinerary of Greece*. London: T. Payne.
Gladstone, W. E.
1878 Preface. In H. Schliemann, *Mycenae: A Narrative of Researches and Discoveries at Mycenae and Tiryns*: vi–xl. New York: Scribner, Armstrong & Company.
Griebel, C.
1993 *Archaeological Evidence for a Dark Age Settlement at the Palace of Nestor in Messenia, Greece*. MA dissertation, University of Minnesota.
Griebel, C. and M. Nelson
1993 Post-Mycenaean occupation at the Palace of Nestor. *American Journal of Archaeology* 97: 331.
Hatzi-Spiliotopoulou, G.
2001 Ο 6ος τάφος των Ελληνικών Ανθείας στη Μεσσηνία. In V. Mitsopoulos-Leon (ed.), *Forschungen in der Peloponnes: Akten des Symposium anläßlich der Feier '100 Jahre Österreichisches Archäologisches Institut Athen' Athen 5.3–7.3.1998* (Sonderschriften Band 38): 285–98. Athens: Österreichisches Archäologisches Institut.
Hope, R.
1953 Palace of Nestor Excavations. Field Notebook.
Hurwit, J. M.
1985 *The Art and Culture of Early Greece, 1100–480 B.C.* Ithaca: Cornell University Press.
Iakovides, S.
1962 *Ἡ Μυκηναικὴ Ακρόπολις τῆς τῶν Ἀθηνῶν*. Athens: The Archaeological Society at Athens.
1983 *Late Helladic Citadels on Mainland Greece*. Leiden: E.J. Brill.
2006 *The Mycenaean Acropolis of Athens* (The Archaeological Society at Athens Library 240). Athens: The Archaeological Society at Athens.
Jackson, D. and S. Ross
2000 Postpalatial pottery of the Epano Anglianos ridge. *American Journal of Archaeology* 104: 333–34.
Klein, N.
1997 Excavation of the Greek temples at Mycenae by the British School at Athens. *Annual of the British School at Athens* 92: 247–322.

Kostoglou, M.
2003 Iron and steel currency bars in ancient Greece. *Mediterranean Archaeology and Archaeometry* 3: 5–12.
Korfmann, M.
2000 Troia-Wilusa: 1999 Ausgrabungen. *Studia Troica* 10: 1–52.
2001 Troia-Wilusa: 2000 Ausgrabungen. *Studia Troica* 11: 1–50.
Kübler, K.
1943 *Kerameikos* IV: *Ergebnisse der Ausgrabungen. Neufunde aus der Nekropole des 11. und 10. Jahrhunderts.* Berlin: Walter de Gruyter.
LaFayette, S.
2011 *The Destruction and Afterlife of the Palace of Nestor at Pylos: The Making of a Forgotten Landmark.* PhD dissertation, University of Cincinnati.
Lavery, J. and E. French
2003 Early accounts of Mycenae. *Archaeological Atlas of Mycenae*: 1–4. Athens: Archaeological Society.
Malkin, I.
1998 *The Returns of Odysseus: Colonization and Ethnicity.* Berkeley: University of California Press.
Malliaris, A.
1997 *Alessandro Pini: Ἀνέκδοτη περιγραφή της Πελοποννήσου.* Venice: Instituto Ellenico di Studi Bizantini e Postbizantini di Venezia.
McDonald, W. A.
1942 Where did Nestor live? *American Journal of Archaeology* 46: 538–45.
McDonald, W. A. and W. D. E. Coulson
1983 The Dark Age at Nichoria: a perspective. In W. A. McDonald, W. D. E. Coulson and J. Rosser (eds.), *Excavations at Nichoria in Southwest Greece III: The Dark Age and Byzantine Occupation*: 316–29. Minneapolis: University of Minnesota Press.
Maran, J.
2000 Das Megaron im Megaron: zur Datierung und Funktion des Antenbaus im mykenischen Palast von Tiryns. *Archäologischer Anzeiger* 2000: 1–16.
2001 Political and religious aspects of architectural change on the Upper Citadel of Tiryns: the case of Building T. In R. Laffineur and R. Hägg (eds.), *Potnia: Deities and Religion in the Aegean Bronze Age. Proceedings of the 8th International Aegean Conference/8e Rencontre égéenne internationale* (Aegaeum 22): 113–21. Liège/Austin: Université de Liège/University of Texas at Austin.
2006 Coming to terms with the past: ideology and power in Late Helladic IIIC. In S. Deger-Jalkotzy and I. S. Lemos (eds.), *Ancient Greece: From the Mycenaean Palaces to the Age of Homer* (Edinburgh Leventis Studies 3): 123–50. Edinburgh: Edinburgh University Press.
Marinatos, S.
1952 Ανασκαφαί εν Πύλῳ. *Πρακτικά της εν Αθήναις Αρχαιολογικής Εταιρείας* 107: 473-96.
1955 Παλαίπυλος. *Altertum* 1: 140–63.
Morgan, C. and T. Whitelaw
1991 Pots and politics: ceramic evidence for the rise of the Argive state. *American Journal of Archaeology* 95: 79–108.
Mountjoy, P.
1997 The destruction of the Palace of Nestor reconsidered. *Annual of the British School at Athens* 92: 109–37.
Mylonas, G. E.
1966 *Mycenae and the Mycenaean Age.* Princeton: Princeton University Press.
Mylonopoulos, I.
2003 *Πελοπόννησος οἰκητήριον Ποσειδῶνος: Heiligtümer und Kulte des Poseidon auf der Peloponnes* (Kernos Supplement 13). Liège: Centre International d'Etude de la Religion Grecque Antique.

Nelson, M. C.
2001 *The Architecture of Epano Englianos, Greece.* PhD dissertation, University of Toronto.
Nelson, M. C., and C. Griebel
2008 The Englianos hilltop after the Palace. In J. L. Davis (ed.), *Sandy Pylos: An Archaeological History from Nestor to Navarino* (2nd ed.): 97–100. Princeton: American School of Classical Studies at Athens.
Nylander, C.
1962 Die sog. mykenischen Säulenbasen auf der Akropolis in Athens. *Opuscula Atheniensia* 4: 31–77.
Papathanasopoulos, G.
1958 Palace of Nestor Excavations. Field Notebook 1958.
Pemberton, E. G.
1989 *The Sanctuary of Demeter and Kore: Corinth: Results of the Excavations Conducted by the American School of Classical Studies* XVIII.1: 18, part 1: *The Greek Pottery.* Princeton: American School of Classical Studies at Athens.
Popham, M.
1991 Pylos: reflections on the date of its destruction and on its Iron Age reoccupation. *Oxford Journal of Archaeology* 10: 315–24.
Rambach, J.
2012 Από τον Πάμισο έως τον Ταΰγετο: προϊστορικοί χρόνοι. In A. Vlachopoulos (ed.), *Αρχαιολογία: Πελοπόννησος*: 474–79. Athens: Melissa.
Raubitschek, I.
1998 *Isthmia: Excavations by the University of Chicago, under the Auspices of the American School of Classical Studies at Athens. The Metal Objects (1952–1989).* Princeton: American School of Classical Studies at Athens.
Rawson, M.
1955 Palace of Nestor Excavations. Field Notebook 1955.
1956 Palace of Nestor Excavations. Field Notebook 1956.
Robinson, D. M.
1941 *Excavations at Olynthus* X: *Metal and Other Miscellaneous Finds.* Baltimore: Johns Hopkins Press.
Rosser, J.
1983 The small finds. In W. A. McDonald, W. D. E. Coulson and J. Rosser (eds.), *Excavations at Nichoria in Southwest Greece III: The Dark Age and Byzantine Occupation*: 405–20. Minneapolis: University of Minnesota Press.
Schachermeyr, F.
1980 *Die ägäische Frühzeit* IV. *Griechenland im Zeitalter der Wanderungen: von Ende der mykenischen Ära bis auf die Dorier.* Vienna: Österreichische Akademie der Wissenschaften.
Schwandner, E.-L.
1988 Archäische Spolien aus Tiryns. *Archäologischer Anzeiger* 1988: 269–84.
Shaw, J. and M. Shaw
2000 *The Greek Sanctuary. Kommos 4.* Princeton: Princeton University Press.
Sherratt, S.
2004 Feasting in Homeric epic. *Hesperia* 73: 301–37.
Simon, C. G.
1986 *The Archaic Votive Offerings and Cults of Ionia.* PhD dissertation, University of California, Berkeley.
Snodgrass, A. M.
1962 Iron Age Greece and Central Europe. Archaeological notes. *American Journal of Archaeology* 66: 408–10.

2001 *The Dark Age of Greece: An Archaeological Survey of the Eleventh to the Eighth Centuries B.C.* New York: Routledge.

Verdelis, N., M. Jameson and I. Papachristodoulou
1975 Ἀρχαικαὶ ἐπιγραφαὶ ἐκ Τίρυνθος. *Ἀρχαιολογικὴ Ἐφημερίς* 1975: 150–205.

Verfenstein, C. D.
2000 Industrial waste and the evidence for bronze casting at post-Bronze Age Pylos. *American Journal of Archaeology* 104: 337.

Vitale, S.
2006 The LH IIIB-IIIC transition on the Mycenaean mainland: ceramic phases and terminology. *Hesperia* 75: 177–204.

Waterhouse, H.
1996 From Ithaca to the Odyssey. *Annual of the British School at Athens* 91: 301–18.

Whitley, J., S. Germanidou, D. Urem-Kotsou, A. Dimoula, I. Nikolakopoulou, A. Karnava and E. Hatzaki
2006 Archaeology in Greece 2005-2006. *Archaeological Reports* 52: 1–112.

Chapter 6

In the Grip of their Past? Tracing Mycenaean *Memoria*

Diamantis Panagiotopoulos

'... memory is not simply history without footnotes'
—(Winter 2006: 6)

In the second half of the twentieth century, the social sciences experienced a 'memory boom' that had a powerful and lasting impact on several academic disciplines (Olick and Robbins 1998: 105–40; Connerton 2006; Winter 2006: 17–51, 286–88). Notions of 'past' and personal or collective 'remembrance' dominated culture theory and generated many productive debates, creating a vast and still growing body of literature. Despite the justifiable critique against the inflationary use of the term 'memory' and its dubious innovativeness (Klein 2000: 127–29), the new theoretical tenet opened our eyes in many ways to the premises and modes of remembering and forgetting. Scholarly interest shifted from the static concept of the 'past', as a former reality with normative strength, to the dynamic concept of 'memory' as a mental process shaped by human agency. The versatility of the novel theoretical approaches aspired to do full justice to the complexity and wide array of this cultural phenomenon. One of the most crucial insights of this recent awareness is related to the concept of 'shared' or 'collective memory'. Contrary to individual memory, an essentially neurophysiological ability, the memory of collectives has always been a social construction (Klein 2000: 130). In his ground-breaking studies on collective memory, M. Halbwachs vividly demonstrated that shared remembrance was not just an accumulation of individual memories, but a cultural product, which grew in a definite social frame through communication and interaction of a group's members (Halbwachs 1925; 1950). In past and present, societies have formed and activated collective memories not just for preserving a remote past, but primarily as a means of sustaining their corporate identity (see also Lowenthal 1985: 197–200). Halbwachs' main results were later elaborated upon in the seminal works of F. Yates (1966), P. Connerton (1989) and J. Assmann (1997), which represent three of the most influential contributions on the subject in the past years. This intense scholarly inquiry has enhanced our understanding of the social significance of memory and illuminated the modes, motifs and repercussions of communally constructed remembrance.

The new focus on the social processes of shared remembrance has provided a very effective methodological tool in archaeology and related disciplines, generating fresh approaches in the study of prehistoric Europe (Bradley 2002; Williams 2003) the ancient Near East (Jonker 1995), classical antiquity (Foxhall 1995; Small 1997; Gehrke 2001; 2003; Alcock 2002; Flower 2006), or even across disciplinary borders (Van Dyke and Alcock 2003; Fewster 2007). Situated in an archaeological context, the exploration of mnemonic strategies has endeavoured to go beyond the established issues of 'tradition' and tomb or hero cult. The awareness of social memory and the dynamics of its physical, architectural and material setting extended the interests of our discipline in a host of new directions. Scholars have focused on the role of mortuary practices in the construction of the past (Williams 2003), stressed the mnemonic qualities of monuments (Bradley 1998; Cummings 2003; Hope 2003) or highlighted the significance of the past in the ancient present (Bradley 2002; Lucas 2005: 77–92).

Despite its pervasiveness in current cultural studies and its application in archaeological explanation, the concept of collective memory has acquired only marginal importance in Aegean archaeology so far (Hamilakis 1998; Day and Wilson 2002: 145–47; Blakolmer 2006). There is an obvious reason for this reluctance, which is related to the extent and nature of the pertinent archaeological record. As will be demonstrated below, however, the encounter with issues of collective memory in Mycenaean culture is a methodologically risky but worthwhile venture. Contrary to many theoretical tenets, which dominate recent debates in our discipline, social memory resembles no modern theoretical construct, but refers to a paramount aspect of ancient culture, an existing mental concept, which can provide lucid insight into social behaviour in pre-modern societies. A further advantage of applying this term to the study of Mycenaean and ancient Greek cultures is that it embraces the spheres of both myth and history. The broad semantic field of collective memory seems thus to reflect the way in which Mycenaeans and Greeks experienced their past more accurately, namely as a former reality in which mythological and historical events were intricately intermingled with one another (Eder 2004: 105). The significance of shared remembrance lies in any given event's meaning for living society and not in the historicity or accuracy of a particular remembrance. Consequently, when the boundaries between truth and fiction become blurred in the remembered past, the concept of memory has a semantic advantage which can indeed provide us with a 'therapeutic alternative to historical discourse' (Klein 2000: 145; see also Nora 1989: 8–11). To be more specific, the employment of this theoretical concept in a Mycenaean context might help us to avoid the intricate and possibly fruitless discussion as to whether a narrative image corresponded to the actual past or to a mythical tradition.

The aim of the present paper is to deal not with the Mycenaean past, a term meaning the Mycenaean heritage as seen from the viewpoint of Iron Age Greece, but with the Mycenaeans' past and thus to proceed one step further – or rather deeper – in historical time. After a short comment on the validity of our sources, the paper will follow two major threads. The first section will seek to give an account of Mycenaean commemorative actions as they are reflected in words, things, monuments and images. In the second section, we will situate our perspective in the city of Mycenae, attempting a contextual overview of the mnemonic strategies of a single site. This paper will close with a consideration of how the questions addressed here may have some relevance to Homeric studies.

Critique of the Sources

Speaking about the past in past societies, one wonders, first and foremost, whether it is feasible to trace social memory as a collective experience and a conscious social action without the aid of pertinent written information. Linear B tablets show a very narrow temporal frame – including the current and the last year – and cannot be regarded as archives in the strict sense of the term (Driessen 1994–95: 244; 2000: 14; Pluta 1996–97: 238, n. 10; Palaima 2003: 169). This is, of course, not the appropriate place to speculate about the existence of other types of records in perishable materials (see Bennet 2001: 27–29; contra Driessen 1994–1995: 244; 1999: 209; Driessen 2000: 14), although it is obviously crucial to our understanding of Mycenaean mnemotechnics to know whether this culture used writing as an external storage place for historical records that could be retrieved later on. If the Mycenaeans used writing only for a very narrow set of administrative purposes, then commemorative acts, monuments or things would have been the main mode of remembering the past. Since Linear B does not provide any clear evidence about remembrance or the significance of the past for the Mycenaeans, we must rely on archaeology alone. The relevant evidence is scarce and ambiguous when compared with the affluent testimonies of other ancient societies, but the situation is not entirely hopeless. Archaeology is in some cases able to discern different layers of historical time in one and the same archaeological horizon. Old things or monuments surviving in the Mycenaean present resemble a tangible past, sustained, activated or manipulated by a conscious act of remembrance. Based on such testimonies, we can indeed document two kinds of *memoria* in Mycenaean palatial culture: a) a sustained or passive remembrance, that is to say tombs and heirlooms as visible protuberances of the past in the dimension of present, which can be experienced or used in many ways, and b) an active remembrance enshrined in memorials and commemorative images, which represent a conscious and deliberate reference to the past. It must be stressed that the first, and passive, kind of memory is ambiguous. An awareness of past relics demands a dynamic tension between what one sees and what one knows to have existed once. The mere existence of an old monument or tomb in the Mycenaean present cannot be an unequivocal proof of a purposeful encounter with a former reality. The same lack of intentional bias applies also to old words, things or visual images, which are transmitted from generation to generation through the unbroken stream of tradition. In these cases, we can only detect the form and not the substance of collective memory.

A Bird's Eye View of Mycenaean *Memoria*

Let us consider first Mycenaean palatial society as a cultural entity in terms of space and as an historical continuum in terms of time, not because we have any clue about *one* polity or *one* society with a uniform cultural behaviour (Shelmerdine 1999; Deger-Jalkotzy 2006: 19–20, 30–31; Dickinson 2006b: 26–29), but because it is impossible to unravel the rope of history into its separate geographical strands due to our fragmentary evidence. How can we trace earlier strata of time in a given Mycenaean archaeological horizon? We can do so in the realms of words, things, monuments and visual language.

Words

As mentioned above, Linear B texts do not provide any sufficient information about the significance and mechanisms of collective memory. It seems that the only glimpse of a conscious bond with the past is the mentioning of ti-ri-se-ro-e, a 'Thrice Hero', in two Pylian tablets (Fr 1204 and Tn 316), where he appears among divine figures as recipient of cult offerings (Antonaccio 2006: 383–85). Provided that the interpretation of the name is correct, this record is welcome evidence of what we would otherwise suspect, namely that a hero cult did exist in the Mycenaean period. We may even assume, without running the risk of overinterpreting our evidence, that both the *wanax* and the palatial elite promoted the veneration of their ancestors and the construction of heroic descent. The tendency of aristocratic dynasties to carry back their pedigree to a divine or mythical primogenitor is a very common phenomenon throughout history. Unfortunately, there is nothing else that unambiguously points to former times, except perhaps in the case of some recurring Mycenaean personal names in Linear B texts. It has been suggested that Mycenaean high officials (the 'collectors' in particular) adhered to a limited stock of personal names, which they had obviously inherited from former generations (Killen 1979: 177). Once again, this a very common phenomenon in societies with aristocracies. G. Neumann described these personal names as 'piety names' since they bear witness to a respectful attitude towards the ancestors (Neumann 1992: 433; 1994: esp. 128; see also Palaima 1999: 370; Deger-Jalkotzy 2006: 19). This is an attractive hypothesis indeed, but it rests on very weak evidence (Rougemont 2001: 135).

Things

Material culture always comprises the accumulated knowledge of former developments and therefore preserves manifold traces of the past. As stressed above, the transmission of forms and techniques from one generation to another, this 'artifactual route to the past' (Lowenthal 1985: 244), results from a repetitive incorporating practice and cannot be regarded as conscious acts of remembrance (Nora 1989: 13; Lucas 2005: 77–85). An intentional reference to the past can only be detected in cases of a deliberate use or abuse of things produced by former generations. In Mycenaean palatial culture, there are only weak traces of such a dynamic awareness of the past, in other words, old objects that document a community's shared memory of the past as collective action or – at least – collective experience. So far, the archaeological exploration of major Mycenaean centres has uncovered nothing similar to the 'Cenotaph Square' of Akrotiri, where a group of Early Cycladic figurines were ritually deposited in a stone platform by some members of the Late Bronze Age community (Sotirakopoulou 1998; Blakolmer 2006: 19–20). In the Mycenaean period, there is no comparable group of old objects invested with memories and symbolic meaning, which were consciously preserved and placed or exhibited in a public area. The discovery of a Cycladic violin-shaped figurine in a Late Helladic IIIB room in Thebes, which yielded a significant group of inscribed nodules (Piteros 1983: 133), is without doubt a remarkable find, but it is too exceptional to demonstrate a pattern of social behaviour. What remains among Mycenaean artefacts as a reference to the past is the use of heirlooms. Durable objects, used by more than one generation, possessed their own 'personal biographies' and served as a tangible link between present and past (Kopytoff 1986; Rowlands 1993: 144; Hoskins 1998; 2006; Gosden and Marshall 1999; Bradley 2002: 49–52; Bennet 2004: 93–95). But, even in these cases, it is difficult to speak unconditionally about collective memory in the strict sense of the term, since the social context of this appropriation of the past is not society but kinship, since heirlooms are usually a concern of individuals or families. The use of old seals in the palaces of the late thirteenth century BC for administrative purposes (Pini 1990: 115; Bennet 2005: 268) provides a very good example of the employment and symbolic significance of heirlooms in the high echelons of Mycenaean society. High-quality seals and signet rings seem to have survived long after the generation of their manufacturers, not just as treasured items but retaining the same function throughout centuries. Even if the early date of some of these pieces can be disputed (see below), there can be no doubt that many pieces used in Late Helladic IIIB were indeed heirloom seals, demonstrating a very strong bond between past and present, perhaps a family tradition of handing down from father to son the insignia of office and power. But even in this case, we may assess only a social *habitus*, and not a conscious reference to the past as a collective experience.

A further possible indication for the survival of old things in the Mycenaean present may be found in Mycenaean procession frescoes (Fig. 6.1), in which female participants are depicted in Minoan-style costumes (Muskett 2004). The question whether or not these clothes were Minoan remains open. If so, then we are dealing with an archaistic iconographical convention derived from Minoan prototypes, or alternatively with the stipulation of a ritual code, according to which women had to wear clothes of Minoan design on certain ceremonial occasions. In both cases, it

Fig. 6.1: Mycenaean women dressed in 'memory saturated' clothes? Procession fresco from the Mycenaean palace at Ano Englianos (after Lang 1969: pl. O).

would be legitimate to regard these ceremonial clothes as 'memory-saturated fabrics' (Schneider 2006: 204) and therefore as a deliberate reference to the past, either at the level of images or at that of ritual practice.

Places/Monuments

P. Nora's collaborative study on the French *lieux de mémoire* (Nora 1984–92), one of the most ambitious and influential works on collective memory, demonstrated the vital importance of a spatial benchmark or frame for anchoring a group's shared remembrance. The roots of this insight stretch back into antiquity. In ancient mnemotechnics, some text or idea to be remembered by an individual had to be associated with a part of a real or imagined building or with an image of a place (Yates 1966: 27–49). In quite the same manner, collectives need 'places', where memory can be sustained and retrieved (Barrett 1999; Connerton 2006: 318–19; Rowlands and Tilley 2006). We conserve our recollections by linking them to the physical and architectural milieu that surrounds us. Places or monuments as visible points of reference acquire the role of spatial and temporal markers, giving the realm of collective remembrance a structure (Knapp and Ashmore 1999: 13–14; Buikstra and Charles 1999). Such loci not only serve to commemorate a past event, achievement or person by their mere presence; they also provide a social arena for communicative events, in which a community's individuals can collectively remember. For instance, the totemic landscapes of the Australian Aborigines (Taçon 1999) or memorial buildings are spaces in which people could become aware of the past or construct it. There can be little doubt that this two-fold mnemonic role of places and monuments was valid for most ancient societies. A sacred landscape or a memorial acted as a tangible reminder of the past and at the same time as a stage for ritual performances, ceremonies or gatherings, where the diversity of individual recollections was channelled into a single repository of homogenised remembrance. Memorial buildings may further possess a third, prospective, dimension of time, if seen as an attempt by a given societal group 'to formulate the memories of the future' (Bradley 2002: 109). Turning back to the context of Mycenaean culture, we have to face again the problem of a discouraging archaeological record. The evidence for commemorative monuments in Mycenaean cities is very weak. In fact, if we exclude the late stage of Mycenae's history, to which we shall return in the course of our contextual approach (see below), there is virtually no evidence at all. The sporadic re-occupation of old tombs is the only attestation of a conscious reference to the past.[1] Given the absence of structures commemorating former realities, we may assume that this role was fulfilled by cemeteries and tombs or places of memory, which cannot be traced by archaeological means. Funeral monuments or landscapes may have served as the only Mycenaean bridges to the past, acting as backdrops for framing social memory. In that case, the lack of relevant evidence could be meaningful. Mycenaean culture may be regarded as a further example of a pre-modern society, in which collective memory was conveyed and sustained by 'noninscribed' modi, such as ritual performances (Connerton 1989). Unfortunately, the character and symbolic content of these ceremonial events, which are quite often narrated in visual images, remain unknown to us, due to the paucity of relevant written evidence.

Images

In the realm of Mycenaean visual culture, the fresco programmes of the palaces represent our most important source for notions of collective memory. This applies both to a) medium-sized or miniature friezes with narrative intent, which commemorate single events or achievements, and b) stereotypical procession frescoes, which refer to recurring ceremonial occasions (Fig. 6.1). Collective memory was built up not only from former deeds situated in a specific point of the past, but also from rituals whose repetitiveness ensured the coherence of a group in space and time. The difference in size undoubtedly reflected a deliberate difference in visual impact. The procession frescoes, with their almost life-sized proportions, the formal images and the repetitive figures, incarnated what we could describe as 'monumental' in Mycenaean art. On the other hand, narrative friezes with their great wealth of details could have a didactic quality, since they provided a visual reference and starting-point for relating or singing the depicted action. The role of Mycenaean images acting as prompts to the generation of stories is indicated by the well-known fresco of a lyre-player associated with a feasting scene (Fig. 6.2) in the main megaron of the Pylian palace (Bennet 2001: 34; 2004: 96, 100). The difference in size between the lyre-player and the feasting community implies that the first was situated in

Fig. 6.2: The eye and the ear of the beholder: Depiction of a lyre-player in a fresco from the main megaron of the Mycenaean palace at Ano Englianos (after Wright 2003: fig. 13).

a different temporal and spatial sphere. In fact, this figure intervenes between the feasting scene and the viewer. The precise meaning of this unparalleled complex narrative strategy, which appeals both to the eye and ear of the beholder, remains unknown. The lyre-player could have served as a prompt for the viewer to narrate the story or, alternatively, as an allusion to the fact that the depicted feast was the visual translation of an epic poem. Either way, the feasting scene resembled a focal point in the shared remembrance of the Pylian elite, a story that was both visually and orally commemorated. This case demonstrates the significance of the Mycenaean royal court not only as political or administrative institution, but also as intellectual centre, an arena of multimedia communication, where the ties with the past were kept alive through oral performances and visual images (see also Sherratt, this volume).

These observations are, of course, nothing terribly new. What appears to be far more interesting, however, is the fact that these images were always displayed in the interiors of palaces. As such, they addressed only a limited audience, the resident elite and its guests, other elite members of society or high officials. Consequently, the visual perception of collective memory through painted images in Mycenaean times was a privilege of the upper classes. It is important to acknowledge that the absence of commemorative visual images in public contexts is part of the general lack of public images in Mycenaean palace society. Apart from the Lion Gate relief in Mycenae (see below), there are virtually no stelai, reliefs or statues that were displayed in a public sphere. The populace of Mycenaean cities seems to have lived in an aniconic social landscape, which contained only miniature-sized images on seals, signet rings and pictorial pottery. Given this fact, one may wonder to what extent the masses really participated in and identified themselves as a subject of the elite's shared remembrance.

Artistic style

Style as a medium of artistic expression has acquired a two-fold significance in archaeology (Earle 2002: 162–63). First, as vehicle of a passive tradition, style reveals the 'mental template' of ancient craftsmen, the inherited concepts of the proper form of things and visual images. Second, as an active form of communication, style elucidates how individuals or groups negotiated social status and identity. Both dimensions of style, the passive and active one, can be very meaningful when interpreting social mentalities, in this case how Mycenaeans treated their past. As already noted, the unbroken stream of cultural tradition, the commitment to the legacy of previous generations, lacks the intentional character of a commemorative act (Lowenthal 1985: 57–62). What really matters for our purposes is how rigid and conservative the transmission of artistic style from one generation to another was, and how the tension between tradition and innovation developed in the Mycenaean context.

We may all agree that the development of Mycenaean imagery in the course of three to four centuries is predictable and unadventurous. After the Shaft Graves art, there is nothing essentially new in repertoire and style. A single exception worth mentioning in this respect is the development of the Boeotian painted larnakes, which belong to

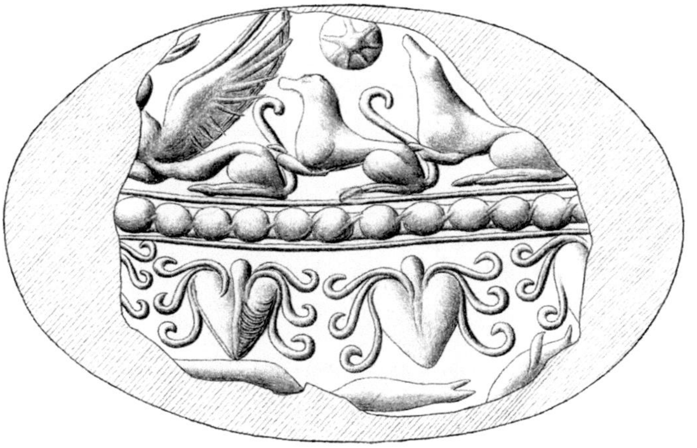

Fig. 6.3: Heirlooms or artistic conservatism? Seal impression from the Mycenaean palace at Ano Englianos (after Pini 1997: pl. 17, no. 39).

a rather different and very difficult chapter of Mycenaean art (Panagiotopoulos 2007) that is beyond our scope here. The conservative and repetitive character of Mycenaean art is clearly visible in virtually all branches of artistic tradition. This conservatism is so extreme, that, beyond pottery decoration, we have serious difficulties in distinguishing and chronologically arranging stylistic phases in most artefact classes, including seals and wall paintings. Who could securely date a Mycenaean signet ring, like the extraordinary example from Pylos, which is unfortunately known to us only through its impression on several nodules, showing a double-frieze composition with griffins, lions and nautili (Fig. 6.3)? The proposed dating of this and similar signet rings in Late Helladic IIIA rests only on stylistic criteria and on the prevailing view that the production of high quality seal engraving ceased by the end of that period (Younger 1981: 270–71; 1987: 58; Rutter 1992: 62; Dickers 2001: 109). This last assumption forces us to accept that at the apex of Mycenaean sealing administration in the thirteenth century BC nearly all officials at the Mycenaean palaces used seals or signet rings which were at that point of time 100 to 200 years old (Palaima 1990: 247; Hallager and Hallager 1999: 311; Hallager 2005: 261–62). Does this make any sense? The existence of heirlooms is unquestionable. But why should we exclude the possibility that a signet ring like the above-mentioned one, which corresponds perfectly to the frescoes of the Pylian palace (Bennet 2001: 34–35), was manufactured in the thirteenth century BC, following a stylistic tradition that remained virtually unchanged over several generations or even centuries? Why should we think that Mycenaean art evolved at the same fast pace as Minoan art? It is therefore possible that the conservatism of Mycenaean art may have been even more acute than we realise.

The passive acceptance of that which former generations of artists created, the concentration on a very narrow and stereotyped repertoire, has received a pejorative evaluation among modern scholars until recent years. Negative assessments dominated modern narratives of material cultural sequence in Mycenaean Greece. As indicated above, this was primarily the result of the inevitable comparison with the dynamic development of Minoan art. The tendency of Minoan art to reinvent itself after a couple of generations, the seemingly effortless creation of new styles and motif types, is actually a very rare phenomenon in the history of ancient art. Pre-modern artists did not strive to be innovative but were bound to follow the path of their predecessors and to perpetuate canonical values. The viewer had exactly the same expectations as for new works of art. He did not seek creativity but variation on traditional themes. The cyclic material of Mycenaean imagery corresponds perfectly to the highly formulaic nature of Homeric verse, in which the listener is addicted to the charm of recurring epithets and expressions (Russo 1997; Edwards 1997; Clark 2004). When embedded in its social context, the conservatism of Mycenaean art, and its limited repertoire of subjects, could be explained not as an inability of Greek mainland artists to be innovative, but as an indication of a deliberate adherence to tradition and an attempt to preserve cultural values unchanged. The repetition of traditional artistic forms, an unbroken continuity which restrained variety and innovation, could be not just a passive adaptation of tradition but a conscious reference to the past. Seen from this angle, Mycenaean art may be understood as an expression of social stability and the legitimisation of the political status quo. This attitude toward artistic tradition is very common among 'cold societies', a term which was coined by C. Lévi-Strauss (1962: 309–10) and later taken up by Assmann (1997: 66–86). A 'cold society' offers desperate resistance against any change of its structure. A typical example is ancient Egypt, a society which throughout its history – apart from the Intermediate Periods – struggled to freeze historical change in the media of literature and visual imagery. In the same vein, the conservative character of Mycenaean art could be a strong indication of the firm fundaments of this social and political system in which former traditions had acquired a canonical value and conveyed the idea of harmony and order.

Summing up this brief overview of the traces of Mycenaean *memoria* we have to admit that the evidence at hand is meagre. This is by no means an indication that Mycenaean society had only weak bonds with its past. It just shows how difficult any future attempt to discern mnemonic strategies in a society can be, in which noninscribed commemorative practices obviously provided the main vehicle for popular recollection. Rituals, ceremonies, feasts and oral performances, in which the community negotiated its past, are not expected to leave any legible archaeological traces. The very traditional and uninspired imagery, however, offers a good argument for the retrospective tendencies of Mycenaean society. Seen through the prism of their visual language, Mycenaeans were indeed in the grip of their past.

A Microarchaeological Perspective

This broad outline of the visible traces of Mycenaean *memoria* is too conventional to be true, since it ignores the dynamics of space and time. Therefore, it would be worthwhile to attempt a closer, contextual look at the extant evidence which enables us to draw a more accentuated and thus accurate picture of shared memory in the given historical context. The following analysis of Mycenaean mnemonic strategies through a microarchaeological perspective (Fahlander 2003: 1–17) focuses on the site of Mycenae and endeavours to apprehend the practices of collective remembrance as a locally rooted social action. Even in this case, we have to begin by acknowledging the gaps in our evidence. A study of shared remembrance in the community of palatial Mycenae is bound to a single context of social activity: the sepulchral sphere. This is a very narrow perspective indeed, yet there is hardly anything else that could be unequivocally related to the collective memory of this social group. Nevertheless, we must keep in mind that the remembrance of the deceased resembles the origin and core of collective memory (Assmann 1997: 60–63). Let us see what happened in Mycenae after the era of the Shaft Graves, the period during which the city became one of the most powerful centres in the Aegean region. The members of this mighty dynasty were buried in one or perhaps both grave circles (Mylonas 1972/73; 1983: 27–61; Mee and Cavanagh 1984: 48–49; Dickinson 1977: 39–58; Graziadio 1991; Cavanagh and Mee 1998: 28–29, 43–44; French 2002: 31–40) at the edges of the so-called Prehistoric Cemetery (Alden 2000; Iakovides and French 2003: 53). What follows after the abandonment of both grave circles is a long period of latent remembrance. There is no archaeologically visible action pointing to a special significance of these elite tombs in later generations. They were respected, since they remained untouched, but they did not acquire the character of an 'active' place of remembrance, a memorial for the veneration of a glorious or even divine dynasty. The only exception to this rule was the erection of the built tomb Rho above an earlier shaft grave in Grave Circle B, a couple of generations after the end of its use (Mylonas 1972/73: 211–25; Cavanagh and Mee 1998: 47). A powerful family chose as burial place for the deceased not a spot outside the city, in one of the various cemeteries surrounding Mycenae, but within the city borders, and – more important still – on the inside of a distinct burial plot. This late intervention in a highly sensitive sepulchral area was a very cautious operation, since the builders of the new burial monument took over the place of an older shaft grave. The usurpation of a former elite tomb within the well-marked terrain of Grave Circle B was without doubt an audacious act; audacious, because up to that point the community of Mycenae had respected the place, avoiding the construction of a new tomb. The fact that this built grave type is unknown in Mycenaean Greece, having its best parallels in the tombs of Ugarit (Schachermeyr 1967: 39; Mylonas 1972/73: 221–22), underlines the uniqueness of the monument and makes the matter of interpretation even more perplexing. In search of a plausible explanation for this behaviour, we might conjecture that the reoccupation of a burial place reserved for some very distinguished ancestors resembled an explicit attempt to appropriate a 'heroic' past or even to fabricate an ancestral lineage with the members of a glorious dynasty. Even if we are not able to establish the motives for this single action with certainty, we do know that it found no followers. Beside this exceptional event, both grave circles remained unchanged for several generations down to the middle of the thirteenth century. The less important tombs of the Prehistoric Cemetery (Fig. 6.4) experienced a quite

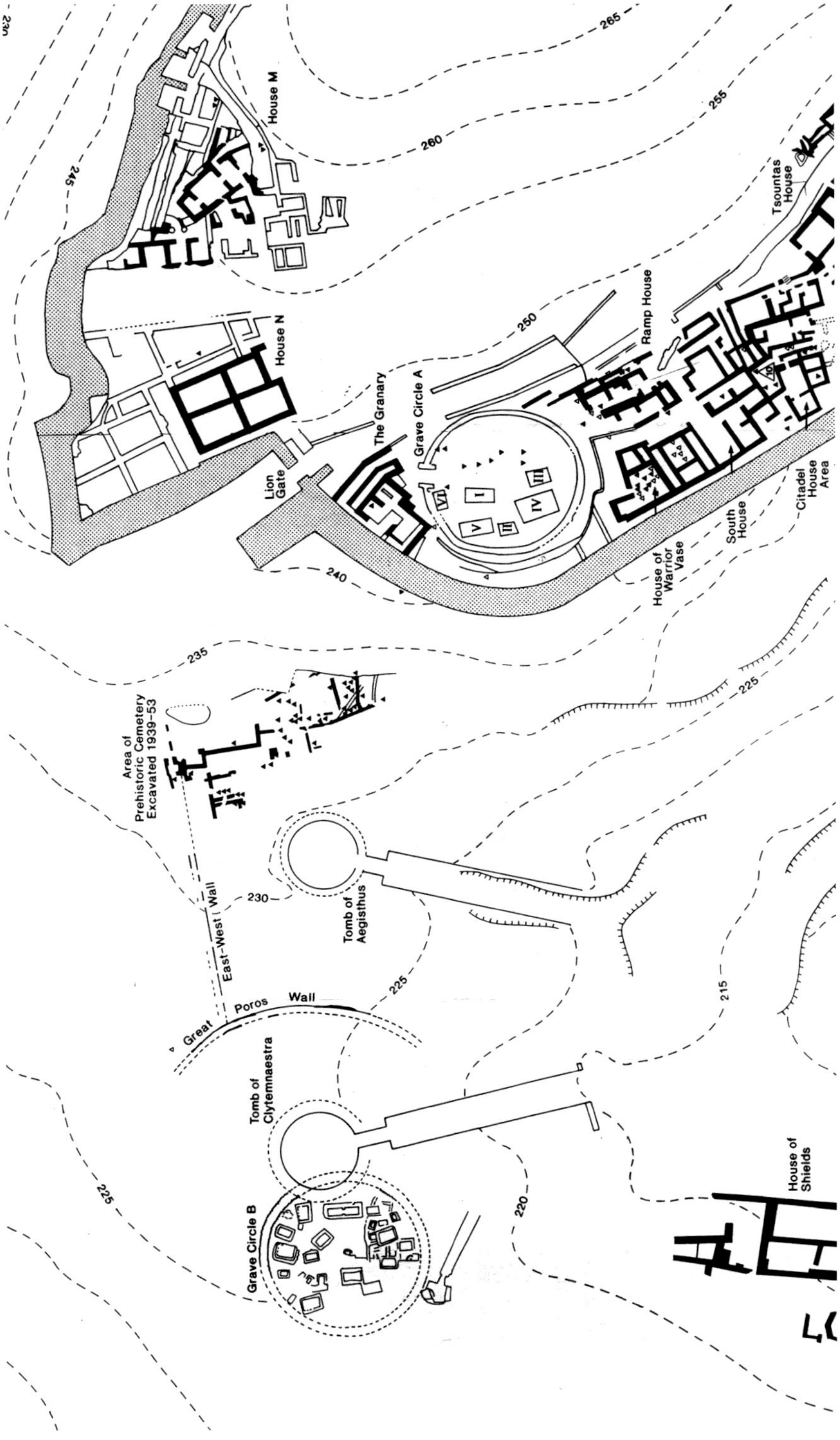

Fig. 6.4: Remembering and forgetting: Mycenae's Prehistoric Cemetery (after Alden 2000: foldout).

different fate, since they fell into limbo. The old burial ground was gradually covered by private houses or other buildings and thus became invisible. Since there was no cultural break between the time of use of the Prehistoric Cemetery and the time of its erasure from the surface of Mycenae's urban landscape, it is really difficult to understand the indifference of Mycenae's community towards these tombs, which must have belonged to their direct ancestors.

This period of latent remembrance ended suddenly in the thirteenth century BC with the initiation of a new building programme at and around the citadel, in the course of which, according to J. Wright's excellent analysis (Wright 1987: 171–84), conglomerate masonry seems to have been employed as a key visual element. This ambitious construction plan included the extension of the massive defensive walls of the citadel, the refurbishment of Grave Circle A (Antonaccio 1995: 49–51; Cavanagh 2001: 129–30; Iakovides and French 2003: 18; Gallou 2005: 21) and the building of the two greatest tholos tombs in Mycenae, that of Clytemnestra and Atreus (Wright 1987: 171–84; Rehak 1992: 40–41; Iakovides 1983: 29–35). It is likely that the entire building programme was the realisation of a single 'master plan', initiated by a ruler who strove to occupy evocative 'nerve' points in Mycenae's urban space with monuments demonstrating his power (Wright 1987: 177–82; Gallou 2005: 24–25, 138).

The most remarkable aspect of the tholos tombs, beyond their admirable size and construction, is the fact that they were erected not outside the city, in one of the thirty cemeteries surrounding Mycenae, but within its urban territory, occupying a public space. The tomb of Atreus, the biggest of all Mycenaean tholoi, lies in a very prominent place on the left side of the road leading from the Argolic plain to the acropolis and is visible from the palace and the acropolis (Iakovides and French 2003: 56). It is likely that its dromos and lavishly decorated façade were not filled up after burial but remained visible for a period of time (Wright 1987: 183). This huge monument was certainly not just a tomb but a mausoleum for a great ruler or his family, a sepulchre founded not among other tombs, but embedded in Mycenae's cityscape. The monument's distance and isolation from the city's burial grounds stressed the significance of the deceased.[2] In the same manner, the slightly later tomb of Clytemnestra was erected within the city boundaries, under the section of the Cyclopean wall, in the area which was previously occupied by the Prehistoric Cemetery (Iakovides and French 2003: 51–52). The huge tumulus that covered this tomb must have had an overwhelming effect upon Mycenae's people (Taylour 1955: 221). The proximity of this tholos to Grave Circle B cannot but be meaningful.[3] In both cases, we can detect an attempt at deliberate association with the old burials which was, however, much more subtle than the transgressive character of the built tomb Rho (Antonaccio 1995: 50). The fact that, during the construction of the Clytemnestra tholos, a part of the Circle B ring wall was damaged, does not really indicate a disrespectful treatment of the old monument. Not only did the old shaft graves within Circle B remain untouched, but the new huge tumulus apparently covered both monuments, thus stressing their intended symbolic nexus.

While the final sleep of the persons buried in Grave Circle B was twice disturbed by later generations, Grave Circle A experienced a quite different fate. The old burial place was transformed into a memorial c. 250 years after it ceased to be used for burials (Fig. 6.5).[4] A new circular parapet of conglomerate blocks was constructed and – in the course of an authentic restoration of the old condition – the old grave stelai were re-erected. The royal burial ground was architecturally and symbolically upgraded to a memorial space and certainly became a focal point in social interaction at Mycenae, since the new arrangement provided an ideal place for congregations (Cavanagh 2001: 129–30; Gallou 2005: 28–29). This massive encroachment on an old monument, which until then had been left untouched, could have been more than a decent act of preserving a remote or neglected past. The likelihood of a cruel manipulation of memory gains credence when viewing this restoration as a part of an orchestrated attempt to construct a politically expedient commemoration in Late Helladic IIIB Mycenae. Only a couple of metres away from Grave Circle A, the monumental entrance of Mycenae received its adequate emblem, the famous Lion Gate relief (Fig. 6.6). The striking similarity in material and construction between the

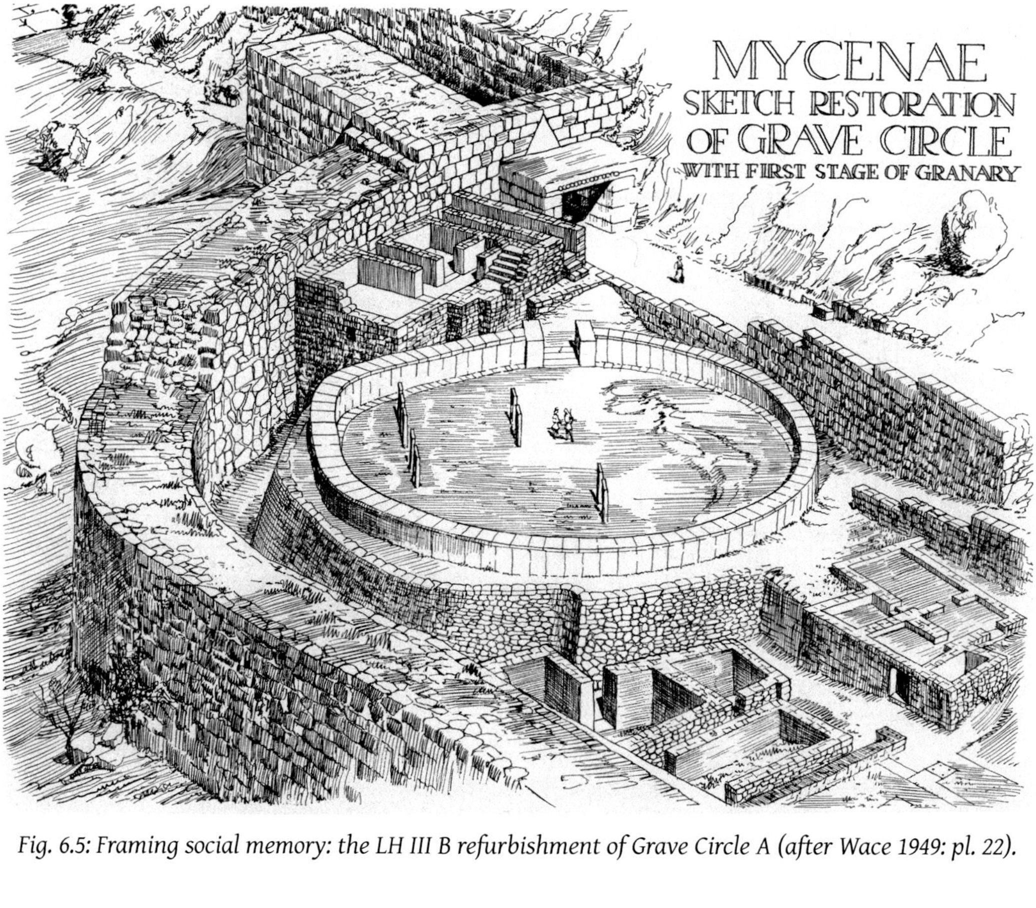

Fig. 6.5: Framing social memory: the LH III B refurbishment of Grave Circle A (after Wace 1949: pl. 22).

Fig. 6.6: A conscious reference to the past? The Lion Gate relief in the citadel of Mycenae (photo by author).

Lion Gate and the monumental tombs of Atreus and Clytemnestra was certainly hard to overlook. The visual appearance and texture of conglomerate stone were probably invested with a symbolic aura. The impressive gate relief (Wace 1949: 51–54; Iakovides 1983: 30–33; Mylonas 1983: 78–84; Iakovides and French 2003: 11–12) may have been the only Mycenaean visual image displayed in a public space. This exceptional work of art has puzzled several generations of archaeologists due to its archaistic style. There can be no doubt that composition and stylistic expression are very close to the art of the fifteenth century BC, so close that it has been suggested that the relief was a spoil from an early Mycenaean monument (see Blakolmer 2006: 21 with further references).[5] If this archaistic style is not the result of an experimental work in a vacuum of artistic traditions of monumental sculpture, we might argue that it deliberately copies earlier works as a means of paying homage to the glorious period of the Shaft Graves dynasty. If so, then we are dealing here with a systematic attempt to manipulate collective memory by a) adopting an archaistic style, b) restoring the tombs of a great dynasty and perhaps using them as a theatre for ritual or commemorative action and c) occupying prominent points of the urban landscape of Mycenae with funerary monuments.

The fact that the desire to establish a genealogical connection with a glorious dynasty comes some 250 years later and only one to two generations before the violent destruction of the citadel might help us to shed some light on the historical background of this project. Curiously, access to the restored Grave Circle A was made impossible by the construction of the Granary House, only a couple of years after the refurbishment work (Laffineur 1990: 202; Gallou 2005: 29). When placed into the historical trajectory of Mycenae, the temporal asymmetry of this restoration becomes striking: it is too remote from the end of use of the burial ground and too close to the final destruction of the acropolis. How can we interpret the belated attempt of a state-directed appropriation of the past? It is a truism that the use or abuse of the past is a favoured political strategy for the establishment of political authority. Ruling elites always try to construct narratives of shared memory, claiming for themselves the role of an eternal order. More important still, mnemonic strategies are activated especially in periods of political or socio-economic crisis. The crucial point is in our case that the need for status legitimisation came for the first time more than two centuries after Grave Circle A fell out of use. The ephemeral character of its 'second life' as a commemorative place at the heart of the city points to a politically motivated plan that was doomed to failure. It is therefore tempting to suggest that this very conscious reference to former times, the attempt to fabricate a heroic pedigree through the veneration of glorious ancestors, was initiated by the first royal dynasty at Mycenae which felt the need to demonstrate a connection to the splendid past, a dynasty which probably did not have any bonds with the royal lineage of this centre at all.

The Question of Relevance

It can scarcely be doubted that the collapse of the Mycenaean palace system at the end of Late Helladic IIIB caused a sharp cultural break and must have triggered a dramatic shift in collective memory (Dickinson 2006a). We do know that the destructions of the palatial centres affected the elite more profoundly than the lower classes. After the collapse of the palatial system, centralised economic structures ceased to function and the local cultures moved down to a lower level of socio-political organisation. We also know that in the period following these destructions (Late Helladic IIIC) the central places of the former Mycenaean citadels in Tiryns, Midea and possibly in Mycenae were reoccupied (Maran 2006: 124–28). It has been suggested that this reoccupation should be understood as a conscious revival of the old palatial system for the legitimisation of those families or groups which now came to power (Maran 2006: 143–44). This interpretation does offer a plausible explanation for the re-enactment of palatial ideology in postpalatial times, yet it is not congruent with all historical scenarios relating to the collapse of Mycenaean culture. If we accept that the main difference between Late Helladic IIIB and Late Helladic IIIC is the absence of the palatial elite, while the lower classes continued to populate the key regions of

Mainland Greece, then it is tempting to ascribe the collapse of the palaces not to a natural catastrophe or foreign invaders, but to a class struggle leading to the expulsion of the royal dynasties (Halstead 1988, 527; see, however, the critical comments of Deger-Jalkotzy 1996b: 716–17, 728 and Dickinson 2006b: 41, 54–55). Following this line of argument, we must pose the question why the Late Helladic IIIC society should adopt the palatial past as the core of its shared remembrance and demonstrate a common bond with the expelled elites? One would rather expect that the *basileis* or other local potentates after the decline of the palatial system would condemn and not adopt it. The reoccupation of the Mycenaean palaces in Late Helladic IIIC is an archaeological fact, but may simply represent the filling of a power vacuum, and not necessarily a deliberate claim of descent from the palatial elites and the creation of a succession of power.

This is exactly the point where the Homeric poems come into play. The combined study of the Mycenaean and Greek Iron Age material culture on the one hand, and Homer on the other, has great potential to answer the new questions which arise in the context of collective memory. The *Iliad*, this 'oral monument' of Greek collective memory, offers us, as an 'official' historical narrative, good insight into the selective strategies of this intellectual process, which included not only remembering but also forgetting. The suggestion of a class struggle at the end of the Mycenaean period – and perhaps even earlier – and the appearance of a new elite in Late Helladic IIIC show how complex the issues of collective memory in this specific cultural context can be. In such a case, it would be reasonable to expect not one but several collective memories. Consequently, if we take a good look at different viewpoints of shared remembrance, and thus different collective memories, we may be able to obtain a fresh perspective on the basis of old evidence. What did Greek Iron Age society actually remember? The Mycenaean palatial system or its short-lived follow-up in the Late Helladic IIIC period (Deger-Jalkotzy 1996a: 23–29; Eder 2004: 113–19)? Why is the Greek remembrance of these dynasties so ambiguous, ascribing to them not only glorious deeds, but also crimes, betrayals, deceptions, murder and incest (Deger-Jalkotzy 1996b: 728)? Could it be possible that the latter derive from the recollections of a Mycenaean population who suffered long enough under a repressive political system? This would explain the quite paradoxical fact that writing in the *Iliad* is actually only once attested, in the legend of Bellerophon and – more important still – receives here a sinister characterisation as 'malevolent signs' (*Iliad* 6. 168; see also Heubeck 1979: 128–42). This passage could be understood as a distant echo of Linear B, a writing system which the dependent population of the Mycenaean palatial centres may have experienced as an instrument of oppressive power. And finally, what about the absence of Thebes from the Homeric ship catalogue, an absence which can be regarded as a 'monumental' *damnatio memoriae* of one of the most important Mycenaean centres? These are some of the questions generated by notions of social memory, which may guide future studies and provide a new sidelight on Mycenaean and Early Greek societies.

Epilogue

The overlapping terms 'social memory', 'collective memory' or 'cultural memory', which have been monopolising the interest of cultural studies for the last two decades, refer to the recollection of the past by a collective as a deliberate, socially embedded action. Groups fabricated their own narratives of collective remembrance and built upon them a collective identity, the consciousness concerning their unity and singularity in time and space. The aim of the present paper was to employ this influential concept on a major branch of Aegean archaeology and to explore its interpretative potential. The overview of the Mycenaean evidence attempted to scan testimonies of the various realities that can be taken on by the word memory, such as old words and things, commemorative images and monuments. It has been demonstrated how difficult it is to extract a Mycenaean past from the Mycenaean present due to the lack of pertinent written information. We are compelled to rely only on the material residues of Mycenaean *memoria*. In the first part of the paper, in which Mycenaean palatial culture was regarded as a social entity, it became apparent that a conscious drift towards the past can be detected only sporadically in Mycenaean art, architecture and ritual action. A serious methodological problem arose with the need to clearly distinguish between 'tradition' and 'collective memory' or what Connerton (1989: 25) so aptly described as the tension between the 'compulsion to repeat and the capacity to remember'. The rather unconscious repetition of habitual practices in art, technique and daily life resembles indeed a strong bond with the past. In this case, though, there is little that merits the term 'collective memory', a concept which presupposes an intentional act of remembering based on social interaction. The second part of the paper was dedicated to a contextual approach, which, for obvious reasons, focused on the city of Mycenae. Here, the large-scale building programme around 1250 BC provides the most evident example of appropriating the past in a Mycenaean context. A key element of the entire project, the refurbishment of Grave Circle A, can be regarded as a conscious reconstitution of a heroic past. One or two generations before the collapse of the palatial system, Mycenae's ruling elite employed meticulous restorative devices in order to 'mantle' the glorious past of the city and invest it with a new meaning. The restored burial ground undoubtedly became an emblematic public space of intensive communal interaction, since it could serve both as a marker and a theatre of memory. Finally, a cursory look beyond the era of the Mycenaean palaces has shown that notions of collective memory may be proven very fruitful for understanding the trajectory of Greek oral tradition in the Iron Age. The likelihood of social unrest as the major agent for the collapse of the Mycenaean palatial system forces us to assume a multivocality of social memory, which may enlighten actions of inconsistent remembering, selective retention and deliberate forgetting in the shared remembrance of early Greek society.

Notes

1. See for instance Voidokoilia, where a Late Helladic I tholos tomb was cut into the centre of a Middle Helladic tumulus, which in turn covered an Early Helladic settlement: Antonaccio 1995: 50 n. 171, 80–81 (with further references); Cavanagh and Mee 1998: 42.
2. For distance and isolation as expressions of social distinctiveness in the sepulchral sphere see Wells 1990: 128.
3. The same applies to the nearby tholos tomb of Aigisthos and a chamber tomb immediately to the south of Grave Circle B excavated by Papademetriou in 1952–53. The latter is the only chamber tomb erected within the city boundaries, after the Prehistoric Cemetery came out of use: see Antonaccio 1995: 47–48, 50–51; Iakovides and French 2003: 35, 51.
4. The Late Helladic IIIB date of this refurbishment has been questioned by Gates (1985) and Laffineur (1990; 1995: 86–93), who propose a later date, without providing, however, any sound arguments.
5. A similar suggestion has been made for the gypsum blocks carved in relief from the Atreus tomb: see Blakolmer 2006: 21–22.

Bibliography

Alcock, S. E.

2002 *Archaeologies of the Greek Past. Landscape, Monuments, and Memories.* Cambridge: Cambridge University Press.

Alden, M.

2000 *The Prehistoric Cemetery. Pre-Mycenaean and Early Mycenaean Graves* (Well Built Mycenae. The Helleno-British Excavations Within the Citadel at Mycenae, 1959–1969, Fascicule 7). Oxford: Oxbow.

Antonaccio, C.

1995 *An Archaeology of Ancestors. Tomb Cult and Hero Cult in Early Greece.* Lanham, MD: Rowman & Littlefield.

2006 Religion, basileis and heroes. In S. Deger-Jalkotzy and I. S. Lemos (eds.), *Ancient Greece: From the Mycenaean Palaces to the Age of Homer* (Edinburgh Leventis Studies 3): 381–95. Edinburgh: Edinburgh University Press.

Assmann, J.

1997 *Das kulturelle Gedächtnis. Schrift, Erinnerung und Identität in frühen Hochkulturen* (2nd ed.). München: C.H. Beck.

Barrett, J. C.

1999 The mythical landscapes of the British Iron Age. In W. Ashmore and A. B. Knapp (eds.), *Archaeologies of Landscape. Contemporary Perspectives*: 253–65. Oxford: Blackwell.

Bennet, J.

2001 Agency and bureaucracy: thoughts on the nature and extent of administration in Bronze Age Pylos. In S. Voutsaki and J. Killen (eds.), *Economy and Politics in the Mycenaean Palace States. Proceedings of a Conference held on 1–3 July 1999 in the Faculty of Classics, Cambridge* (Cambridge Philological Society Suppl. 27): 25–37. Cambridge: Cambridge Philological Society.

2004 Iconographies of value: words, people and things in the Late Bronze Age Aegean. In J. C. Barrett and P. Halstead (eds.), *The Emergence of Civilisation Revisited* (Sheffield Studies in Aegean Archaeology 6): 90–106. Oxford: Oxbow.

Blakolmer, F.

2006 'Historical memory' in der ägäischen Bronzezeit: das Beispiel der Kykladenidole. In G. Koiner, M. Lehner, Th. Lorenz and G. Schwarz (eds.), *Akten des 10. Österreichischen Archäologentages in Graz, 7. –9. November 2003*: 17–23. Wien: Phoibos Verlag.

Bradley, R.
1998 *The Significance of the Monuments. On the Shaping of Human Experience in Neolithic and Bronze Age Europe*. London and New York: Routledge.
2002 *The Past in Prehistoric Societies*. London and New York: Routledge.
Buikstra, J. E. and D. K. Charles
1999 Centering the ancestors: cemeteries, mounds, and sacred landscapes of the North American midcontinent. In W. Ashmore and A. B. Knapp (eds.), *Archaeologies of Landscape. Contemporary Perspectives*: 201–28. Oxford: Blackwell.
Cavanagh, W.
2001 Empty space? Courts and squares in Mycenaean towns. In K. Branigan (ed.), *Urbanism in the Aegean Bronze Age* (Sheffield Studies in Aegean Archaeology 4): 119–34. Sheffield: Sheffield Academic Press.
Cavanagh, W. and C. Mee
1998 *A Private Place: Death in Prehistoric Greece* (Studies in Mediterranean Archaeology 125). Jonsered: Paul Åström.
Clark, M.
2004 Formulas, metre and type-scenes. In R. Fowler (ed.), *The Cambridge Companion to Homer*: 117–38. Cambridge: Cambridge University Press.
Connerton, P.
1989 *How Societies Remember*. Cambridge: Cambridge University Press.
2006 Cultural memory. In C. Tilley, W. Keane, S. Küchler, M. Rowlands and P. Spyer (eds.), *Handbook of Material Culture*: 315–24. London, Thousand Oaks, New Delhi: SAGE Publications.
Cummings, V.
2003 Building from Memory. Remembering the Past at Neolithic Monuments in Western Britain. In H. Williams (ed.), *Archaeologies of Remembrance. Death and Memory in Past Societies*: 25–43. New York: Kluwer Academic/Plenum Publishers.
Day, P. M. and D. E. Wilson
2002 Landscapes of memory, craft and power in Prepalatial and Protopalatial Knossos. In Y. Hamilakis (ed.), *Labyrinth Revisited. Rethinking 'Minoan' Archaeology*: 143–66. Oxford: Oxbow.
Deger-Jalkotzy, S.
1996a 'Hier können wir Achäer nicht alle König sein'. Zur Geschichte des frühgriechischen Königtums. In W. Leschhorn, A. V. B. Miron and A. Miron (eds.), *Hellas und der griechische Osten. Studien zur Geschichte und Numismatik der griechischen Welt. Festschrift für Peter Robert Franke zum 70. Geburtstag*: 13–30. Saarbrücken: SDV Saarbrücker Druckerei und Verlag.
1996b On the negative aspects of the Mycenaean palace system. In E. de Miro, L. Godart and A. Sacconi (eds.), *Atti e Memorie del Secondo Congresso Internazionale di Micenologia, Roma-Napoli, 14–20 ottobre 1991*, vol. II: Storia (Incunabula Greca XCVIII, 2): 715–28. Roma: Gruppo Editoriale Internazionale.
2006 Theben und Pylos: terminologische und onomastische Korrespondenzen? In S. Deger-Jalkotzy and O. Panagl (eds.), *Die neuen Linear B-Texte aus Theben. Ihr Aufschlusswert für die mykenische Sprache und Kultur. Akten des Internationalen Forschungskolloquiums an der Österreichischen Akademie der Wissenschaften, 5. –6. Dezember 2002* (Österreichische Akademie der Wissenschaften, Philosophisch-Historische Klasse, Denkschriften 338, Veröffentlichungen der Mykenischen Kommission 23, Mykenische Studien 19): 19–35. Wien: Verlag der Österreichischen Akademie der Wissenschaften.
Dickers, A.
2001 *Die spätmykenischen Siegel aus weichem Stein. Untersuchungen zur spätbronzezeitlichen Glyptik auf dem griechischen Festland und in der Ägäis* (Internationale Archäologie 33). Rahden: Leidorf.

Dickinson, O.

1977 *The Origins of Mycenaean Civilization* (Studies in Mediterranean Archaeology 49). Göteborg: Paul Åströms.

2006a The Mycenaean heritage of Early Iron Age Greece. In S. Deger-Jalkotzy and I.S. Lemos (eds.), *Ancient Greece: From the Mycenaean Palaces to the Age of Homer* (Edinburgh Leventis Studies 3): 115–22. Edinburgh: Edinburgh University Press.

2006b *The Aegean from Bronze to Iron Age. Continuity and Change between the Twelfth and Eighth Centuries BC*. London and New York: Routledge.

Driessen, J.

1994-95 Data storage for reference and prediction at the dawn of civilization? A review article with some observations on 'Archives Before Writing'. *Minos* 29–30: 239–56.

1999 The Northern Entrance Passage at Knossos. Some preliminary observations on its potential role as 'Central Archives'. In S. Deger-Jalkotzy, S. Hiller and O. Panagl (eds.), *Floreant Studia Mycenaea. Akten des X. Internationalen Mykenologischen Colloquiums in Salzburg vom 1. –5. Mai 1995* (Österreichische Akademie der Wissenschaften, Philosophisch-Historische Klasse, Denkschriften 274 (Veröffentlichungen der Mykenischen Kommission 18): 205–26. Wien: Verlag der Österreichischen Akademie der Wissenschaften.

2000 *The Scribes of the Room of the Chariot Tablets at Knossos. Interdisciplinary Approach to the Study of a Linear B Deposit* (Minos Supplement 15). Salamanca: Ediciones Universidad de Salamanca.

Earle, T.

2002 *Bronze Age Economics. The Beginnings of Political Economies*. Boulder, CO: Westview Press.

Eder, B.

2003 Noch einmal: der homerische Schiffskatalog. In Chr. Ulf (ed.), *Der neue Streit im Troia. Eine Bilanz*: 287–308. München: C. H. Beck.

Edwards, M.

1997 Homeric style and 'oral poetics'. In I. Morris and B. Powell (eds.), *A New Companion to Homer*: 261–83. Leiden, New York, Köln: Brill.

Fahlander, F.

2003 *The Materiality of Serial Practice. A Microarchaeology of Burial*. Göteborg: Department of Archaeology, Göteborg University.

Fewster, K. J.

2007 The role of agency and material culture in remembering and forgetting: an ethnoarchaeological case study from Central Spain. *Journal of Mediterranean Archaeology* 20.1: 89–114.

Flower, H. I.

2006 *The Art of Forgetting. Disgrace and Oblivion in Roman Political Culture*. Chapel Hill: The University of Carolina Press.

Foxhall, L.

1995 Monumental ambitions: the significance of posterity in Greece. In N. Spencer (ed.), *Time, Tradition and Society in Greek Archaeology: Bridging the 'Great Divide'*: 132–49. London: Routledge.

French, E.

2002 *Mycenae. Agamemnon's Capital. The Site in its Setting*. Stroud: Tempus Publishing.

Gallou, Chr.

2005 *The Mycenaean Cult of the Dead* (BAR International Series 1372). Oxford: Archaeopress.

Gates, C.

1985 Rethinking the building history of Grave Circle A at Mycenae. *American Journal of Archaeology* 89: 263–74.

Gehrke, H.-J.

2001 History and collective identity: uses of the past in ancient Greece and beyond. In N. Luraghi (ed.), *The Historian's Craft in the Age of Herodotus*: 286–313. Oxford: Oxford University Press.

2003 Was ist Vergangenheit? oder: die 'Entstehung' von Vergangenheit. In Chr. Ulf (ed.), *Der neue Streit im Troia. Eine Bilanz*: 62–81. München: C. H. Beck.
Gosden, C. and Y. Marshall
1999 The cultural biography of objects. *World Archaeology* 31: 169–78.
Graziadio, G.
1991 The process of social stratification at Mycenae in the Shaft Grave period: a comparative examination of the evidence. *American Journal of Archaeology* 95: 403–40.
Halbwachs, M.
1925 *Les cadres sociaux de la mémoire*. Paris: Librairie Félix Alcan.
1950 *La mémoire collective*. Paris: Presse Universitaire de France.
Hallager, E.
2005 The uniformity in seal use and sealing practice during the LH/LM III period. In L. D'Agata and J. Moody (eds.), *Ariadne's Threads. Connections between Crete and the Greek Mainland in Late Minoan III (LM IIIA2 to LM IIIC). Proceedings of the International Workshop held at Athens, Scuola Archeologica Italiana, 5–6 April 2003*: 243–65. Atene: Scuola Archeologica Italiana di Atene.
Hallager, E. and B.-P. Hallager
1999 Nodules and LM IIIB Kydonian pottery from the Little Palace at Knossos. In P. Betancourt, V. Karageorghis, R. Laffineur and W.-D. Niemeier (eds.), *MELETEMATA. Studies in Aegean Archaeology Presented to Malcolm H. Wiener as he Enters his 65th Year* (Aegaeum 20): 309–16. Liège and Austin: Université de Liège and University of Texas at Austin.
Halstead, P.
1988 On redistribution and the origin of Minoan-Mycenaean palatial economies. In E. B. French and K. A. Wardle (eds.), *Problems in Greek Prehistory. Papers Presented at the Centenary Conference of the British School at Athens, Manchester, April 1986*: 519–29. Bristol: Bristol Classical Press.
Hamilakis, Y.
1998 Eating the dead: mortuary feasting and the politics of memory in the Aegean Bronze Age societies. In K. Branigan (ed.), *Cemetery and Society in the Aegean Bronze Age* (Sheffield Studies in Aegean Archaeology 1): 115–32. Sheffield: Sheffield Academic Press.
Heubeck, A.
1979 *Schrift* (Archaeologia Homerica III, X). Göttingen: Vandenhoeck & Ruprecht.
Hope, V. M.
2003 Remembering Rome. Memory, funerary monuments and the Roman soldier. In H. Williams, (ed.), *Archaeologies of Remembrance. Death and Memory in Past Societies*: 113–40. New York: Kluwer Academic/Plenum Publishers.
Hoskins, J.
1998 *Biographical Objects: How Things Tell the Stories of People's Lives*. London: Routledge.
2006 Agency, biography and objects. In C. Tilley, W. Keane, S. Küchler, M. Rowlands and P. Spyer (eds.), *Handbook of Material Culture*: 74–84. London, Thousand Oaks, New Delhi: SAGE Publications.
Iakovides, S.
1983 *Late Helladic Citadels on Mainland Greece* (Monumenta Graeca et Romana 4). Leiden: E.J. Brill.
Iakovides, S. and E. B. French
2003 *Archaeological Atlas of Mycenae* (The Archaeological Society of Athens Library 229). Athens: Archaeological Society of Athens.
Jonker, G.
1995 *The Topography of Remembrance. The Dead, Tradition and Collective Memory in Mesopotamia* (Studies in the History of Religions 68). Leiden, New York, Köln: Brill.
Killen, J.
1979 The Knossos Ld(1) tablets. In E. Risch and H. Mühlestein (eds.), *Colloquium Mycenaeum. Actes du Sixième Colloque international sur les textes mycéniens et égéens tenu à Chaumont sur Neuchâtel du 7 au 13 septembre 1975*: 151–81. Geneva : Librairie Droz.

Klein, K. L.
2000 On the emergence of memory in historical discourse. *Representations* 69: 127–50.
Knapp, A. B. and W. Ashmore
1999 Archaeological landscapes: constructed, conceptualized, ideational. In W. Ashmore and A. B. Knapp (eds.), *Archaeologies of Landscape. Contemporary Perspectives*: 1–30. Oxford: Blackwell.
Kopytoff, I.
1986 The cultural biography of things. Commoditization as process. In A. Appadurai (ed.), *The Social Life of Things. Commodities in Cultural Perspective*: 64–91. Cambridge: Cambridge University Press.
Laffineur, R.
1990 Grave Circle A at Mycenae: further reflections on its history. In R. Hägg and G. Nordquist (eds.), *Celebrations of Death and Divinity in the Bronze Age Argolid. Proceedings of the Sixth International Symposium at the Swedish Institute at Athens, 11–13 June, 1988* (Skrifter Utgivna av Svenska Institutet i Athen 4o, 40): 201–05. Stockholm: Paul Åströms.
1995 Aspects of rulership at Mycenae in the Shaft Grave period. In P. Rehak (ed.), *The Role of the Ruler in the Prehistoric Aegean. Proceedings of a Panel Discussion Presented at the Annual Meeting of the Archaeological Institute of America, New Orleans, Louisiana, 28 December 1992, with Additions* (Aegaeum 11): 81–94. Liège and Texas: Université de Liège, Histoire de l'art et archéologie de la Grèce antique and University of Texas at Austin, Program in Aegean Scripts and Prehistory.
Lang, M. L.
1969 *The Palace of Nestor at Pylos in Western Messenia II. The Frescoes*. Princeton, NJ: Princeton University Press.
Lévi-Strauss, C.
1962 *La pensée sauvage*. Paris: Plon.
Lowenthal, D.
1985 *The Past is a Foreign Country*. Cambridge: Cambridge University Press.
Lucas, G.
2005 *The Archaeology of Time*. Routledge: London and New York.
Maran, J.
2006 Coming to terms with the past: ideology and power in Late Helladic IIIC. In S. Deger-Jalkotzy and I. S. Lemos (eds.), *Ancient Greece: From the Mycenaean Palaces to the Age of Homer* (Edinburgh Leventis Studies 3): 123–50. Edinburgh: Edinburgh University Press.
Mee, C. B. and W. G. Cavanagh
1984 Mycenaean tombs as evidence for social and political organisation. *Oxford Journal of Archaeology* 3(3): 45–64.
Muskett, G.
2004 Colour coding and the representation of costumes in Mycenaean wall painting. In L. Cleland and K. Stears (eds.), *Colour in the Ancient Mediterranean World* (BAR International Series 1267): 68–73. Oxford: Archaeopress.
Mylonas, G. E.
1972/73 Ο ταφικός κύκλος Β των Μυκηνών, vols. 1–2 (The Archaeological Society of Athens Library 73) Athens: Archaeological Society of Athens.
1983 Πολύχρυσοι Μυκήναι. Athens: Ekdotike Athenon.
Neumann, G.
1992 Deutungsvorschläge zu mykenischen Namen. In J.-P. Olivier (ed.), *MYKENAÏKA. Actes du IXe Colloque international sur les textes mycéniens et égéens organisé par le Centre de l'Antiquité Grecque et Romaine de la Fondation Hellénique des Recherches Scientifiques et l'École française d'Athènes, Athènes, 2–6 Octobre 1990* (Bulletin de Correspondance Hellénique Supplement XXV): 433–41. Athens: École française d'Athènes.

1994 Wertvorstellungen und Ideologie in den Personennamen der mykenischen Griechen. *Anzeiger der phil.-historischen Klasse der Österreichischen Akademie der Wissenschaften* 131: 127–66.

Nora, P.

1989 Between memory and history: Les Lieux de Mémoire. *Representations* 26 (Spring): 7–25.

Nora, P. (ed.)

1984–92 *Les Lieux de Mémoire*, vols. 1–3. Paris : Gallimard.

Olick, J. K. and J. Robbins

1998 Social memory studies: from 'collective memory' to the historical sociology of mnemonic practices. *Annual Review of Sociology* 24: 105–40.

Palaima, T. G.

1990 *Aegean Seals, Sealings and Administration. Proceedings of the NEH-Dickson Conference of the Program in Aegean Scripts and Prehistory of the Department of Classics, University of Texas at Austin, January 11–13, 1989* (Aegaeum 5). Liège: Universitè de Liège.

1999 Mycenaean militarism from a textual perspective. Onomastics in context: lāwos, dāmos, klewos*. In R. Laffineur (ed.), *POLEMOS. Le Contexte Guerrier en Égée à l'Age du Bronze. Actes de la 7e Rencontre égéenne internationale, Université de Liège, 14–17 avril 1998* (Aegaeum 19): 367–78. Liège and Austin: Université de Liège and University of Texas at Austin.

2003 'Archives' and 'scribes' and information hierarchy in Mycenaean Greek Linear B records. In M. Brosius (ed.), *Ancient Archives and Archival Tradition. Concepts of Record-keeping in the Ancient World*: 153–94. Oxford: Oxford University Press.

Panagiotopoulos, D.

2007 Mykenische Trauerbilder. Zu den Anfängen der griechischen funerären Ikonographie. In F. Lang et al. (eds.), *ΣΤΕΦΑΝΟΣ ΑΡΙΣΤΕΙΟΣ. Archäologische Forschungen zwischen Nil und Istros. Festschrift für Stefan Hiller zum 65. Geburtstag*: 205–14. Wien: Phoibos Verlag.

Pini, I.

1990 Some considerations on the use of seals for administrative purposes in Mycenaean Greece. *Studi Micenei ed Egeo-anatolici* 28: 107–16.

Pini, I. (ed.)

1997 *Die Tonplomben aus dem Nestorpalast von Pylos*. Mainz: Philipp von Zabern.

Piteros, Chr.

1983 Θ΄ Εφορεία Προϊστορικών και Κλασικών Αρχαιοτήτων. Θήβα. Οδός Οιδίποδος 1 (οικόπεδο Δ. Λιάγκα). *Archaiologikon Deltion* 38 (Chronika): 131–34.

Pluta, K. M.

1996–97 A reconstruction of the archives complex at Pylos: a preliminary report. *Minos* 31–32: 231–50.

Rehak, P.

1992 Tradition and innovation in the Fresco from Room 31 in the 'Cult Center' at Mycenae. In R. Laffineur and J. L. Crowley (eds.), *EIKON. Aegean Bronze Age Iconography: Shaping a Methodology. Proceedings of the 4th International Aegean Conference, University of Tasmania, Hobart, Australia* (Aegaeum 8): 39–62. Liège: Université de Liège, Histoire de l'art et archéologie de la Grèce antique.

Rougemont, F.

1998 Quelques problèmes liés à l'étude des 'collecteurs' dans les tablettes en linéaire B. *Bulletin de Correspondance Hellénique* 122 : 431–34.

Rowlands, M.

1993 The role of memory in the transmission of culture. *World Archaeology* 25 (2): 141–51.

Rowlands, M. and C. Tilly

2006 Monuments and memorials. In C. Tilley, W. Keane, S. Küchler, M. Rowlands and P. Spyer (eds.), *Handbook of Material Culture*: 500–15. London, Thousand Oaks, New Delhi: SAGE Publications.

Russo, J.

1997 The formula. In I. Morris and B. Powell (eds.), *A New Companion to Homer*: 238–60. Leiden, New York, Köln: Brill.

Rutter, J.

1992 Cultural novelties in the post-Palatial Aegean world: indices of vitality or decline?, In W. A. Ward and M. Sharp Joukowsky (eds.), *The Crisis Years: The 12th Century B.C. From Beyond the Danube to the Tigris*: 61–78. Dubuque: Kendall/Hunt.

Schachermeyr, F.

1967 *Ägäis und Orient. Die überseeischen Kulturbeziehungen von Kreta und Mykenai mit Ägypten, der Levante und Kleinasien unter besonderer Berücksichtigung des 2. Jahrtausends v. Chr.* (Österreichische Akademie der Wissenschaften, Philosophisch-Historische Klasse, Denkschriften 93). Wien: Hermann Böhlaus Nachf.

Schneider, J.

2006 Cloth and clothing. In C. Tilley, W. Keane, S. Küchler, M. Rowlands and P. Spyer (eds.), *Handbook of Material Culture*: 203–20. London, Thousand Oaks, New Delhi: SAGE Publications.

Shelmerdine, C. W.

1999 A comparative look at Mycenaean administration(s). In S. Deger-Jalkotzy, S. Hiller and O. Panagl (eds.), *Floreant Studia Mycenaea. Akten des X. Internationalen Mykenologischen Colloquiums in Salzburg vom 1.-5. Mai 1995* (Österreichische Akademie der Wissenschaften, Philosophisch-Historische Klasse, Denkschriften 274, Veröffentlichungen der Mykenischen Kommission 18): 555–76. Wien: Österreichische Akademie der Wissenschaften.

Small, J. P.

1997 *Wax Tablets of the Mind. Cognitive Studies of Memory and Literacy in Classical Antiquity*. London and New York: Routledge.

Sotirakopoulou P.

1998 The Early Bronze Age stone figurines from Akrotiri on Thera and their significance for the Early Cycladic settlement. *Annual of the British School at Athens* 93: 107–65.

Taçon, P. S. C.

1999 Identifying ancient sacred landscapes in Australia: from physical to social. In W. Ashmore and A. B. Knapp (eds.), *Archaeologies of Landscape. Contemporary Perspectives*: 33–57. Oxford: Blackwell.

Taylour, W. D.

1955 Mycenae 1939–1954. Part IV. The Perseia Area. *Annual of the British School at Athens* 50: 199–237.

Van Dyke, R. M. and S. E. Alcock (eds.)

2003 *Archaeologies of Memory*. Malden, Mass.: Blackwell.

Wace, A. J. B.

1949 *Mycenae. An Archaeological History and Guide*. Princeton, NJ: Princeton University Press.

Wells, B.

1990 Death at Dendra. On mortuary practices in a Mycenaean community. In R. Hägg and G. Nordquist (eds.), *Celebrations of Death and Divinity in the Bronze Age Argolid. Proceedings of the Sixth International Symposium at the Swedish Institute at Athens, 11-13 June, 1988* (Skrifter Utgivna av Svenska Institutet i Athen 4o, 40): 125–40. Stockholm: Paul Åström.

Williams, H.

2003 *Archaeologies of Remembrance. Death and Memory in Past Societies*. New York: Kluwer Academic/ Plenum Publishers.

Winter, J.

2006 *Remembering War. The Great War Between Memory and History in the Twentieth Century*. New Haven and London: Yale University Press.

Wright, J.
1987 Death and power at Mycenae: changing symbols in mortuary practice. In R. Laffineur (ed.), *Thanatos. Les coutumes funéraires en Égée à l'âge du Bronze. Actes du colloque de Liège, 21–23 avril 1986* (Aegaeum 1): 171–84. Liège: Université de l'Etat à Liège, Histoire de l'art et archéologie de la Grèce antique.
2004 A survey of evidence for feasting in Mycenaean society. *Hesperia* 73 (2): 133–78.
Yates, F.
1966 *The Art of Memory*. London: Routledge and Kegan Paul.
Younger, J. G.
1981 The Island Sanctuaries Group: date and significance. In I. Pini (ed.), *Studien zur minoischen und helladischen Glyptik. Beiträge zum 2. Marburger Siegel-Symposium, 26. –30. September 1978* (CMS Beiheft 1): 263–72. Berlin: Gebr. Mann.
1987 Aegean seals of the Late Bronze Age: stylistic groups VI. Fourteenth-century Mainland and later fourteenth-century Cretan workshops. *Kadmos* 26: 44–73.

Chapter 7

Heroes in Early Iron Age Greece and the Homeric Epics

Alexander Mazarakis Ainian

The phenomenon of the rise of hero cults in the eighth century BC has been the subject of numerous studies. Nevertheless, the long-lasting controversy over whether these cults were generated in one way or another by the spread of the Homeric epics has not been settled. In past decades many eminent scholars dealt with this issue, and even though several argued in favour of this opinion (Farnell 1921; Coldstream 1976), most of them reached the conclusion that the epics had a small impact on this phenomenon, arguing that it was existing practices, such as funerary rituals, that inspired the epics, rather than *vice-versa* (Rohde 1894; Hadzisteliou-Price 1973; 1979; Nagy 1979; Antonaccio 1994; Crielaard 1995).

The development of hero cults coincides with a series of other phenomena, such as the re-appearance of images and narrative scenes in art, especially in vase painting, the recovery of literacy, the rise of sanctuaries and temples and the formation of the polis (Polignac 1995: esp. 41–92, 127–50). The spread of the Homeric poems, partly thanks to the recovery of literacy which enabled their recording (Powell 1991), doubtless played a significant role in the rise of these cults and the shape they took. Likewise, the choice of the figured scenes on vases was also largely conditioned by the wide circulation of the epic and mythic cycles (Snodgrass 1998, with earlier literature).

One question that I will try to clarify here is that of who were involved in the practice of hero cults and what may have been their motives. At the same time, I will investigate the possible connection of the dissemination of the epic poems with the various forms of hero cults in the Early Iron Age, while attempting to connect this development with the social, political and artistic changes of the second half of the eighth century BC.

Sanctuaries of Epic Heroes

The founding of sanctuaries dedicated to the cult of epic heroes, such as those of Agamemnon at Mycenae (Cook 1953a; 1953b; Deoudi 1999: 113; Mazarakis Ainian 2000: 192;

Boehringer 2001: 173–78), Menelaos at Sparta (Antonaccio 1995: 155–66; Deoudi 1999: 124f.; Mazarakis Ainian 2000: 192), Odysseus in Ithaca (Benton 1934/35; 1938/39; 1936; Coulson 1991; Polignac 1994: 11, n. 23; Malkin 1998: 94–119; Deoudi 1999: 119; Mazarakis Ainian 2000: 193), and Phrontis at Sounion (Stais 1917; Picard 1940; Calligas 1993; Abramson 1979; Antonaccio 1995: 166–69; Deoudi 1999: 113–15; Mazarakis Ainian 2000: 193; Boehringer 2001: 64–66; Theodoropoulou-Polychroniadis 2015), could indeed be related to the dissemination of the epics. Yet, here one is faced with a possible circular argument: epigraphic or literary evidence for worship of these heroes does not antedate the seventh century BC, and usually appears much later, creating uncertainty as to the identity of the figures worshipped at these places at the moment of the inauguration of the cult. Moreover, in several cases the exact location of the sanctuary is still a matter of debate (for example, that of Phrontis at Sounion) or highly contested (the enclosure of the 'Seven against Thebes' at Eleusis, mentioned by Pausanias I, 39.2 [see G. Mylonas, *Praktika* 1953: 81 ff.]). The case of the 'Odysseion' at the Polis cave in Ithaca stands out as a good example illustrating the above mentioned ambiguity: which came first - the story which generated the cult, or the cult which was adapted to the story? (Malkin 1998: 94–119; Papalexandrou 2005: 22–23).

All the above mentioned sanctuaries, and several minor, less famous ones (especially in and around Sparta: Antonaccio 1995: 182–83; Deoudi 1999: 119–24), were founded rather early, certainly within the eighth century BC, if not earlier (notably the cult in the Polis cave in Ithaca), and lasted for several centuries. It is quite possible that the cults were from the beginning addressed to the same heroes, as suggested by the early graffiti of the Menelaion. This idea is further supported by the new discoveries at Thebes by V. Aravantinos, which confirm that mythical heroes, such as Heracles, were worshipped already by the end of the eighth century BC (Aravantinos 2010: 152ff.). As for the 'Odysseion', even if the epics were inspired by the existing knowledge of a sacred cave of non heroic nature on the island, it is most probable that the cult in it would have shifted towards the veneration of the epic hero some time after the circulation of the *Odyssey*. By analogy one could assume that some of the known landmarks connected with epic and mythic heroes, such as the supposed remains of a wooden pillar from Oinomaos' dwelling at Olympia, could have been established very early too (Herrmann 1980; Kyrieleis 1992; Brulotte 1994; Antonaccio 1995: 170–76; Deoudi 1999: 118f.).

The long-lasting nature of these hero sanctuaries, and their character, suggest that they were founded (or alternatively rapidly appropriated) by organised communities, perhaps by the decision-making members of the rising poleis, and that, apart from serving specific goals directly related to cult, they also conveyed certain clear political messages related to territorial claims, as in the case of the Argolid (Polignac 1995) or Messenia (Snodgrass 1982: 118).

Prominent Individuals who were Honoured after their Death

The geographical areas where prominent individuals were venerated after their death (defined also as 'true hero cults' by van den Eijnde [2010: 397]) are not the same as those where the more widely attested practice of 'tomb cult' at Late Bronze Age tombs is attested (see below). Thus, provided that this is not a simple coincidence, it could be argued that there may be no direct connection between these two different sorts of cult. Euboea (Lefkandi?, Eretria, Viglatouri?) and the immediately adjacent geographical area (Oropos) is such an area, and the Cyclades another (Naxos, Paros, Amorgos) (see in general Mazarakis Ainian 2004; 2007–2008). Attica seems to be an exception to this pattern. Nevertheless, the 'hero cults' associated with the recently deceased here are either ambiguous or exceptional. The case of the Sacred House at Eleusis stands out as very unusual, since it concerns a male individual who was exceptionally honoured after his death at the fringes of the rising sanctuary of Demeter (Antonaccio 1995: 190–91; Mazarakis Ainian 1997: 150–54; 1999b; 2000: 189–91; Deoudi 1999: 71–72; van den Eijnde 2010: 168–85). Within Athens, at the Areopagus, it is far from certain that there existed some form of veneration of the dead during the Geometric period (Burr 1933; Mazarakis Ainian 1997: 86f.; Deoudi 1999: 68–70; D'Onofrio 2001; van den Eijnde 2010: 113–17).

Such cults are often connected with places where residential areas of the elite were subsequently turned into formal cult areas of the rising polis. Eretria is perhaps the best example of this kind of transition; the inauguration of the cult at the Heroon by the West Gate follows a generation or so after the erection of the *hekatompedon* which marks the foundation of the poliad sanctuary of Apollo (Bérard 1970; 1972: 219–27; 1978: 89–95; 1982: 89–105; 1983: 43–59; Deoudi 1999: 77–80; Mazarakis Ainian 2000: 187–89; Blandin 2007: 35–58; Verdan 2013). Oropos fits into this pattern too: the 'heroon' there (a cenotaph of the early seventh century BC) seems to mark a drastic change in the function of the area, from a residential area of the elite to a cult place dedicated to a seafarer who perished at sea (Mazarakis Ainian 1997: 47–77; Mazarakis Ainian 2002; 2004: 136; 2006–2007: 91–92). Within Athens, at the Areopagus, the oval edifice was presumably a dwelling, forming part of a larger complex, within an elite residential area, in close proximity to which burials were also made, subsequently converted into a cult complex perhaps associated with a hero (D'Onofrio 2001: 257–320, with all the previous bibliography; now see also van den Eijnde forthcoming). Likewise, the peribolos, east of the subsequent 'Tholos' lies in a similar residential quarter of the eighth and seventh centuries BC, which in the sixth century BC became the focal point of the Agora (van den Eijnde 2010: 106–10, with earlier literature). At Eleusis too, the inauguration of the hero cult at the so-called Sacred House marked radical transformations in the use of the existing buildings and the beginnings of intensive cult activities in the specific area, as well as in the neighbouring sanctuary of Demeter (Travlos 1983; Kokkou-Vyridi 1991).

Cults at Ancient Tombs ('Tomb Cults')

Based on the available archaeological evidence, the cult at tombs of the Bronze Age must have been much more widespread than the other two forms of cult described above. The role that the spread of the epics may have played in the popularity of these particular 'tomb cults' is contested. J. N. Coldstream was the first to argue that such cults were indeed dictated by the spread of the epics (Coldstream 1976), but most scholars subsequently followed a different line of approach. Indeed, various other explanations have been given: tomb cults are usually thought to have a complex sociopolitical background, reflecting the wish of the ruling class – or alternatively that of the emerging ruling class – to emphasise its ties with legendary heroes or past rulers, respectively, justifying by this act its own privileged or aspired position. In other instances, especially in the case of less formal tomb cults, these activities would have been instigated for social or more complex political reasons, by which the people living in the Early Iron Age attempted to establish a link with past generations (for a summary of these opinions see Mazarakis Ainian 2004); for instance, the so called 'place of burning' at the Late Bronze Age necropolis outside the walls of Troy has also been interpreted as an attempt of the inhabitants of Troy to express territorial claims and reinforce the power of the local elite (Chabot Aslan 2011); likewise, in the case of Messenia, where there was no free peasantry, the reason for the practice of tomb cults may have been nostalgia for the period of autonomy (Snodgrass 1982: 118).

It is usually thought that tomb cults attested in association with chamber and tholos tombs of the Late Bronze Age were addressed to 'anonymous' heroes or ancestors (Whitley 1994: 221–22; Antonaccio 1995), but this may not have been so: it will be argued that in some instances local myths, and by analogy even the epic poems, may lie behind their inauguration. Furthermore, I would like to elaborate on the impact that these 'rediscoveries' may have played in the revival of figurative art in the Greek World.

'Eponymous' Tomb Cults?

A fairly recent discovery south of the dromos of a Late Helladic IIIB tholos tomb at Georgiko near Xironeri, 5.5 km south-west of Karditsa in Thessaly, is important in the attempt to understand the beneficiaries of tomb cults in the pre-classical period (Intzesiloglou 1995; 2002a; see also Morgan 2003: 190, 192).[1] In an extensive area of 530 sq.m. in front of the Mycenaean tholos tomb there were numerous concentrations of stones on top of which plentiful offerings were found, mostly terracotta figurines of horsemen and iron knives (and miniature vases, judging by the finds exhibited in the new Museum of Karditsa). Two bases for stone stelae were also brought to light. In one area, burnt soil remains and calcined animal bones were investigated, suggesting the presence of an ash altar. The dromos of the tholos was blocked by a cross wall. A channel dug into the rock was identified, starting near this wall, continuing into the dromos and leading at the back of the round chamber of the tomb, following the curved west side of the chamber. The most evocative find from the area outside the tomb was a Laconian roof tile bearing an inscribed inscription of the seventh or, more probably, the sixth century BC, reading AIATIION (accusative) or AIATIIO (genitive) (Intzesiloglou 1995: 11–18; 2002a: 289–95; 2003: 233; see also Mili 2015: 226–227, 255, 334). The excavator, B. Intzesiloglou, has convincingly argued that this name is probably that of Aiatos, a mythical hero of the area, the father of Thessalos; he and his sister Polykleia, after crossing the Acheloos river, pushed the Boeotians southward and were established as rulers in the area (Polyenos, *Strategemata* 8.44). The importance of this discovery lies not only in its context, but also in its early date: the first votives, judging by the inscribed tile, but also by the earliest (Corinthian) pottery, dating, according to the excavator, in the seventh and sixth centuries BC (B. Inzesiloglou personal communication), prove that the cult of Aiatos was established here sometime in the Early Archaic period. Aiatos was not simply a common hero, but the ancestor of all the Thessalians. It is not coincidental that the tholos tomb lies in the confines of the necropolis of the town of Metropolis, which lies c. 1 km to the north. There an Archaic temple of Apollo has been excavated (Intzesiloglou 2002b), the uniqueness of which is indicated not only by its architectural details, but also by the character of its patron divinity: against the prevailing tradition, Apollo was worshipped here as a war deity. According to B. Intzesiloglou, the cult at the tholos tomb and the erection of the Apollo temple should be regarded as parallel phenomena, closely relevant to the foundation of the polis of Metropolis, created after the synoecism of the three communities of the surroundings (Strabo 9.5.17; Intzesiloglou 2002a: 291, n. 8). It is beyond doubt that at Metropolis the inauguration of cult activities, both in the Archaic sanctuary of Apollo and at the Mycenaean tholos tomb nearby, represents a conscious decision by the local community, or probably its aristocracy, to claim ancestral legitimacy in respect of land and a common ethnic identity.

The recently added evidence from Georgiko draws attention to the identification of early manifestations of tomb cult in Thessaly during the Early Iron Age, as in the cases of the tholos tombs excavated by Verdelis at Pteleon and especially at Pharsalos (Antonaccio 1995: 137, with references to Verdelis, *Praktika*). The idea advanced long ago by J.N. Coldstream (1976) that tomb cult in Thessaly was not practised due to the fact that the Late Bronze Age built tombs did not significantly differ from those constructed during the Early Iron Age, and thus did not create a similar impression to that experienced by the Greeks living in the south, has to be slightly re-evaluated. The available evidence shows now that Thessaly belongs to the geographical area where tomb cult was practised since the end of the Geometric period, while there are positive grounds for suggesting that the recipients of such cults may have been from the very beginning eponymous heroes of the mythic cycles. The latter remark is of great importance for the understanding of the nature of the long lasting cults at tholos tombs in other areas, as for instance in Attica, where it has been argued that the 'heroes' in question may not have been anonymous to the worshippers (see van den Eijnde 2010: 219–26 and in general Kearns 1989). If this is indeed so, then we should perhaps reassess the importance that the epic poems may also have had in the development of this phenomenon, even if direct evidence in favour of this is sill lacking.

The Search for Traces of Heroes and Antiques and the Re-Appearance of Figured Scenes

The spread of tomb cult from the second half of the eighth century BC onwards was probably one of the manifestations of the wish of individuals, families or communities to establish a link with their past. This phenomenon roughly coincides with the dissemination of the Homeric epics, which praised the heroic deeds of the ancestors who also lived in the past. The general 'heroic' character of the society at the close of the eighth century BC could have had as a side effect the search for *realia* belonging to this glorious heroic past (Boardman 2003). Indeed, from the middle of the eighth century BC a conscious 'search for heroes' can be claimed, which resulted in the rediscovery of chamber and tholos tombs of the earlier Bronze Age and the establishment often of long lasting cults at them, as in the case of Solygeia (Verdelis 1958; 1962; Antonaccio 1995: 65f.; Mazarakis Ainian 1997: 65–67; Deoudi 1999: 85–86; Lorandou-Papantoniou 1999), Menidi (Lolling *et al.* 1880; Whitley 1994, 222–26; Antonaccio 1995: 102–09; Deoudi 1999: 103–05; 2005), Thorikos (Devillers 1988; Antonaccio 1995: 109–12; Deoudi 1999: 105f.) or Georgiko (Intzesiloglou 2002a, and see above). In most cases, however, the rediscovery of a tomb (basically a rock-cut chamber) resulted in a momentary act of veneration which usually, though not always (see, for instance, Solygeia above), did not develop into a long-lasting cult. On some such occasions it cannot be ruled out that the rediscovery of old burials may have resulted in acquiring wealth, by appropriating the more precious burial offerings, i.e. 'antiques' belonging to alleged heroes or distinguished ancestors. Antiques both from the Aegean area and also from far distant lands were already in circulation from the eleventh century BC in the Aegean (at Knossos for instance: Catling 1995), and were acquired basically through gift exchange and trade. Such heirlooms were occasionally positioned over tombs, as at Grotta on Naxos (Lambrinoudakis 1988: 235, a Late Helladic IIIC hydria was set as a *sema* over the cover slabs of a Protogeometric tomb), served some ritual (Hägg 1974: 96; Wells 1983: 31, 88–90, a Mycenaean vase served for libations over a Protogeometric grave at Asine), or, more often, placed inside tombs, as at Lefkandi (H. W. Catling in Coulton and Catling 1993: 81–92; Catling 1994: 138; Popham 1994; Popham and Lemos 1995). Likewise, and following the same exchange networks, strange and attractive 'exotic' contemporary objects, several bearing figured scenes, were already circulating in the Aegean from the Protogeometric period, for instance at Lefkandi and Crete (Kourou 1990–1991).

It is beyond doubt that such antiques on the one hand and exotic contemporary imports on the other appear to have played some role in the creation of the first images and had an impact in the formative stages of Greek figured art (Benson 1970). It must not be totally unrelated that the majority of the earliest images in Greek art occur in areas where such objects were indeed circulating during the tenth century BC (Knossos, Lefkandi). Yet, despite the fact that there is no doubt that vases and other objects of earlier periods which bore figured decoration would have been known by the communities living in the earlier Iron Age, these did not lead artists to copy them in a systematic way (see also Lemos 2000: 160). The reason may be that such objects, as soon as they found their way into the aristocratic households, were not set on display widely and therefore may have been viewed by a small minority of the population, mostly other members of the elite. Indeed, such rare and prized acquisitions were not set on 'public' display: they were rarely offered as dedications in sanctuaries before the eighth century BC, and were acquired mainly as objects of value denoting wealth and status and ended as burial offerings in wealthy tombs. They may have been kept within the household for a longer or shorter period, or may have been acquired shortly before deposition in the grave of a wealthy individual. From the middle of the eighth century BC onwards, however, an interest in the heroic past appears to have been the concern of many; this interest resulted in the discovery, and often the exploration, of tombs of the past, with numerous people inevitably finding themselves for the first time facing various valued antiques, including old vases, some bearing figured decoration, which may have provided a source of inspiration to contemporary artists.

Indeed, a general 'heroic' feeling emerges when one examines the various manifestations of interest concerning the past in the eighth century BC, including the 'heroic' burial customs, and the newly invented figured scenes of the Late Geometric period. To what extent, however, were Homer's epics responsible for such attitudes and innovations? Snodgrass convincingly argued that the artists of this period were not well acquainted with the epics and that few of the 'Homeric' scenes can be definitely proven to have been inspired by Homer (Snodgrass 1998). This seems to indicate that the poems were not well known in their details, but only in their general lines. Indeed, very few people would have been able to read and write (though the recent discovery of numerous graffiti of the eighth century BC at Methoni in Pieria, an Eretrian foundation, should incite caution, especially concerning the level of illiteracy of the Euboeans: see Bessios, Kotsonas and Tzifopoulos 2012), fewer would have undertaken the task of reciting the poems to wider audiences based on a written version of them, and even fewer would have been bards reciting the poems by heart. Snodgrass argued that the painted inscriptions on later vases of the Archaic period served as a means for wider illiterate audiences to approach the epics and myths, through those few who were able to read and identify the scenes for them. In an earlier era, when literacy was in its initial stages, such inscriptions would have been almost meaningless, not to mention that very few of the actual artists would have been literate and thus few of them would have been able to add 'captions' to the scenes they were painting. Originally, these limitations may have conditioned artists, as well as those who made the commissions, to stick to well-understood scenes, such as those involving funerals and fighting. Some scenes may have become more popular because they could be given a series of interpretations, in accordance with the context that the vase or object would be used in, or depending on the meaning that its owner would wish to give to it. Independent images or narrative scenes may have acquired an obvious meaning by the end of the eighth century BC, though not always as obvious for us, the modern readers of these icons. Moreover, while some images would have been widely recognised all over the Greek world, others may have had a more restricted 'audience' which could understand them, and in several cases they could 'speak' only to those who commissioned the item, and perhaps to those very close to them.

Hero Cults Performed by Whom?

Having said this, we need to ask a further essential question: who were practising the cults at Late Bronze Age tombs? Were they members of the elite or of the middle or lower classes? Furthermore, were they related to the members of the communities who were responsible for the commissioning of narrative 'heroic' painted scenes on vases? If we opt for the former hypothesis, this would fit well with Hurwit's line of thought, according to which the aristocrats of the Late Geometric period aimed at underlining through narrative art the deeds of heroes and through them their own 'heroic descent', which gave them the right to manage communal affairs and to maintain power in a society which was rapidly developing towards the *isonomia* of the polis (Hurwit 1985: 124). Yet, it is well known that the re-invention of figured scenes in vase-painting antedates the phenomenon of tomb cult and thus cannot be related to it (Coldstream 1974: 273–78). The large numbers of tomb cults suggest that behind them stood a large portion of the population, presumably the middle classes rather than the elites. If we accept this hypothesis, we might perhaps imagine that this was the first time that those among the less privileged encountered objects from the past in significant numbers, including figured images: images that they could observe at ease and thus be inspired from, unlike those similar items circulating among the established elites, which were either restricted to households to which few had access, especially during drinking parties, or destined to be buried within the tomb, and thus taken out of circulation. It is roughly at the same period that offerings at sanctuaries start not only to multiply in numbers but also to be more diversified. Until then we find mostly figurines and everyday pottery, with the exception of the most prized dedications, the tripod cauldrons (Papalexandrou 2005). It is at that time that objects bearing figured scenes were displayed in sanctuaries, and people of all social levels could view them. As a consequence of this, vases decorated with narrative scenes soon entered the repertoire of dedications in sanctuaries.

Thus, behind the rise of tomb cults we could seek for a reflection of the pressure exercised upon the existing social system (Morris 1986: 129; 1988). This may have been one of the means through which the new emerging classes aspiring to elite status competed with the previous ruling decision-making classes (Antonaccio 1995: 70–102; Deoudi 1999: 108–11; Whitley 1988). They must have been those who practised cults at prehistoric tombs and perhaps those responsible for a change in deposition strategies at sanctuaries as well as at tombs. This hypothesis brings us closer to Snodgrass's opinion, according to which it was the small but free landowners, who were threatened by the new elite which was being shaped, who were trying to establish connections with their estates through tracing their ownership of land to legendary ancestors (Snodgrass 1982: 107–19; 1988: 19–26; 1987/89: 60–62). On the other hand, it does not conform to the idea that those practising tomb cults would have been aristocrats who felt that their estates were threatened by the rising lower social classes (Whitley 1988). It should be noted, however, that the latter assumption can be applied to Attica, which witnessed during the late eighth and seventh centuries, as Coldstream argued, an 'internal colonisation' (Coldstream 1977/2003: 135).

On the other hand, behind the cults of prominent individuals who were honoured like heroes after their death we could perhaps envisage the actual ruling members of the elite, who wished to reinforce their threatened position. Several of these 'true heroes' of the eighth century BC did not need to claim their heroic descent through a connection with a prehistoric tomb; their status was acknowledged not only by their family but also by a wider portion of the community, and they were subsequently honoured as such for several generations. It is perhaps not a coincidence either that, in several areas where such cults are observed, there were intense antagonisms between the rising states, for instance Eretria (Bérard 1970; 1978: 89–95; 1972: 219–27; 1982: 89–105; 1983: 43–59; Deoudi 1999: 77–80; Mazarakis Ainian 2000: 187–89) and Chalcis (Hesiod, *Works and Days*, 654 ff.), Lelantine war (Jeffery 1976: 63–68; Parker 1997) or Paros and Naxos (in the case of Mitropolis Square in Naxos, it seems that private family cults at the tombs of relatives gradually merged and finally evolved into a communal hero cult of the rising polis of Naxos [Lambrinoudakis 1988: 235–46; Mazarakis Ainian 1997: 188–89], while at Paros the rising polis paid exceptional honours to its numerous warrior-citizens who fell in the battlefield [Zapheiropoulou 1999; 2006; Croissant 2008]).

Conclusion

The above examination brings us back to the question posed at the beginning: was there any impact of the Homeric epics on the rise of hero cults? In other words can the poems be related to the awakening of interest in the past and the honouring of heroes? Since it is today widely accepted that the Homeric epics were not conceived in the eighth century BC, but were orally transmitted from generation to generation throughout the Early Iron Age, it would be fair to assume that the rise of hero cults is not an unrelated phenomenon. By the Late Geometric period the epics would have reached a wider audience and their impact on the formation of these cults would have become significant. They may have even stimulated the founding of sanctuaries devoted to epic heroes and the practice of tomb cults and cults of 'true heroes'. It is perhaps also at that point (from the mid eighth century BC onwards) that the Greeks became fully aware that the long period that had elapsed since the fall of the Mycenaean civilisation had ultimately resulted in deeply affecting their lives and beliefs, and consequently it was only then that they experienced for the first time a feeling of 'distance' regarding their 'heroic' past (Mazarakis Ainian 2004).

We cannot deny, therefore, that the general 'heroic' way of life reflected in several warrior burial customs and specific iconographical scenes was significantly promoted by the end of the eighth century BC thanks to the growing interest in the epics. The better acquaintance with the poems which now started reaching wider audiences belonging to different social strata must have had a significant impact on attitudes; the honouring of prominent individuals after their death and the conscious search for physical evidence of past heroes were two manifestations of this heroic ideal.

Towards the end of the eighth century BC the ruling nobility gradually started losing its exclusivity in the management of communal matters, as it was apparently challenged by a rising elite, perhaps the 'semi-aristocrats' (as defined by C. Starr [1977: 123–28]), who were steadily and systematically shaping a new ideology. One after effect of this change was that ritual activities, once performed inside dwellings and involving a restricted number of participants, were transferred inside 'urban' temples, some of them monumental (e.g. Eretria, Verdan 2013), suggesting that the participants in these cults were now much more numerous than before. Additionally, a new trend emerged, that of honouring mythical or remote ancestors, alongside 'true heroes' who had earned distinction through their deeds during their lifetime. The former cults were perhaps initiated by the rising elites in order to legitimate their aspired-to position, while the latter may have characterised a threatened nobility, which had held power until then. The rising polis appropriated a number of such cults in the course of the Archaic and later periods (for instance the cults at certain tholos tombs [e.g. Georgiko, Menidi], the Heroon by the West Gate at Eretria, the tumulus at Mitropolis Square at Naxos, the Heraion of Argos [Wright 1988: esp. 193–94; Van Leuven 1994] etc). Within the new frame of the polis the age of heroes became the past. However, they were remembered through the spread of tales narrating their deeds. More importantly, the establishment of sanctuaries, where epic heroes were now worshipped, and the appropriation and maintenance of a restricted number of hero or ancestral cults in several places of the Greek world could safeguard and promote the developing polis ideology.

Acknowledgements

I wish to thank Sue Sherratt and John Bennet for inviting me to participate in the symposium, as well as for their warm hospitality in Sheffield in 2007. I wish to thank Babis Intzesiloglou for discussing with me his excavations at the site of Georgiko in Thessaly and clarifying questions related to the chronology of the material. I also thank Alexandra Alexandridou for fruitful discussions.

Note

1. The tomb was excavated in 1917 by Arvanitopoulos. Intzesiloglou, M. G. *Archaiologiko Deltio* 52 (1997), B2: 478–80; 53 (1998), B2: 439; 54 (1999), B1: 408–409.

Bibliography

Abramson, H.
1979 A hero shrine for Phrontis? *California Studies in Classical Antiquity* 12: 1–19.
Antonaccio, C.
1995 *An Archaeology of Ancestors, Tomb and Hero Cult in Early Greece*. Lanham: Rowman and Littlefield.
Aravantinos, V.
2010 *The Archaeological Museum of Thebes*. Athens: John Latsis Benefit Foundation.
Benson, J. L.
1970 *Horse, Bird and Man: the Origins of Greek Painting*. Amherst: University of Massachusetts Press.
Benton, S.
1934/35 Excavations in Ithaca III, The Cave at Polis I. *Annual of the British School at Athens* 35: 45–73.
1938/39 Excavations in Ithaca III, The Cave of Polis II. *Annual of the British School at Athens* 39: 1–51.
1936 A votive offering to Odysseus. *Antiquity* 10: 350.
Bérard, C.
1970 *Eretria: fouilles et recherches III. L'Hérôon à la porte de l'Ouest*. Bern: Francke.
1972 Le sceptre du prince. *Museum Helveticum* 29: 219–27.
1978 Topographie et urbanisme de l'Erétrie archaïque: L'Héroon. In *Eretria VI*: 89–95. Bern: Francke.
1982 Récuperer la mort du prince: héroïsation et formation de la cité. In G. Gnoli and J.-P. Vernant (eds.), *La Mort, les morts dans les sociétés anciennes*: 89–105. Cambridge and Paris: Cambridge University Press and Edition de la Maison des sciences de l'homme.
1983 L'héroisation et la formation de la cité: Un conflit idéologique. In *Architecture et société de l'archaïsme grec à la fin de la république romaine. Actes du colloque international organisé par le CNRS et l'Ecole Française de Rome, Rome, 2–4 Dec., 1980*: 43–62. Paris and Rome: Centre National de la Recherche Scientifique and Ecole française de Rome.
Bessios, M., A. Kotsonas and Y. Tzifopoulos
2012 *Μεθώνη Πιερίας Ι. Επιγραφές, χαράγματα και εμπορικά σύμβολα στη Γεωμετρική και Αρχαϊκή κεραμική από το 'Υπόγειο'*. Thessaloniki: Centre for the Greek Language.
Blandin, B.
2007 *Eretria: fouilles et recherches XVII. Les pratiques funéraires d'époque géométrique à Erétrie*. Gollion: Ecole suisse d'archéologie en Grèce.
Boardman, J.
2003 *The Archaeology of Nostalgia. How the Greeks Re-Created Their Mythical Past*. London: Thames & Hudson.
Boehringer, D.
2001 *Heroenkulte in Griechenland von der geometrischen bis zur klassischen Zeit. Attika, Argolis, Messenien* (Klio Beihefte 3). Berlin: Akademie Verlag.
Brulotte, E. L.
1994 The 'Pillar of Oinomaos' and the location of Stadium I at Olympia. *American Journal of Archaeology* 98: 53–64.
Burr, D.
1933 A Geometric house and a proto-Attic deposit. *Hesperia* 2: 542–640.
Calligas, P.
1993 Πρώιμη ιστορία των ιερών του Σουνίου. In *Πρακτικά Δ' Επιστημονικής Συνάντησης ΝΑ. Αττικής*: 301–12. Athens: Επιμορφώτικος Σύλλογος Καλυβιών.
Catling, H.
1976 New excavations at the Menelaion, Sparta. In U. Jantzen (ed.), *Neue Forschungen in griechischen Heiligtümern*: 77–90. Tübingen: Wasmuth.
1976–77 Excavations at the Menalaion, Sparta, 1973–76. *Archaeological Reports* 23: 24–42.

1992 Sparta: a Mycenaean palace and a shrine to Menelaus and Helen. *Current Archaeology* 130: 429–31.

1994 Cyprus in the 11th century B.C. – An end or a beginning? In V. Karageorghis (ed.), *Cyprus in the 11th Century B.C.*: 133–41. Nicosia: A.G. Leventis Foundation.

1995 Heroes returned? Subminoan burials from Crete'. In J. B. Carter and S. P. Morris (eds.), *The Ages of Homer. A Tribute to Emily Townsend Vermeule*: 123–36. Austin: Texas University Press.

Chabot Aslan, C.

2011 A place of burning: hero or ancestor cult at Troy. *Hesperia* 80: 381–429.

Coldstream, J. N.

1974 Review of J. L. Benson, Horse, Bird and Man. The Origins of Greek Painting (Amherst, 1970). *Gnomon* 46: 273–78.

1976 Hero cults in the age of Homer. *Journal of Hellenic Studies* 96: 8–17.

1977/2003 *Geometric Greece*. London: Benn/Routledge.

Cook, J. M.

1953a The Agamenoneion. *Annual of the British School at Athens* 48: 30–68.

1953b The cult of Agamemnon at Mycenae. In Γέρας Α. Κεραμόπουλλου: 112–18. Athens: Typographeion Myrtide.

Coulson, W.

1991 The Protogeometric from *Polis* reconsidered. *Annual of the British School at Athens* 86: 42–64.

Coulton, J. and H. W. Catling

1993 *Lefkandi II. The Protogeometric Building at Toumba. Part 2: The Excavation, Architecture and Finds*. London: British School of Archaeology at Athens.

Crielaard, J. P.

1995 Homer, history and archaeology. In J. P. Crielaard (ed.), *Homeric Questions. Essays in Philology, Ancient History and Archaeology, Including the Papers of a Conference Organized by the Netherlands Institute at Athens (15 May 1993)*: 266–273. Amsterdam: J.C. Gieben.

Croissant, F.

2008 Batailles géométriques pariennes. In *Alba de la città, alba delle immagine? Da un suggestione di Bruno d'Agostino* (Tripodes 7): 31–62. Athens: Scuola Archeologica Italiana di Atene.

Deoudi, M.

1999 *Heroenkulte in homerischer Zeit*. (BAR International Series 806). Oxford: Archaeopress.

2005 Keramik und Kult im dromos der Tholos bei Menidi. *Thetis* 11–12: 33–44.

Devillers, M.

1988 *An Archaic and Classical Votive Deposit from a Mycenaean Tomb at Thorikos* (Miscellanea Graeca 8). Gent: Belgian Archaeological School in Greece.

D'Onofrio, A. M.

2001 Immagini di divinità nel materiale votivo dell'edificio ovale geometrico Ateniese e indagine sull'area sacra alle pendici settentrionali dell' Areopago. *Mélanges de l'École française de Rome, Antiquité* 113: 257–320.

Eijnde, F. van den

2010 *Cults and Society in Early Athens*. PhD thesis, University of Utrecht.

forthcoming The Areopagus oval building and Athenian ancestor worship. In A. Mazarakis Ainian, A. Alexandridou and X. Charalambidou (eds.), *Regional Stories Towards a New Perception of the Early Greek World, Acts of an International Symposium in honour of Professor Jan Bouzek, Volos 18–21 June 2015*. Volos: University of Thessaly Press.

Farnell, L. R.

1921 *Greek Hero Cults and Ideas of Immortality*. Oxford: Clarendon Press.

Hadzisteliou-Price, Th.

1973 Hero cult and Homer. *Historia* 22: 129–44.

1979 Hero cult in the age of Homer and earlier. In G.W. Bowersock, W. Burkert and M.C.J. Putnam (eds.), *Arktouros. Mélanges B.W.W. Knox*: 219–28. Berlin and New York: W. de Gruyter.

Hägg, R.

1974 *Die Gräber der Argolis in submykenischer, protogeometrischer und geometrischer Zeit 1. Lage und Form der Gräber*. Uppsala: Universitas Uppsaliensis.

Herrmann, V.

1980 Pelops in Olympia. In *Στήλη. Τόμος εις μνήμην Νικολάου Κοντολέοντος*: 59–74. Athens: Σωματείο φίλων του Νικολάου Κοντολέοντος.

Hurwit, J.M.

1985 *The Art and Culture of Early Greece, 1100–480 B.C.* Ithaca and London: Cornell University Press.

Intzesiloglou, M. G.

1995 Ο μύθος του Αιάτου και της Πολύκλειας. *Καρδιτσιωτικά Χρονικά* 1: 11–18.

2002a Aiatos et Polycléia. Du mythe à l'histoire. *Kernos* 15: 289–95.

2002b The Archaic temple of Apollo at ancient Metropolis (Thessaly). In M. Stamatopoulou and M. Yeroulanou (eds.), *Excavating Classical Culture: Recent Archaeological Discoveries in Greece*, Oxford, Somerville College, 23–27 March 2001 (BAR International Series 1031): 109–15. Oxford: Archaeopress.

2003 Η Ιτωνία Αθηνά και το Θεσσαλικό Ομοσπονδιακό Ιερό της στη Φίλια Καρδίτσας. In *Αρχαιολογικό Έργο Θεσσαλίας και Στερεάς Ελλάδας* 1: 221–237.

Jeffery L. H.

1976 *Archaic Greece*. London: Methuen.

Kearns, E.

1989 *The Heroes of Attica*. London: Institute of Classical Studies, University of London.

Kokkou-Vyridi, K.

1991 *Πρώιμες πυρές θυσιών στο Τελεστήριο της Ελευσίνας*. Athens: Athens Archaeological Society.

Kourou, N.

1990–91 Εύβοια και Ανατολική Μεσόγειος στις αρχές της πρώτης χιλιετίας. *Archäologisch epigraphische Mitteilungen aus Österreich-Ungarn* 29: 237–79.

Kyrieleis, H.

1992 Neue Ausgrabungen in Olympia. In W. Coulson and H. Kyrieleis (eds.), *Proceedings of an International Symposium on the Olympic Games*: 19–24. Athens: Deutsches Archäologisches Institut Athen.

Lambrinoudakis, V.

1988 Veneration of ancestors in Geometric Naxos. In R. Hägg and N. Marinatos (eds.), *Early Greek Cult Practice. Proceedings of the Fifth International Symposium at the Swedish Institute at Athens, 26–29, June, 1986*: 235–46. Stockholm: Svenska Institutet i Athen.

Lemos, I. S.

2000 Songs for heroes: the lack of images in early Greece. In N. K. Rutter and B. A. Sparkes (eds.), *Word and Image in Ancient Greece*: 11–21. Edinburgh: Edinburgh University Press.

Lolling, H. et al.

1880 *Das Kuppelgrab bei Menidi*. Athens: Deutsches Archäologisches Institut.

Lorandou-Papantoniou, R.

1999 *Σολυγεία : η ανασκαφή του 1957–1958*. Athens: Athens Archaeological Society.

Malkin, I.

1998 *The Returns of Odysseus. Colonization and Ethnicity*. Berkeley: University of California Press.

Mazarakis Ainian, A.

1997 *From Rulers' Dwellings to Temples. Architecture, Religion and Society in Early Iron Age Greece* (Studies in Mediterranean Archaeology 121). Jonsered: Paul Åströms Förlag.

1998 Oropos in the Early Iron Age. In M. Bats and B. D'Agostino (eds.), *Euboica. L'Eubea e la presenza Euboica in Calcidica e in Occidente, Atti del Convegno internazionale Napoli 13–16 novembre 1996*: 173–209. Napoli: Centre Jean Bérard.

1999a Reflections of hero cult in Early Iron Age Greece. In R. Hägg (ed.), *Ancient Greek Hero Cult, Proceedings of the 5th International Seminar on Ancient Greek Cult* (Göteborg University 21–23 April 1995): 9–36. Göteborg: Svenska Institutet i Athen.

1999b Νέα στοιχεία για την «Ιερά Οικία» της Ελευσίνας από το αρχείο Ι. Τραυλού. *Αρχαιολογική Εφημερίς* 1999: 43–65.
2000 *Όμηρος και Αρχαιολογία*. Athens: Kardamitsas.
2002 Recent excavations at Oropos (northern Attica). In M. Stamatopoulou and M. Yeroulanou (eds.), *Excavating Classical Culture: Recent Archaeological Discoveries in Greece*, Oxford, Somerville College, 23–27 March 2001 (BAR International Series 1031): 149–78. Oxford: Archaeopress.
2004 From the beginnings to the Archaic Age. Hero cults of Homeric society. In *Thesaurus Cultus et Rituum Antiquorum* (ThesCRA), II, 3.d. *Heroisierung und Apotheose*: 131–40. Basel and Los Angeles: Fondation pour le lexicon iconographicum mythologiae classicae and Getty Publications.
2006–2007 I primi Greci d'Occidente? Scavi nella Graia Omerica (Oropos). *Annali di archeologia e Storia antica* 13–14: 81–110.
2007–2008 Buried among the living in Early Iron Age Greece: some thoughts. In G. Bartoloni and M. Gilda Benedettini (eds.), *Sepolti tra i vivi. Atti del convegno internazionale, Roma, 26–29 Aprile 2006* (Scienze dell'Antichità. Storia, Archeologia, Anthropologia 14): 365–98. Roma: Quasar.

Mili, M.
2015 *Religion and Society in Ancient Thessaly*. Oxford: Oxford University Press.

Morgan, C.
2003 *Early Greek States Beyond the Polis*. London: Routledge.

Morris, I.
1986 The use and abuse of Homer. *Classical Antiquity* 5: 81–129.
1988 Tomb cult and the 'Greek Renaissance': the past in the present in the 8th century B.C. *Antiquity* 62: 750–61.

Nagy, G.,
1979 *The Best of the Achaeans: Concepts of the Hero in Archaic Greece*. Baltimore: John Hopkins University Press.

Papalexandrou, N.
2005 *The Visual Poetics of Power. Warriors, Youths and Tripods in Early Greece*. Lanham: Lexington Books.

Parker, V.
1997 *Untersuchungen zum Lelantischen Krieg und verwandten Problemen der frühgriechischen Geschichte* (Historia Einzelschriften 109). Stuttgart: F. Steiner.

Picard, Ch.
1940 L'heroon de Phrontis au Sounion. *Revue Archéologique* 16: 1–28.

Polignac, F. de
1994 Mediation, competition, and sovereignty. The evolution of rural sanctuaries in Geometric Greece. In S.E. Alcock and R. Osborne (eds.), *Placing the Gods. Sanctuaries and Sacred Space in Ancient Greece*: 3–18. Oxford: Clarendon Press.
1995 *Cults, Territory, and the Origins of the Greek City-State*. Chicago and London: University of Chicago Press.

Popham, M. R.
1994 Precolonization: early Greek contact with the east. In G.R. Tsetskhladze and F. De Angelis (eds.), *The Archaeology of Greek Colonisation. Essays Dedicated to Sir John Boardman*: 11–34. Oxford: Oxford University School of Archaeology.

Popham, M. R. and I. S. Lemos
1995 A Euboean warrior trader. *Oxford Journal of Archaeology* 14: 151–57.

Powell, B. B.
1991 *Homer and the Origin of the Greek Alphabet*. Cambridge: Cambridge University Press.

Rohde, E.
1894 *Psyche. Seelencult und Unsterblichkeitsglaube der Griechen*. Freiburg: J.C.B. Mohr.

Snodgrass, A.
1982 Les origines du culte des héros dans la Grèce antique. In G. Gnoli and J.-P. Vernant (eds.), *La Mort, les morts dans les sociétés anciennes*: 107–19. Cambridge and Paris: Cambridge University Press and Edition de la Maison des sciences de l'homme.
1987/89 The rural landscape and its political significance. *Opus* 6/7: 60–62.
1988 The archaeology of the hero. Annali del Seminario di studi del mondo classico: *Sezione di archeologia e storia antica* 10: 19–26.
1998 *Homer and the Artists. Text and Picture in Early Greek Art*. Cambridge: Cambridge University Press.
Stais, V.
1917 Σουνίου Ανασκαφαί. *Αρχαιολογική Εφημερίς* 1917: 168–213.
Starr, C.
1977 *The Economic and Social Growth of Early Greece, 800–500 B.C.* New York: Oxford University Press.
Theodoropoulou-Polychroniadis, Z.
2015 *Sounion revisited: The sanctuaries of Poseidon and Athena at Sounion in Attica*. Oxford: Archaeopress.
Travlos, J.
1983 Η Αθήνα και η Ελευσίνα στον 8ο και 7ο π.Χ. αι. *Annuario della Scuola archeologica di Atene e delle Missioni italiane in Oriente* 61: 323–37.
Van Leuven, J.
1994 Tombs and religion at Mycenaean Prosymna. *Journal of Prehistoric Religion* 8: 42–60.
Verdan, S.
2013 *Le Sanctuaire d'Apollon Daphnéphoros à l'époque géométrique*, Eretria XXII. Lausanne: Gollion.
Verdelis, N.
1958 Σολυγεία. *Πρακτικά της Αρχαιολογικής Εταιρείας* 1958: 135–45.
1962 A sanctuary at Solygeia. *Archaeology* 15: 184–92.
Wace, A. J. B., M. S. Thompson and J. P. Droop
1908/09 The Menelaion. *Annual of the British School at Athens* 15: 108–57.
Wells, B.
1983 *Asine II: Results of the Excavations East of the Acropolis 1970–1974, fasc. 4: The Protogeometric Period. Part 2: An Analysis of the Settlement*. Stockholm: Svenska Institutet i Athen.
Whitley, J.
1988 Early states and hero cults: a re-appraisal. *Journal of Hellenic Studies* 108: 173–82.
1994 The monuments that stood before Marathon: tomb cult and hero cult in Archaic Attica. *American Journal of Archaeology* 98: 213–30.
Wright, J.
1988 The Old Temple Terrace at the Argive Heraeum and the early cult of Hera in the Argolid. *Journal of Hellenic Studies* 102: 186–201.
Zapheiropoulou, Ph.
1999 I due 'Polyandria' dell'antica necropolis di Paros. *Annali dell'Istituto universitario orientali di Napoli* (sezione archeologia) N.S. 6: 13–24.
2006 Geometric battle scenes on vases from Paros. In E. Rystedt and B. Wells (eds.), *Pictorial Pursuits*: 271–77. Stockholm: Svenska Institutet i Athen.

Chapter 8

Gilgamesh and Heroes at Troy: Myth, History and Education in the Invention of Tradition

Stephanie Dalley

Many books and articles claim to show connections between Homeric epic and that of ancient Mesopotamia, particularly the *Epic of Gilgamesh* (e.g. West 1997: 335, n.3). Some likenesses consist of narrative themes, others of motifs and phrases. But all types of similarities can be dismissed as coincidental, without the need to invoke contact or influence, by those who reject a diffusionist model in the belief that similar phases of development can trigger similar inspirations. What is needed in order to convert the sceptics is, to find mechanisms of contact that led to the demonstrated result. The aim of this paper is to look at evidence, much of it recently discovered in cuneiform texts, for the role of international education as a mechanism, and to show how newly published pieces of the *Epic of Gilgamesh* have radically changed our understanding of its transmission. The period from which evidence can be found is mainly the Middle and Late Bronze Ages, with some transition into alphabetic scripts and into the early Iron Age.

Ancient education, in particular the Mesopotamian school curriculum from its earliest known stages to its latest, provides a key. This area of explanation is different from that of Lord, who mainly assumed that the movement of peoples, whether through migration, deportation or individual travel, caused the spread of mythic patterns orally (Lord 1990). This may well be true in some instances, but I hope to show that it may not be the main type of contact between Mesopotamia and Greece for literary influence. Closer connections came through a system of educational training in cuneiform, now attested among the Egyptians, the Hittites of Anatolia and the Levant in the Bronze Age, and adapted for, or supplanted by, alphabetic scripts from the Late Bronze Age into the Iron Age.

In recent decades it has become apparent that both Middle and Late Bronze Age scribes throughout the literate world were trained to write the Babylonian language in non-alphabetic cuneiform script. Far beyond the limits of the Mesopotamian empires,

Babylonian was the common language of diplomacy in writing. Even in Egypt the records of Tell el-Amarna include not only the well known diplomatic letters but also less well known lexical lists which functioned as dictionaries, and epic literature used in extracts for advanced study by apprentice scribes (Izreel 1997). What is true for Amarna is true also for Ugarit on the North Syrian coast, and for the Hittite capital Hattusha, as well as for other Egyptian, Anatolian and Canaanite cities. The tradition of scribal training in cuneiform, well known for the Late Bronze Age, extends back in time from the Early Bronze Age at Ebla in Syria (Archi 1992), with less well-known evidence from Byblos (Sollberger 1976–80); from the Middle Bronze c. 1800 BC at Kültepe in Anatolia (Hecker 1993); in Palestine, according to evidence from Hebron, Hazor, Megiddo, Aphek, including trilingual dictionary fragments with Sumerian, Babylonian and West Semitic (Horowitz and Oshima 2006: 29–32, 42); two fragments dated c. 1550–1450 from Transjordanian Pella (Black 1992), some Middle or Late Bronze Age school tablets, such as those from Hazor (Horowitz and Oshima 2006: 73) and many lexical texts from Ugarit and Emar at the end of the Late Bronze Age. Those lexical pieces disclose a widespread and long-standing training in cuneiform Babylonian. From the several official letters found on the same sites it is clear that the training was put into practice for official letters in the Middle and Late Bronze Ages. The same is true for several administrative texts written in cuneiform on clay. A chance find from Megiddo gives an extract from the *Epic of Gilgamesh* in Middle Bronze Age Palestine, and tablets with versions from parts of the *Epic of Gilgamesh* from Ugarit and Emar date to the end of the Late Bronze Age (Cavigneaux 2007: 319–20; George 2007b: 239–42).

Even before the rise of the Hittite kingdom in central Anatolia, when stories about Gilgamesh were definitely diverse in Mesopotamia – for instance in the case of Sumerian stories about Gilgamesh and Huwawa (Edzard 1993; George 1999: 149–66) – Assyrian merchants at Kanesh not only used a simplified repertoire of cuneiform signs and limited vocabulary for business records, but also possessed a copy of a literary text that used a more extensive range of signs, grammar and syntax (Günbatti 1997; van de Mieroop 2000). This discovery was a surprise, because it had previously been supposed that writing was used there purely for commercial purposes. Thus literacy was not restricted to business. The discovery also gives some background into how the city of Kanesh came to play a part in epics about kings of Agade c. 2300 BC (Röllig 2004: 206–07).

It may seem surprising that evidence is so scarce. Two reasons may be suggested. Clay tablets are cheap, easily discarded, often re-used for new texts (Faivre 1995) or for patching holes in walls and floors, ideal for school work. Contrary to a common misconception, they were not baked, only sun-dried, and so dissolved if they were not protected from water. Wooden or ivory writing boards with inscribed waxed surfaces are much more expensive, therefore prestigious, and likely to have been used for certain kinds of archives and collections of literature that we cannot yet call libraries in the Early and Middle Bronze Age. There are many textual references to such writing boards in Hittite and Babylonian texts (Symington 1991). Owing to their perishable fabric, we can be sure that absence of material evidence – with the lucky exception of the one found in the Late Bronze Age shipwreck at Ulu Burun off the southern coast of Turkey (Pulak 2008: 294, 367–68) and two from a hinged set of sixteen found in a Neo-Assyrian well at Nimrud (Howard 1955; Curtis and Reade 1995: fig. 198) – is certainly not evidence for material rarity. Even in the marshy area of southern Mesopotamia writing boards were in common use around 1500 BC by the First Sealand Dynasty (Dalley 2009: 15–16); and letters incised in alphabetic script on the edges of three of the clay tablets from that Sealand archive are almost certainly genuine (Colonna d'Istria 2012), and imply the use of a still undiscovered medium, presumably an organic material that does not survive. In the Yemen the central ribs from fronds of the date-palm are incised in alphabetic script with official correspondence, the earliest known examples dated by C14 going back to the ninth century (Stein 2010), but presumably beginning at an earlier date. The new evidence, both from the First Sealand Dynasty and from the palm ribs of the Yemen, shows that the variety of scripts and materials used within Mesopotamia from the middle of the second millennium into the Iron Age is greater than was appreciated before. Full versions of the *Epic of Gilgamesh* were available to members of the elite, not necessarily on clay, whereas extracts written by school children were perhaps put on clay tablets in the Bronze Age more often than in the Iron Age. Alphabetic versions of literature written on long-perished other materials are not out of the question, at least from the Late Bronze Age onwards.

Recent discoveries in Hittite studies have shown that Hittite control of some sort extended in the Late Bronze Age to Miletus, Ephesus and Troy / Hisarlık (Hawkins 1998; Latacz 2004: 80, 86). That control was reinforced through treaties and diplomatic correspondence which, like that of Tell el-Amarna, was written in cuneiform script by scribes who had been trained by experts from Mesopotamia. At the Hittite capital scribes with Babylonian and Assyrian names took charge of teaching (Beckman 1983). In one clear example a Sumerian hymn, known from the Mesopotamian Middle Bronze Age, was adapted for a Hittite version (Metcalf 2011). At Ugarit an Assyrian scribe named Nahiš-šalmu, who can be identified by his name as an Assyrian working abroad, taught the locals cuneiform (van Soldt 2001); and at Emar on the bend of the Euphrates in northern Syria a North Babylonian scribe named Kidin-Gula gave instruction in lexical lists (Cohen 2004), at a time when the Hittite Empire was dissolving. The dissolution was far from absolute: it left behind remnant kingdoms in Carchemish and in Cilician Tarhuntassa whose rulers' descendants established their own dynasties in cities such as Kinalua, modern Tell Tayinat. The Dark Age, long thought to break the link between the Late Bronze Age and the Early Iron Age, is no longer a valid concept (Hawkins 2011), and the idea that travelling heroes occasionally transmitted oral stories (Lane Fox 2008: 38, 179) is of less consequence than the presence of well-trained teachers at the heart of foreign powers, responsible for producing professionals who could compose a treaty, list a valuable dowry, enumerate military chariotry or compose a royal seal inscription. Specifically in the case of the Greek-speaking world, direct contact between the people of Ahhiyawa and the Middle Assyrian empire may be attested in the Hittite treaty of Tudhaliya IV with the kingdom of Amurru under king Shaushga-muwa, in which an attempt was made to block contacts between Ahhiyawa and Assyria in the late thirteenth century BC (Latacz 2004: 127; Bryce 2004: 315–16; Beckman *et al.* 2011: 50–68). Scholarship consisting of instruction in cuneiform writing was thus exported from Mesopotamia, although not from a single base.

From Egypt recent evidence has shown that the cuneiform from Amarna of the 18th Dynasty was not an isolated intrusion into native writing tradition. More than a century earlier than the Amarna archive is the fragment of a cuneiform Babylonian letter that was found in a palace well at Tell el-Dab'a in the eastern Delta. The well was filled up in the late 15th Dynasty of the Hyksos kings, and the clay tablet must have come from Babylonia in the latter part of the Old Babylonian dynasty to which Hammurabi belonged, thus in archaeological terms towards the end of the Middle Bronze Age (Van Koppen and Radner 2009: 115–18). Another fragment of a clay tablet was found at the adjacent site of Qantir, written in Babylonian cuneiform from the Hittite court to the Egyptian court of Rameses II of the 19th Dynasty, several decades later than the Amarna tablets (Pusch and Jakob 2003: 143–54). Although it was found in a secondary context, the date to the reign of Rameses II or soon after was clear from the text. These finds give a minimum of 300 years during which cuneiform Babylonian was practiced in Egypt. The royal courts from which these fragments came must have employed scribes trained in cuneiform Babylonian, extracts from the *Epic of Gilgamesh* included; but the depth of Egyptian mythology was sufficient, presumably, to discourage the composition of a local version of the *Epic* such as was produced in Hittite and Hurrian.

From Mesopotamian sites, very many of the tablets bearing extracts of the *Epic of Gilgamesh* in Babylonian have been recognised as school exercises: almost all the Middle and Late Bronze Age tablets are extracts written by pupils, according to the listings in George's 2003 edition, but this is not true of most of the Iron Age tablets. At first it might seem perplexing that we have so few school texts from the Iron Age, from the many centuries during which tablets inscribed with text from the *Epic of Gilgamesh* mainly come from Ashurbanipal's library at Nineveh, or from the Seleucid library at Uruk. School work must have been prolific to have produced the many scribes known from clay tablets, and we can only suppose that there was a shift from clay to perishable materials, or ostraca with writing scrubbed off by energetic excavators. The use of wooden writing boards is now quite well known, as already mentioned; but there is now evidence not just for texts written with alphabetic scripts but also in cuneiform, on scrolls of parchment, Babylonian *magallatu*, though they are only attested so far from the Hellenistic period (Frahm 2005). School texts written on clay are, however, found at Sultantepe in south-east Turkey, dating to the late Assyrian period, and they give good evidence for continuation of the Bronze Age tradition of school work.

Current research among Assyriologists is concentrating on identifying the curriculum of apprentice scribes at different periods (e.g. Veldhuis 1997). Babylonian cuneiform script is complicated because it uses so many different signs, both as logograms and as syllabic signs, so they began with exercises based on individual signs. Until recently it was supposed that they learned their *Epic of Gilgamesh*, at least from the Late Bronze Age onwards, from a fixed, canonical version that had been established from earlier material, perhaps 'essentially the masterpiece of a single, anonymous poet' (George 1999: xxi), an author-scribe named Sin-lēqi-unninni who made many major changes in the story to mould it into the great work which we now call the Standard Babylonian Version. He was a lamentation priest (*kalû*), not an incantation priest (*mašmaššu / āšipu)* as was thought earlier (Beaulieu 2000).

There were already several reasons to discard that model of single authorship together with a named author. The fragmentary tablets from Hattusha, the Hittite capital, made it clear that the *Epic of Gilgamesh* was not just translated into Hittite and Hurrian (Beckman 2003), but retold for its new environment in a free, creative way, very different from the stilted and word-for-word translation of, for example, some Amarna letters which imply a pedantic reliance on those dictionary texts already mentioned. Since paraphrases or adaptations of the *Gilgamesh Epic* were made in Hittite and Hurrian, we might infer that similar creative paraphrases were made in Canaanite and Phoenician, using a trilingual dictionary of the kind that came to light in Tell Aphek. Even within George's magisterial work on the *Babylonian Epic of Gilgamesh* in 2003, he deliberately omitted from his edition a Middle Bronze Age fragment relating the episode of the bull-of-heaven from Nineveh (George 2003: 23, n.62) and an Iron Age school text probably from Kish (George 2003: 395, n.46) because they did not fit his model. Since then he has modified his opinion, based on new evidence, notably from three texts.

The first, a well-written text, certainly not a school exercise, is probably from the First Sealand Dynasty of the mid-second millennium BC, now in the Schøyen private collection (George 2007a: 75). It describes Gilgamesh as king of Ur rather than Uruk, and includes episodes that George had originally assigned to the genius of Sin-lēqi-unninni who is dated later. This shows, among other things, that the city which the hero ruled was not fixed.

The second consists of fragments from a library excavated at Ugarit in the house of Urtenu, dating to the end of the Late Bronze Age. They included a much altered version of the prologue to the *Epic of Gilgamesh* which had previously been considered the beginning to the narrative established by Sin-lēqi-unninni and thereafter fixed and canonical (George 2007b). The alterations were far more than minor variants and included the insertion of new lines and different ordering of others. George thought that the coherence of the text was damaged by them, and attributed the confusion to oral transmission. In part this opinion was the result of his division of text into quatrains and couplets (George 1999: liii–liv, e.g. 23, lines iii 26–27), but there is much subjectivity in his divisions; compare e.g. George 1999: 23–24, where 'I shall face a battle I know not' is separated from the next line 'I shall ride a road I know not', but not separated when they are repeated in the third person on the next page. His division into 4-line stanzas is thus imposed arbitrarily by him on the text and is inconsistent; no ancient evidence exists to justify it.

A third new text, identified in the Sulaimaniyah Museum in Iraqi Kurdistan, appears to show that the neo-Assyrian version of the *Epic* such as was recognised by George in 2003 but supposed to have been discontinued in the late seventh century, far from dying out, was known in Babylonia after the fall of the Assyrian empire, and existed alongside the supposedly canonical Babylonian text (Al-Rawi and George 2014). The differences between the Assyrian and Babylonian versions can be substantial, showing that a speech from one character could be transferred to the mouth of another, at a different stage of the story. For instance, the *carpe diem* speech of Siduri to Gilgamesh, a passage in an Old Babylonian version, was remodelled and transferred to Ut-napishtim in an Assyrian, later version best attested from seventh century Nineveh (George 2003: 32). This text in particular refutes the concept of a single canonical text in Babylonia after the fall of the Assyrian empire around 612 BC.

We know that the Greek alphabet is derived from the Phoenician, and that Phoenicians were trading in the Late Bronze and Early Iron Ages in the East Mediterranean; their formal inscriptions on stone at Zincirli dated roughly 825 BC (Gibson 1982: 30–39), at Karatepe and at Çineköy, both in Cilicia, dated to the second half of the eighth century (Röllig in Çambel 1999: 50–81; Tekoglu and Lemaire 2000). All these inscriptions bear witness to the widespread use and prestige of the Phoenician script in the ninth and eighth centuries, around the time when the adaptation of the script from Phoenician to Greek took place. These are not the work of locally trained, peripheral scribes, but were made 'by a scribe / by scribes educated in a centre of standard Phoenician writing' (Röllig *apud* Çambel 1999: 79). Some of the inscriptions from north-west Syria and Cilicia have versions in the Luwian language, written with Hittite hieroglyphs, so Luwian too is likely to have played a part in the adaptation and transmission of epic tales.

Those inscriptions date from a time when the Assyrians, as recorded in the inscriptions of Sargon II, were in direct contact with kings of Cypriot cities, whose names are certainly Greek (Radner 2010: 436–40). They, or their representatives, travelled to Babylon, over which Sargon had recently established direct rule, roughly in 709 BC:

> And seven kings of Ya$^{\underline{o}}$, a region of the land Yadnana which is situated 7 days' journey to the west in the middle of the sea, and so their residences are distant, whose names none of the kings my fathers, kings of Assyria and Babylonia had heard from distant days til now; from the midst of the sea they heard the deeds I had done in Chaldea (Babylonia) and the Hittite land (Syria), and their hearts palpitated and fear fell upon them. Gold, silver, vessels of ebony and boxwood, their country's craftsmanship they brought to me, to my presence in Babylon, and they kissed my feet. (Fuchs 1994: 232)

From iconography it appears that men in Greek armour, whether Cypriot, Ionian or other, were serving in the Levant around that time (Luraghi 2006).

These observations have implications for interpreting the fact that both the *Iliad* (Morgan 1998: 69) and the *Epic of Gilgamesh* were used in extracts for schoolboys: the adoption of a script goes hand-in-hand with the structure and contents of a school curriculum, not only in the Iron Age (Gesche 2000: 61–198) but also now established for the Late Bronze Age at Ugarit. There tablets combine the use of the traditional Mesopotamian logo-syllabic script with texts in the local alphabet. The traditional Mesopotamian curriculum is modified for local conditions; scribes were trained in both languages and both scripts. They made extracts from Mesopotamian myths in Mesopotamian script but their local Ugaritic myths in alphabetic script. Their model epistolary letters written in alphabetic script follow the general layout of Mesopotamian practice but adapted to local usages (Hawley 2008). This group of information clarifies the way that transition was made from non-alphabetic to alphabetic, and seems, on lesser evidence, to apply also to the Iron Age in Palestine, where a symbiosis between script and curriculum has recently been set out in the context of a tenth century BC abecedary from southern Palestine (Tappy *et al.* 2006), giving an early date which is relevant for the Philistine evidence described below.

A well-dated ostracon of the mid tenth century from Khirbet Qeiyafa, on the border between Philistia and Judah (see Fig. 8.1 for sites mentioned in text), has drawn from Na'aman the statement that the inscription 'is tightly connected to the literary

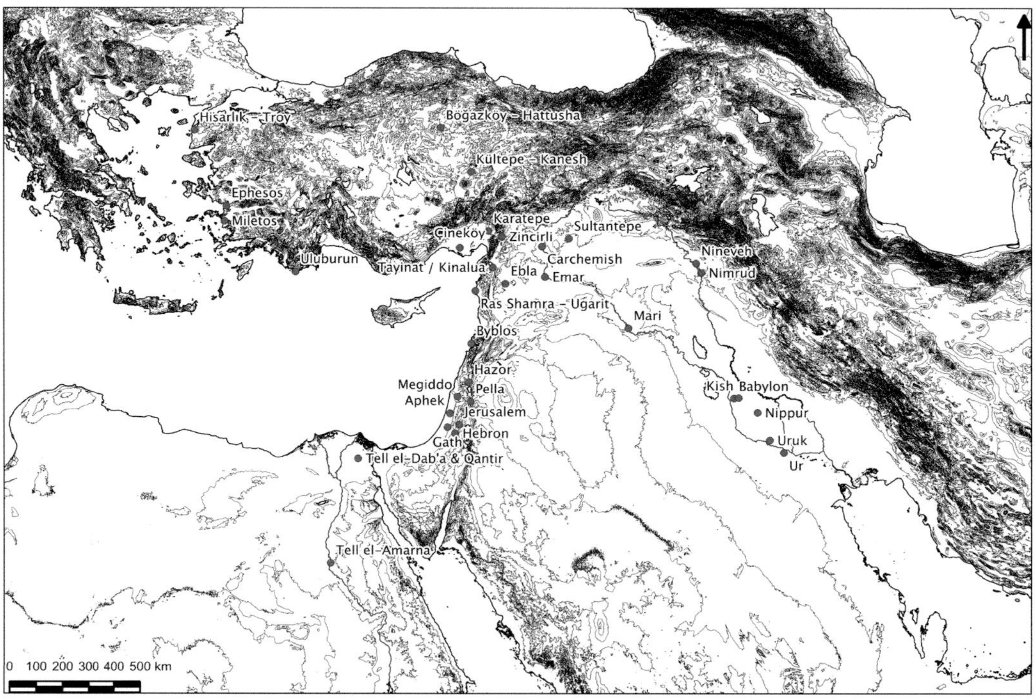

Fig. 8.1: Map showing places mentioned in the text.

tradition that developed in the Shephelah during the transitional period from the Late Bronze Age to Iron II A' (Na'aman 2010: 513). The royal name Achish, Babylonian Ikausu, interpreted as 'the Achaean' (Gitin, Dothan and Naveh 1997), 'an appellation intending to declare the ancestral nationality of the king', has been found at Ekron in a late-eighth/early-seventh-century context, and is thought to be a more-or-less dynastic name, since it occurs for the ninth century king of Gath in the Old Testament (I Sam 27–29; I Kings 2:39); but the interpretation has been questioned. If these two names are correctly analysed – which is not certain without supporting evidence – they would complement archaeological evidence for Minoan/Mycenaean customs during the early phase of Philistine settlement in southern Palestine (Stager 2004; Maeir 2003–05: 535), seeming to imply that the Philistines understood themselves to be Greeks and preserved the word Achaean outside the archaic context of Homeric poetry. This would tie in with the interpretation of the greaves worn by Goliath, which seems to retroject Greek sixth-century (or earlier) armour into an ostensibly local battle in Palestine (Yadin 2004).

In the case of the curriculum for Greek, the existence of exercises in writing syllables as well as single letters (Morgan 1998: 42–43) is probably derived from the teaching of syllabic writing when ligatures are not in question (cf. Thomas 1992: 55). As far as the late eighth century and the Phoenicians are concerned, we can assume that the Phoenicians, as direct neighbours and descendants of Bronze Age Canaanites, inherited the type of curriculum that had been used earlier for training Canaanite and Hittite scribes in cuneiform, beginning with individual signs, progressing to syllabaries, and using trilingual dictionaries; and we now know that apprentice scholars, having learnt the script, went on to practise with a set curriculum. This consisted of lists of words and phrases relevant to legal and business terminology; proverbs – often found on the obverse of school tablets that have mathematical calculations on the reverse – (e.g. Robson 1999: 245); and extracts from particular literary works. This is likely the right explanation for how Archilochus in the mid seventh century BC came to quote in Greek a proverb attested a thousand years earlier in a cuneiform Babylonian text of Middle Bronze Age Mari (Moran 1978), expressing a general sentiment with identical imagery.

A comparable use of fables for school work (Morgan 1998: 121; Tinney 1999: 167) presumably underlies the close relationship between writings attributed to Ahiqar in Aramaic and those attributed to Aesop in European languages (Perry 1952). Proverbs had short sentences ideal for dictation, and fables were suited likewise for a slightly longer exercise as trainees improved their skills. The extract of lines from the *Epic of Gilgamesh*, identified in Hebrew translation in the *Book of Ecclesiastes* can be explained in a similar way (Tigay 1982: 167–68; George 2003: 275). The existence of commentaries on Babylonian texts from the eighth to the second century BC may also belong to a school tradition that was inherited, eventually, in Ionian and Hellenistic Egyptian schools (Frahm 2011: 3). It was not limited to any specific language family; indeed, Sumerian and Babylonian with which the tradition began, do not belong to the same linguistic group. The system could be adapted for Hittite, Luwian, Egyptian, Canaanite, etc.

Admittedly the evidence for schools and curriculum in the Early Iron Age is scant, and the transition from the cuneiform system of writing to an alphabetic system with the changes of curriculum involved in that transition is barely traceable. In Israel it is debatable whether the abecedaries, with various ordering of letters, indicate the existence of school training; but the standard shapes of alphabetic letters throughout Palestine, and the templates for writing epistolary letters based on older templates, show a consistency that implies a centralised control. The content of extant early inscriptions too, largely economic and military, supports that implication (Rollston 2006).

At what point in time we can begin to speak of libraries is hard to establish. In the Middle Bronze Age at Mari on the middle Euphrates, rituals and heroic epic-type compositions seem to have been written for one specific occasion, without any attempt to create a universal application or a template for the future, implying a very fluid tradition. Moreover, they were quite carelessly written, as drafts to accompany a ceremony or ritual; such a text could be imported from another city, but again, for a specific, single event (Durand and Guichard 1997: 19–24). So when literary texts are found, they probably belong within the category of archives as defined by Pedersén (1998: 3–4). Most of the so-called libraries of the second millennium are found alongside archival records and teaching texts such as lexical lists. On the other hand, the looting of literary texts from Babylon by Tukulti-Ninurta I (1244–1208 BC), as recorded in his epic (not in his 'historical' inscriptions), implies the collection of older works written elsewhere, perhaps not primarily intended for teaching purposes; the deliberate baking of such texts in antiquity, and the drawing up of catalogues, also indicate a more than ephemeral purpose. We cannot assume that texts from the earliest libraries were fixed and canonical from then onwards, although texts distributed among a few different cities by collecting and copying may sometimes give that impression.

Claims for oral transmission are hard to verify: the evidence speaks mainly for a written tradition, although king Shulgi of Ur (2094–47) in the Early Bronze Age claimed to have collected and written down oral narratives and songs, and to have established scribal schools at Ur and Nippur (Klein 1981:46–47). As far as the Homeric epics are concerned, we can say that influence from the *Epic of Gilgamesh* was not only possible but likely, no matter what versions of the *Gilgamesh Epic* were known in the Late Bronze Age. Some of the additions and changes made to the Babylonian *Epic* are very similar to those noted in the *Iliad*, although West ascribes such changes in the latter to the one poet progressively altering his own written work (West 2011: 3, 11). So we can suggest one line of contact, through training for scribes.

It would be easy to suppose that oral tradition is responsible for both the diversity and for the deliberate changes. But we cannot take this for granted in the literate, centralised and hierarchical society of Assyria. A recent study of a highly rhetorical yet historical Assyrian text which is ostensibly a letter written by the king Esarhaddon to a god, shows that one of the two extant texts contains blank spaces, to be filled in at a later date (Eph'al and Tadmor 2006). This is very direct and unequivocal evidence for the cut-and-paste technique of written composition that has been deduced from occasional blatant disjunctions in single texts.

For a 'cut-and-paste' technique which can lead to anomalies or disjunctions in a text, I would like to cite a Mediaeval parallel from England. In statutes for benefactions in the fifteenth century, John Goodall writes: 'Like most mediaeval documents, statutes tend to follow standardized formulae ... they share much in common, and occasionally even phrases or whole regulations, with other, roughly contemporary statutes. ... (A) model was expanded, added to or tailored to suit their respective needs'. He found that this phenomenon was recognisable even though one text was in Latin and another in colloquial English (Goodall 2001: 219–21).

Can iconography be used to prove the existence of a story, presumably as oral tradition, before the cuneiform texts become available? The answer depends to some extent on how specific the image is. There is a growing body of opinion that the motif of a man ascending on the back of an eagle while his sheep look up at him may not necessarily represent an antecedent to the *Epic of Etana* as was long supposed (Buchanan and Moorey 1966: no. 332; Green 1997: 137–39), because an early Sumerian text seems to refer to an episode in which Gilgamesh as a child abandoned at birth and adopted, was later rescued from harm by an eagle. This substantiates the story told by Aelian, long dismissed as an non-authentic Mesopotamian tale (Henkelman 2006; Frayne in Steymans 2010: 168–75). On the ninth century BC gold beaker found at Hasanlu in western Iran several episodes from traditions about Gilgamesh are portrayed, according to recent interpretations (Steymans 2010: 361 and 415 for drawings). They include the handing over for adoption and the flight on the eagle which are not narrated in any extant text; and episodes well-known from extant text including the wrestling of Gilgamesh with Enkidu, the forging of new weapons, the killing of Humbaba, Ishtar's attempt at seduction, the snorting of the bull of heaven, and the wearing of lion-skins.

So far there is no evidence that the export of educators teaching cuneiform Babylonian continued after the Late Bronze Age, during the neo-Assyrian Empire period. What little evidence there is from neo-Assyrian texts, shows that singers or musicians and lamentation priests (who also sang), came to Assyria from abroad: in the early eighth century singers from Tabal (upland Cilicia) and Kummuh (Commagene) received rations in Nimrud (Dalley and Postgate 1984 no.184) in 784 BC; in the late eighth century lamentation priests from Samaria and from Syria ('Hatti') feasted at Nimrud (Watanabe 1989: 272); and Sennacherib deported Judaean musicians from Jerusalem in 701 BC (Luckenbill 1924: 34 ll.46–48). The visit of those foreign lamentation priests to Nimrud early in the eighth century, feasting with the royal family, would have provided an ideal opportunity for the reception of the *Gilgamesh Epic* by foreigners and subsequent dissemination beyond Assyria.

The question of whether Gilgamesh was once an historical character can be put alongside the question whether the heroes at Troy and their war were fictional or real, with a view to finding out whether a comparison can be made in that respect. We may need to separate the war located at Troy from the named heroes and their homelands, for we cannot assume that the same understanding is true on both accounts.

Many scholars have thought that the hero Gilgamesh was historical (Jacobsen 1976: 195; Moran 1995: 2327; Lambert 1998: 58), all supposing that he was king of Uruk c. 2700 BC as the *Sumerian King List* says. Among some of the opinions quite recently expressed in the *Blackwell Companion to Epic*, we find Noegel (2005: 235–36) implying that we know for certain that Gilgamesh was historical, whereas Nagy (2005: 85), supporting Hendel (1987), regards him as a generic embodiment of an ideal. Of course he is there in the *Sumerian King List*, but Wilcke has shown that the early Sumerian kings' names and parentage were designed to demonstrate legitimate succession derived from the great gods, and can be understood as an invented tradition (Wilcke 1989). Extensive excavations at Uruk, Ur and Kish have yielded not a single dedicatory inscription of Gilgamesh or his 'father' Lugalbanda on any material object. An analysis of the hero's name and the names of his relatives Lugalbanda and Enmerkar seems to point in the same direction (Falkenstein 1957–71: 357; Glassner 2003: 211). Gilgamesh himself is included in a list of gods from Abu Salabikh around 2600 BC (Mander 1986: 86); and the great cities of early antiquity were considered to have been built by gods – Kish according to the *Epic of Etana* was built by the gods in general; and Mari was built by 'the god' according to an inscription of the nineteenth century BC (Sollberger and Kupper 1971: 246; Frayne 1990: 605 line 35). Likewise the wall of Troy was said to have been built by the gods Poseidon and Apollo (*Iliad* 7.446–53). I have changed my mind since writing an introduction to the myths of Mesopotamia, and now think that Gilgamesh was almost certainly *not* a historical man (Dalley 1989: 40).

An invented tradition which promoted the kingship of a specific city may be a useful way to understand Gilgamesh and his traditions. What is perhaps just as important, as agreed by several scholars quoted by Niditch (2005: 280), is that audience and tellers of the tale both believed that their epic described real historical events. As far as Gilgamesh is concerned, this belief was entrenched by the time king Anam ruled Uruk in the nineteenth century BC, for he recorded that he had restored a temple built by the two divinised but definitely historical kings Ur-Nammu and Shulgi, but also restored the wall of Uruk which was the ancient work of divine Gilgamesh (Sollberger and Kupper 1971: 233; Frayne 1990: 474). His predecessor Sin-kašid, who claimed to be born of the same mother as Gilgamesh, was married to the daughter of a king of Babylon (Frayne 1990: 464), making him well placed to ensure that his version succeeded in dominating the curriculum of apprentice scribes.

Whether historical or not, Gilgamesh changed from legendary king to ruler of the Underworld; this is a transition that has notable parallels in the Egyptian myth of Osiris and the Cretan–Greek legend of Minos.

For various versions of the *Epic of Gilgamesh*, locations other than the king's royal city could be changed too. We know from Sumerian tales of Gilgamesh that his great adventure with Enkidu was to travel eastwards into the Zagros mountains of Iran; whereas the Babylonian epic places the same adventure in the west, in the mountains of Lebanon. This shift reflects the focus of royal campaigns, which were conducted mainly eastwards in the late third millennium, but mainly westwards thereafter. One senses the influence of a royal patron on the evolution of the epic, and one is reminded of the situation in Mari, when all rituals and poems were composed for one particular occasion. Changes in the place named where the Ark came to rest after the Flood seem also to reflect the deeds of particular kings or periods of activity: Mt Nimush in the Standard version, as in the inscriptions of the ninth century king Ashurnasirpal II, but Mt Ararat as in Achaemenid Persian inscriptions, according to the Seleucid priest Berossus in the fourth century; and Mt Parnassus in Ovid's account of the Flood. Shifts of location in these examples make it very unlikely that a supposedly historical king Gilgamesh could be connected with particular deeds in a particular location. The deduction to be drawn from the Gilgamesh material is, that the use of geographical information does not prove a historical origin for the story or its hero, but reflects a time when a particular version was made.

The *Gilgamesh Epic* concerns kingship first and foremost, and was not linked to the rituals of temples as the *Epic of Creation* was. Different royal patrons had an effect on what changes occurred, particularly in the locations of certain episodes. Therefore the longer the epic takes to evolve, the less likely it is to preserve 'original' locations, hence the change from the Zagros to the Lebanon, from Uruk to Ur, from Mt Nimush to Mt Ararat. Stories about Gilgamesh in Mesopotamia outlived several huge changes of empire: the Third Dynasty of Ur, the First Dynasty of Babylon, the Middle Assyrian empire, the Neo-Assyrian empire, the Neo-Babylonian empire, and the Achaemenid empire. Perhaps in all of these periods, powerful patrons influenced changes in the *Gilgamesh Epic* to reflect their own achievements.

As for the *Iliad*, the Achaean Wall in *Iliad* 7.442–64, linked by West to Sennacherib's siege of Babylon in 689 BC, is firmly tacked on to the topography of Troy (West 1997: 377–80). Although what applies to the *Epic of Gilgamesh* is not necessarily applicable to the *Iliad*, a possibility has recently arisen that the composition of the *Iliad* has transformed an episode with a historical kernel located in North Syria. The text, known as the *Song of Release*, was found at Hattusha in the same building as fragments of the Middle Babylonian version of the *Gilgamesh Epic* (Bachvarova 2005: 131–54). It is a type of text used in schools, recognisable for having two different genres of text on a single clay tablet: not only the *Song of Release*, but also parables. It narrates the anger of the Storm-god Teshub, who caused the fall of the city of Ebla because of a refusal to free captives from the town Ikinkalis. The fall of Ebla seems to relate to a campaign c. 1600 BC by either Hattusilis I or Mursilis I. The text states that the song was performed by a singer or musician. Whether the claim that it contributes to the *Iliad* stands up to scrutiny remains to be seen.

This suggestion can be set alongside a Babylonian tradition of narrating at a triumphal ceremony a genuinely historical event recreated in epic form as a poetic composition (Grayson 1975: 7–9; Villard 2008). The type is now known from five separate works with dates extending from the Middle Bronze Age (the still unpublished *Epic of Zimri-Lim* from Mari) through into the Iron Age, from Adad-nirari I (1305–1274) through Tukulti-Ninurta I, Tiglath-pileser I, Assurnaṣirpal II to Shalmaneser III (858–824) (Hurowitz and Westenholz 1990). In the late eighth and seventh century this tradition sometimes blends into annalistic and epistolary types of royal inscription, such as Sargon II's letter describing his eighth campaign to Urartu, Sennacherib's account of the Battle of Halule, and Esarhaddon's letter describing his campaign to Shubria (Villard 2008). The victory ceremonies included a dramatic recreation of a battle, the display of trophies, and music.

Efforts to date parts of Homeric epic have led scholars in the past to invoke archaeological evidence, particularly when metal technology and weapons are described. That approach is now contrasted with the understanding that Homer sought to evoke an earlier, heroic age by using archaisms and anachronisms, especially by referring to materials and objects from the distant past (Bennet 1997: 531–32; Morris 1997: 558). Here comparisons with the *Gilgamesh Epic* and with Assyrian royal inscriptions of the eighth to seventh centuries are informative. If we think that much of the content of Homeric epic dates to the Late Bronze Age but was written in the form in which we know it in the first half of the first millennium, we have a similar track through time as is certain for development of the *Gilgamesh Epic* from its scantily known early fragments into the much more nearly complete Babylonian standard version. However, in certain late eighth-century Assyrian royal inscriptions, written in epic style, there is a nostalgic reference to the use of bronze or even copper for tools and weapons, as if to ignore the introduction of iron and hark back to a better age when copper and bronze were universally used. This is overt, for instance, in the letter to the gods recounting Sargon II's eighth campaign against Urartu, in which the sappers cut roads through the mountains with copper axes (Thureau-Dangin 1912: lines 24, 329) – an unrealistic endeavour in the Iron Age. The archaism is all the more striking when we look at similar contexts in inscriptions of Sargon's son Sennacherib, whose axes are almost always made explicitly of iron (see e.g. Oppenheim *et al.* 1956: s.v. hesû D).

Something similar by way of nostalgia seems to happen with chariotry, which was the preserve of the rich and aristocratic warriors of the Late Bronze Age, but was gradually reduced to a ceremonial role by 600 BC due to the effectiveness of cavalry. Assyrian records make it clear that chariotry belonged to the expertise of sophisticated Levantine cities such as Samaria, whereas cavalry was the speciality (in breeding, training and harnessing of horses) of hardy mountain people to the north and east of Assyria. In the *Gilgamesh Epic* there is only a passing reference to chariotry, when Ishtar tries to seduce Gilgamesh with the promise of 'a chariot of lapis lazuli and gold harnessed for you, with wheels of gold', rather than a swift and spirited steed in the mould of Pegasus or Bucephalus. This is an image from the Late Bronze Age elite of charioteers, and would have been seen as such when the *Epic of Gilgamesh* was recited even in the Seleucid period.

Acknowledgements

I would like to thank John Bennet and Susan Sherratt for the invitation to speak at an event that was both a gastronomic and an intellectual pleasure; and Oliver Dickinson for some insights in discussion and the reference to Bachvarova's work. An extended version of the paper delivered in Sheffield was presented at the Advanced Seminar in the Humanities held at Venice International University, September 2007, by kind invitation of Lucio Milano and Ettore Cingano. The paper was extensively revised in late 2013 for publication, to take much new evidence into account, along with the perceptive comments of the editors.

Bibliography

Al-Rawi, F. and A. R. George

2014 Back to the Cedar Forest: the beginning and end of Tablet V of the Standard Babylonian Epic of Gilgamesh. *Journal of Cuneiform Studies* 66: 69–90.

Archi, A.

1992 Transmission of the Mesopotamian lexical and literary texts from Ebla. In P. Fronzaroli (ed.), *Literature and Literary Language at Ebla* (Quaderni di semitistica 18): 1–39. Florence: Dipartimento di Linguistica, Università di Firenze.

Bachvarova, M. R.

2005 The Eastern Mediterranean epic tradition: from Bilgames and Akka to the Song of Release to Homer's Iliad. *Greek, Roman, and Byzantine Studies* 45: 131–54.

Bagg, A.

2007 *Die Orts- und Gewässernamen der neuassyrischen Zeit. Teil 1: Die Levante* (Répertoire Géographique des Textes Cunéiformes 7/1). Wiesbaden: Dr. Ludwig Reichert Verlag.

Beaulieu, P-A.

2000 The descendants of Sin-lēqi-unnini. In J. Marzahn and H. Neumann (eds.), *Assyriologie et Semitica, Festschrift für Joachim Oelsner anlässlich seines 65. Geburtstages* (Alter Orient und Altes Testament 252): 1–16. Münster: Ugarit-Verlag.

Beckman, G.

1983 Mesopotamians and Mesopotamian learning at Hattusa. *Journal of Cuneiform Studies* 35: 97–114.

2003 Gilgamesh in Hatti. In G. Beckman, R. Beal and G. McMahon (eds.), *Hittite Studies in Honor of Harry A. Hoffner, Jr.: on the Occasion of his 65th Birthday*: 37–58. Winona Lake: Eisenbrauns.

Beckman, G. M., T. R. Bryce and E. H. Cline

2011 *The Ahhiyawa Texts* (Writings from the Ancient World 28). Atlanta: Society of Biblical Literature.

Bennet, J.

1997 Homer and the Bronze Age. In I. Morris and B. Powell (eds.), *A New Companion to Homer*: 511–34. Leiden/New York/Cologne: Brill.

Black, J. A.

1992 Appendix 11. In A. W. McNicoll, P. C. Edwards, J. Hanbury-Tenison, J. B. Hennessy, T. F. Potts, R. H. Smith, A. Walmsley and P. Watson (eds.), *Pella in Jordan 2, The Second Interim*

Report of the Joint University of Sydney and College of Wooster Excavations at Pella 1982-1985 (Mediterranean Archaeology Supplement 2): 299–301. Sydney: Meditarch.

Bryce, T.

2004 Relations between Hatti and Ahhiyawa in the last decades of the Bronze Age. In G. Beckman *et al.* (eds.), *Hittite Studies in Honor of Harry A. Hoffner Jr*: 59–72. Winona Lake: Eisenbrauns.

Buchanan, B. and R. Moorey

1966 *Catalogue of Ancient Near Eastern Seals in the Ashmolean Museum vol. 1. Cylinder Seals.* Oxford: Clarendon Press.

Çambel, H.

1999 *Karatepe - Arslantaş. The Inscriptions* (Corpus of Hieroglyphic Luwian Inscriptions vol. 2). Berlin: Walter de Gruyter.

Cavigneaux, A.

2007 Les oiseaux de l'arche. *Aula Orientalis* 25: 319–20.

Cohen, Y.

2004 Kidin-Gula: the foreign teacher at the Emar scribal school. *Revue d'Assyriologie* 98: 81–100.

Colonna d'Istria, L.

2012 Épigraphes alphabétiques du pays de la Mer. *Nouvelles Assyriologiques Brèves et Utilitaires* 2012(3): 61–62.

Curtis, J. E. and J. E. Reade

1995 *Art and Empire: Treasures from Assyria in the British Museum.* London: British Museum Press.

Dalley, S.

1989 *Myths from Mesopotamia.* Oxford: Oxford University Press.

2009 *Texts from the First Sealand Dynasty.* Maryland: CDL Press.

Dalley, S. and J. N. Postgate

1984 *The Tablets from Fort Shalmaneser* (Cuneiform Texts from Nimrud III). London: British School of Archaeology in Iraq.

Durand, J-M. and M. Guichard

1997 Les rituels de Mari. In D. Charpin and J.-M. Durand (eds.), *Recueil d'études à la mémoire de Marie-Thérèse Barrelet* (Florilegium marianum III):19–78. Paris: SEPOA.

Edzard, D.-O.

1993 *Gilgameš und Huwawa, zwei Versionen der sumerischen Zedernwaldepisode nebst einer Edition von Version 'B'* (Bayerische Akademie der Wissenschaften, Sitzungsberichte). Munich: Verlag der Bayerischen Akademie der Wissenschaften.

Eph'al, I. and H. Tadmor

2006 Observations on two inscriptions of Esarhaddon: Prism Nineveh A and the Letter to the God. In Y. Amit *et al.* (eds.), *Essays on Ancient Israel in its Near Eastern Context, A Tribute to Nadav Na'aman*: 155–70. Winona Lake: Eisenbrauns.

Faivre, X.

1995 Le recyclage des tablettes cuneiformes. *Revue d'Assyriologie* 89: 57–66.

Falkenstein, A.

1957–71 Gilgameš. In *Reallexikon der Assyriologie*, Band 3: 357–63. Berlin & New York: De Gruyter.

Foley, J. (ed.)

2005 *A Companion to Ancient Epic.* Oxford: Blackwell.

Frahm, E.

2005 On some recently published Late Babylonian copies of royal letters. *Nouvelles Assyriologiques Brèves et Utilitaires* 2005(2): 43–46.

2011 *Babylonian and Assyrian Text Commentaries. Origins of interpretation.* Münster: Ugarit Verlag.

Frayne, D.

1990 *The Royal Inscriptions of Mesopotamia. Early Periods, vol. 4. Old Babylonian Period.* Toronto: Toronto University Press.

2010 Gilgameš in Old Babylonian glyptic. In H.U. Steymans (ed.), *Gilgamesch. Ikonographie eines Helden*: 165–208. Fribourg/Göttingen: Academic Press/Vandenhoeck and Ruprecht.

Fuchs, A.

1994 *Die Inschriften Sargons II aus Khorsabad*. Göttingen: Cuvillier Verlag.

George, A. R.

1999 *The Epic of Gilgamesh, a New Translation*. London: Allen Lane.

2003 *The Epic of Gilgamesh*. Oxford: Oxford University Press.

2007a The civilizing of Ea – Enkidu: an unusual tablet of the Babylonian Gilgameš Epic. *Revue d'Assyriologie* 101: 59–80.

2007b The Gilgamesh Epic at Ugarit. *Aula Orientalis* 25: 237–54.

Gesche, P.

2000 *Schulunterricht in Babylonien im ersten Jahrtausend v. Chr*. (Alter Orient und Altes Testament 275). Münster: Ugarit-Verlag.

Gibson, J. C. L.

1982 *Syrian Semitic Inscriptions vol. III. Phoenician Inscriptions*. Oxford: Oxford University Press.

Gitin, S., T. Dothan and J. Naveh

1997 A royal dedicatory inscription from Ekron. *Israel Exploration Journal* 47: 1–16.

Glassner, J.-G.

2003 *The Invention of Cuneiform: Writing in Sumer*. Baltimore: Johns Hopkins University Press.

Goodall, J. A. A.

2001 *God's House at Ewelme*. Farnham: Ashgate.

Grayson, A. K.

1975 *Babylonian Historical-Literary Texts*. Toronto: Toronto University Press.

Green, A.

1997 Myths in Mesopotamian art. In I. L. Finkel and M. J. Geller (eds.), *Sumerian Gods and their Representations*: 135–58. Groningen: Styx.

Günbatti, C.

1997 Kültepe'den Akadlı Sargon'a ait bir Tablet. *Archivum Anatolicum* 3: 131–55.

Hawkins, D.

1998 Tarkasnawa, King of Mira, 'Tarkondemos'. Bogazköy sealings and Karabel. *Anatolian Studies* 48: 1–31.

2011 The inscriptions of the Aleppo temple. *Anatolian Studies* 61: 35–54.

Hawley, R.

2008 On the alphabetic scribal curriculum at Ugarit. In R. Biggs, J. Myers and M. Roth (eds.), *Proceedings of the 51st Rencontre Assyriologique Internationale* (Studies in Ancient Oriental Civilizations): 57–68. Chicago: Oriental Institute.

Hecker, K.

1993 Schultexte vom Kültepe. In M. J. Mellink, E. Porada and T. Özgüç (eds.), *Aspects of Art and Iconography: Anatolia and its Neighbours. Studies in Honor of Nimet Özgüç*: 281–91. Ankara: Türk Tarih Kurumu Basımev.

Hendel, R. S.

1987 *The Epic of the Patriarch: The Jacob Cycle and the Narrative Traditions of Canaan and Israel* (Harvard Semitic Monographs 42). Atlanta: Scholar Press.

Henkelman, W.

2006 The Birth of Gilgameš (AEL. NA XII.21). A case-study in literary receptivity. In R. Rollinger and B. Truschnegg (eds.), *Altertum und Mittelmeerraum: die antike Welt diesseits und jenseits der Levante: Festschrift für Peter W. Haider zum 60. Geburtstag*: 807–56. Stuttgart: F. Steiner.

Horowitz, W. and T. Oshima

2006 *Cuneiform in Canaan: Cuneiform Sources from the Land of Israel in Ancient Times*. Jerusalem: Israel Exploration Society.

Howard, M.
1955 Technical description of the ivory writing boards from Nimrud. *Iraq* 17: 14–20.
Hurowitz, V. and J. G. Westenholz
1990 LKA 63: a heroic poem in celebration of Tiglath-pileser I's Muṣru – Qumanu campaign. *Journal of Cuneiform Studies* 42: 1–49.
Izreel, S.
1997 *The Scholarly Amarna Tablets.* Groningen: Styx.
Jacobsen, T.
1976 *The Treasures of Darkness.* New Haven: Yale University Press.
Klein, J.
1981 *Three Shulgi Hymns. Sumerian Royal Hymns Glorifying King Šulgi of Ur.* Ramat-Gan: Bar-Ilan University Press.
Lambert, W. G.
1998 Kingship in ancient Mesopotamia. In J. Day (ed.), *King and Messiah in Israel and the Ancient Near East*: 54–71. Sheffield: Sheffield Academic Press.
Lane Fox, R.
2008 *Travelling Heroes: Greeks and their Myths in the Epic Age of Homer*. London: Allen Lane.
Latacz, J.
2004 *Troy and Homer. Towards a Solution of an Old Mystery*. Oxford: Oxford University Press.
Lord, A. B.
1990 Gilgamesh and other epics. In T. Abusch, J. Huehnergard and P. Steinkeller (eds.), *Lingering over Words. Studies in Ancient Near Eastern Literature in Honor of William Moran*: 371–80. Atlanta: CDL Press.
Luckenbill, D. D.
1924 *Annals of Sennacherib* (Oriental Institute Publications 2). Chicago: Chicago University Press.
Luraghi, N.
2006 Traders, pirates, warriors: the proto-history of Greek mercenary soldiers in the Eastern Mediterranean. *Phoenix* 60: 21–47.
Maeir, A.
2003–05 Philister-Keramik. In *Reallexikon der Assyriologie* Band 10: 535. Berlin & New York: De Gruyter.
Mander, P.
1986 *Il pantheon di Abu-Ṣalābīkh*. Naples: Istituto universitario orientale, Dipartimento di studi asiatici.
Metcalf, C.
2011 New parallels in Hittite and Sumerian praise of the Sun. *Welt des Orients* 41: 168–76.
Moran, W.
1978 An Assyriological gloss on the new Archilochus fragment. *Harvard Studies in Classical Philology* 82: 17–19.
1995 The Gilgamesh Epic: a masterpiece from ancient Mesopotamia. In J. M. Sasson *et al.* (eds.), *Civilizations of the Ancient Near East* IV: 2327–36. New York: Simon and Shuster.
Morgan, T.
1998 *Literate Education in the Hellenistic and Roman Worlds*. Cambridge: Cambridge University Press.
Morris, I.
1997 Homer and the Iron Age. In I. Morris and B.Powell (eds.), *A New Companion to Homer*: 513–34. Leiden: Brill.
Na'aman, N.
2010 Khirbet Qeiyafa in context. *Ugarit Forschungen* 42: 497–526.
Nagy, G.
2005 The epic hero. In J. M. Foley (ed.), *A Companion to Ancient Epic*: 71–89. Oxford: Blackwell.

Noegel, S. B.
2005 Mesopotamian epic. In J. M. Foley (ed.), *A Companion to Ancient Epic*: 233–45. Oxford: Blackwell.
Oppenheim, A. L. *et al.* (eds.)
1956 *The Assyrian Dictionary of the Oriental Institute of the University of Chicago, vol. 6*. Chicago: Oriental Institute.
Pedersén, O.
1998 *Archives and Libraries in the Ancient Near East 1500–300 B.C.* Atlanta: CDL Press.
Perry, B. E.
1952 *Aesopica: A Series of Texts Relating to Aesop*. Urbana: University of Illinois Press.
Pulak. C.
2008 The Uluburun shipwreck and Late Bronze Age trade. In J. Aruz, K. Benzel and J. M. Evans (eds.), *Beyond Babylon: Art, Trade, and Diplomacy in the Second Millennium B.C.*: 288–305. New Haven: Yale University Press.
Pusch, E. B. and S. Jakob
2003 Der Zipfel des diplomatischen Archivs Ramses' II. *Aegypten und Levante* 13: 143–54.
Radner, K.
2010 The stele of Sargon II of Assyria at Kition. In R. Rollinger, B. Gufler, M. Lang and I. Madreiter (eds.), *Interkulturalität in der Alten Welt*: 429–49. Wiesbaden: Harrassowitz.
Robson, E.
1999 *Mesopotamian Mathematics 2100–1600 BC* (Oxford Editions of Cuneiform Texts XIV). Oxford: Clarendon Press.
Röllig, W.
2004 Sprachen und Schriften der Levante. In M. Novák, F. Prayon and A-M. Wittke (eds.), *Die Aussenwirkung des späthethitischen Kulturraumes* (Alter Orient und Altes Testament 323): 205–17. Münster: Ugarit-Verlag.
Rollston, C. A.
2006 Scribal education in ancient Israel: the Old Hebrew epigraphic evidence. *Bulletin of the American Schools of Oriental Research* 344: 47–74.
Sollberger, E.
1980 Ibdati. *Reallexikon der Assyriologie* Band 5: 8.
Sollberger, E. and J.-R. Kupper
1971 *Inscriptions royales sumeriennes et akkadiennes.* Paris: Éditions du Cerf.
Stager, L.
2004 Ashkelon, seaport of the Canaanites and the Philistines. Schweich lectures (British Academy, unpublished).
Stein, P.
2010 *Die altsüdarabischen Minuskelinschriften auf Holzstäbchen aus der Bayerischen Staatsbibliothek in München 1: Die Inschriften der mittel- und spätsabäischen Periode* (Epigraphische Forschungen auf der Arabischen Halbinsel 5). Tübingen: Wasmuth.
Steymans, H. U. (ed.)
2010 *Gilgamesch. Ikonographie eines Helden.* Fribourg/Göttingen: Academic Press/Vandenhoeck and Ruprecht.
Symington, D.
1991 Late Bronze Age writing-boards and their uses: textual evidence from Anatolia and Syria. *Anatolian Studies* 41: 111–23.
Tappy, R. E., P. Kyle McCarter, M. J. Lundberg and B. Zuckerman
2006 An abecedary of the mid-tenth century BCE from the Judaean Shephelah. *Bulletin of the American Schools of Oriental Research* 344: 5–46.

Tekoglu, R. and A. Lemaire

2000 La bilingue royale louvito-phénicienne de Çineköy. *Comptes-rendus de l'Académie des Inscriptions et Belles Lettres* 144: 961–1007.

Thomas, R.

1992 *Literacy and Orality in Ancient Greece*. Cambridge: Cambridge University Press.

Thureau-Dangin, F.

1912 *Une relation de la huitième campagne de Sargon* (Textes cunéiformes du Louvre 2). Paris: Geuthner.

Tigay, J.

1982 *The Evolution of the Gilgamesh Epic*. Philadelphia: University of Pennsylvania Press.

Tinney, S.

1999 On the curricular setting of Sumerian. *Iraq* 61: 159–72.

Van Koppen, F. and K. Radner

2009 Der Hyksospalast bei Tell el-Dab'a. *Aegypten und Levante* 19: 115–19.

van de Mieroop, M.

2000 Sargon of Agade and his successors in Anatolia. *Studi micenei ed egeo-anatolici* 42: 145–57.

van Soldt, W.

2001 Nahiš-šalmu: an Assyrian scribe working in the 'Southern Palace' at Ugarit. In W. van Soldt *et al.* (eds.), *Veenhof Anniversary Volume: Studies presented to Klaas R. Veenhof on the Occasion of his Sixty-Fifth Birthday*: 429–44. Leiden: Nederlands Instituut voor het Nabije Oosten.

Veldhuis, N.

1997 *Elementary Education at Nippur: The Lists of Trees and Wooden Objects*. Groningen: Rijksuniversiteit Groningen.

Villard, P.

2008 Les cérémonies triomphales en Assyrie. In P. Abrahimi and L. Battini (eds.), *Les Armées du Proche-Orient ancien: IIIe - 1er mill. av. J.-C.* (BAR International Series 1855): 257–70. Oxford: Archaeopress.

Watanabe, K.

1989 Review of S. Dalley and J. N. Postgate, *The Tablets from Fort Shalmaneser, Cuneiform Texts from Nimrud III* (London, 1984). *Zeitschrift für Assyriologie* 79: 272–78.

West, M. L.

1997 *The East Face of Helicon*. Oxford: Clarendon Press.

2011 *The Making of the Iliad*. Oxford: Oxford University Press.

Wilcke, C.

1989 Genealogical and geographical thought in the Sumerian King list. In H. Behrens *et al.* (eds.), *DUMU-E-DUB.BA.A: Studies in Honor of Åke Sjøberg*: 557–72. Philadelphia: Samuel Noah Kramer Fund.

Yadin, A.

2004 Goliath's armor and Israelite collective memory. *Vetus Testamentum* 54: 373–95.

Chapter 9

History and the Making of South Slavic Epic

Margaret H. Beissinger

South Slavic epic – narrative poetry that circulated for centuries in the Bosnian-Croatian-Serbian speaking areas of what was formerly Yugoslavia and is now Bosnia, Croatia, Serbia, and Montenegro – is commonly viewed as having strong historical connections and significance. Rarely is the genre discussed without reference to local history. The most noteworthy classifications of South Slavic epic – from the early nineteenth to the latter twentieth century – delineate song types that are categorised as overwhelmingly historical in nature, e.g., by Vuk Stefanović Karadžić (1824; 1841), Pavle Popović (1909), V.M. Jovanović (1922), V. Djurić (1954), and T. Čubelić (1970) (see Kleut 1994). By contrast, songs labelled as ahistorical make up only a small percentage of the standard repertoire. History and historical readings have been invoked over and over as the meanings of South Slavic epic are examined and debated. Historical readings of epic have also profoundly informed questions of South Slavic identity and have frequently been coupled with intense nationalism.

History-related approaches to epic locate historical conditions, events, personages, and places in the text and examine the roles they play in the narratives. Neat connections between 'real' references and the stories in which they are found are identified, and 'historical' meaning is either assigned or even determined, thanks to inferred relationships. Assumptions are made that singers are often inspired by history and consequently compose songs that reflect historical facts. In some readings, the epics are seen to form a set of unique, self-contained, and culturally-specific messages that chart a nation's past and its destiny and that reputedly reflect ancient, sacred, historical truths. Tradition-related interpretations of epic, by contrast, subvert the historical view to some extent, turning it on its head and suggesting a process that moves in a significantly different direction. Oral poets are seen as they compose epic not so much moved by historical events as stirred by the broader narratives of the tradition, which they sometimes embellish with 'history' (names, events and places). Historical details are at times injected into or become embedded in the traditional stories that singers perform, and they even sometimes become part of the larger narrative repertories. But the tradition itself, what Albert B. Lord called 'a melting pot of story elements, ... a tapestry of heroic actions woven on a gigantic loom' (Lord 1994: 7), as opposed to the individual moments of history, provides the singers with the fundamental tales to sing.

In the pages below, I explore relationships between history and South Slavic epic. What is the role of history in the genre? How have historical readings been implemented? How do alternative readings offer other meaningful interpretations of the epic? Throughout this essay I chart how history, combined with oral epic, became a powerful tool in generating nationalist sentiment and nation-building, starting in eighteenth- but particularly in nineteenth-century Serbia as the Ottoman yoke was thrown off. Epic used in the service of nationalism continued during the twentieth century as well – from the Balkan Wars in 1912–1913 to the Yugoslav Wars of Secession during the 1990s. While I recognise the role that history played in the genre, I also suggest that chiefly historical (or pseudo-historical) readings of South Slavic epic – indeed, the seminal readings of the nineteenth century – frequently masked the central role of traditional storytelling within the genre.[1] They often overlooked the importance of the traditional narratives that provided the bedrock for the epic songs that were collected at that time, as well as the traditional characters that performed in them. Viewing epic songs from the point of view of the tradition is based to a large extent on comparative study – within the same tradition (here, South Slavic), as well as in other similar traditions (Romanian, Albanian, Greek, Armenian, Turkic, etc.). As one looks comparatively at the traditional world of stories and the actors who figure in them, it becomes clear that epic is made up of a large body of story elements that are versatile, mobile and fundamentally generic, not historic. Narratives include events and actors that flow from song to song, singer to singer, even tradition to tradition instead of informing one particular culture and historical period. As Lord explained, 'an oral tradition of narrative song consists of a very large number of closely interrelated songs ... a tradition is made up not of discrete songs but of songs, or, preferably, stories about a limited number of heroes, tales that overlap and intertwine' (Lord 1994: 6). A comparative, ahistorical approach – which finds a fluidity and generality of traditional story patterns and heroic traits – cannot really be reconciled with a predominantly historical orientation, which sees epics as distinct, independent, locally significant narratives that inform a nation's past and even its fate. My purpose here is to explore how Serbian epic has been expressly presented and interpreted since the mid-eighteenth century in a historical frame, thereby promoting a strongly nationalist agenda, and to offer additional modes of analysis.

South Slavic Oral Epic

South Slavic oral epic refers to narrative songs that were performed by Serbian, Bosnian, and Croatian traditional singers who all spoke more or less the same language, now called Bosnian-Croatian-Serbian. These singers were either Christian (Orthodox

Serbs or Catholic Croats) or Muslim (Bosnians). Christian epic was usually performed either in informal home settings attended by both genders or at more formal events: family celebrations – especially weddings – and gatherings such as open-air marketplaces. Muslim epic, by contrast, was often heard in all-male settings, including at the *kafanas* (coffee houses), taverns and private homes. South Slavic singers of heroic song were by and large male and accompanied themselves on stringed instruments: the *gusle* (one-stringed and bowed) or the *tambura* (strummed). The poetry is stichic, decasyllabic verse. Christian and Muslim epics fundamentally relate the same stories. They are narratives that tell of capture and rescue, returning heroes, obtaining brides and celebrating weddings, the slaying of dragons or dragon substitutes, and the capture of cities. Yet there are several differences. The first concerns ethno-religious orientation: the Christian epics (Serbian and Croatian) tell of heroes who are fighting an anti-Turkish war, while in the Muslim (Bosnian), heroes uphold the Ottoman Empire as they struggle against Christian infidels. Moreover, the Christian songs are generally shorter and less elaborate than the Muslim. As is well-known, it was the long, developed Muslim epics and their singers that Milman Parry sought, along with Albert Lord, in the 1930s in an attempt to find modern-day analogues to Homer. Finally, South Slavic Christian epic is considerably more historical in content, while Muslim epic is characterised by narratives that are generally ahistorical.[2] Although they were widely sung in the past, by the mid- to late-twentieth century, South Slavic epics in traditional performance had disappeared – the Christian genre by the late nineteenth century and the Muslim after World War II.

The first written evidence of South Slavic epic includes a fragment of a song from 1497; a traveller's account from 1531; and two epic texts from the Croat Petar Hektorović's *Fishing and Fishermen's Conversation* (*Ribanje i Ribarsko Razgovaranje,* 1556). The 1497 fragment is in the *bugarštica* form (traditional poetry composed of 15- and 16-syllable verses), performed by Slavic entertainers in southern Italy (Koljević 1980: 27–30; see Kekez 1991). The earliest commentary on South Slavic epic performed on native soil is from a 1531 travel account of a Slovene, who heard heroic songs performed by the folk in Croatia and Bosnia (Marešić 1966: 28). Hektorović's *Ribanje i Ribarsko Razgovaranje* included two songs (also in the *bugarštica* form) sung by fishermen.

But the most influential early publication of epic was found in *A Pleasant Discourse of the Slavic people* (*Razgovor ugodni naroda slovinskoga*), a history primarily in verse from 1756 by the Croat Andrija Kačić-Miošić. His intention was to glorify South Slavic heroes through a presentation that would reach the common people as well as the literati of society. Kačić-Miošić's efforts were far-reaching. He imitated the style of oral epic in his poetry (e.g., decasyllabic metre) but composed the texts himself, drawing from oral epics but even more from historical accounts. The volume became so popular that several of Kačić-Miošić's songs even entered oral tradition. It marked an important turning point in the history of South Slavic epic. As Mary Coote points out, the work 'foster[ed] among the folk, as well as among observers of the tradition, the persistent notion that heroic songs constitute history in the sense that people with written records understand history' (Coote 1978: 259). It generated immense interest in South Slavic oral traditions, especially in the nineteenth century, and set the stage for the close relationship that epic would share with history.

The 500-year-long Ottoman chapter in South Slavic history was critical to the development of epic song. As Lord aptly noted, the whole South Slavic epic genre 'depends on the Turks' (Lord 1972a: 299). Once the Ottoman Empire established its presence in Serbia and Bosnia in the late fourteenth century, and Turkish rule replaced the earlier local dynasties, an Ottoman upper class emerged and many of the South Slavs in Bosnia converted to Islam. As the powerful and elite in society, they also generated a significant epic tradition. As Lord put it, 'epic normally belongs to the dominant group' (Lord 1972a: 298). Meanwhile, the narrative songs of those who remained Christian (in Serbia and Croatia), which had flourished in the medieval pre-Ottoman Christian courts, persisted, though not in public and not patronised as were those of the ruling Muslims. By the time the Ottoman presence in Serbia drew to a close in the nineteenth century and the native courts were resurrected, the age of courtly epic entertainment had passed. By then, it was performed instead by peasants and the non-elite of society. Moreover, in the interim, the Christian songs lost many of their more mythic elements (which, by contrast, the Muslim songs retained). Many of the Christian songs became, as Lord remarked, 'historical or pseudo-historical oral narrative traditional songs' (Lord 1972a: 299). Indeed, Muslim epic rarely included references to events or figures of the past as did the Christian songs. Thus Muslim and Christian epic developed in significantly different ways. Furthermore, since the Muslim Bosnians were politically powerful in the Ottoman period, they were not stirred to form a national consciousness, to articulate and proclaim – or revive – a national identity as were the Christian South Slavs, especially the Serbs, subject to Ottoman rule for centuries. In Serbia, the Ottoman period had followed the fall of the glorious Serbian Empire, ruled by the great Nemanja family dynasty from the twelfth to the fourteenth century. One could argue that by the nineteenth century, South Slavic Christian epic, unlike the Muslim genre, 'needed' historical references to validate itself.

Serbian 'Historical' Songs

Though Christian epic developed among both the Orthodox Serbs and Catholic Croats, it was the Serbs whose epic formed the heart of the South Slavic Christian heroic song tradition. Serbian epic also became a powerful vehicle for nationalist expression and historical representation during the nineteenth and twentieth centuries. Popular historical understandings of Serbian epic have been oriented around two key topics. They are the historical phenomena that retrospectively characterized fourteenth-century Serbia: the Battle of Kosovo and the hero Marko Kraljević. The Battle of Kosovo, which took place in 1389, eventually developed into a legendary event in

Serbian historiography and cultural mythology. In its legendary meaning, it was the battle at which the Serbs were defeated by the Turks and became victims of Ottoman domination. The battle, it is believed, defined Serbian history and enabled the subsequent centuries of Ottoman occupation. Marko Kraljević figured at the same historical juncture. He was a vassal of the Sultan yet also fought for the Christian Serbs. Marko paradoxically epitomised Serbian Christendom and came to represent the greatest Serbian hero and pan-Balkan champion of the oppressed.

As an emergent Serbian identity was being forged in the nineteenth century, Kosovo and Marko became powerful epic tropes of history and culture and sacred emblems of the Serbian nation. Other 'historical' themes in South Slavic epic include people and stories drawn from the past, outlaws and border raiders during the seventeenth through nineteenth centuries, and the Serbian Uprisings from 1804 to 1813. South Slavic Christian life – from 1389 to the crumbling of the Ottoman Empire in the late nineteenth to early twentieth century – was regarded as one long struggle against the Turks. Thus, most of the epic that was performed during that time was considered 'historical', as conveying a sense of the ongoing opposition by the oppressed and powerless Serbs to the Ottomans. Their epic poetry – performed mainly in private, non-elite circles – thus conveyed their opposition to the Turks. A 'national myth' was perpetuated through epic: for hundreds of years South Slavic Christians declared their resistance in song.

How is history manifest in epic? How do we interpret this 'history'? These questions have been asked by many scholars. Focusing on the narratives of South Slavic epic as history, Vasa Mihailovich asserted that '[m]any if not most of the poems in Vuk's [Karadžić's] collection recount historical events, and ... recount the deeds of the nobility in the years of grandeur of the Serbian feudal state' (Mihailovich 1997: 42). And with a similar message, Zora Devrnja Zimmerman maintains that Serbian epic 'preserves accurate, concrete particulars of real people, places, and events' (Zimmerman 1986: 2). Other scholars have recognized more nuanced degrees of history embedded in epic. Jovan Deretić explained that since 'the facts of macrohistory tend to be reflected far more faithfully in a poem than the individual events of microhistory, [t]he historicity of the Serbo-Croatian epics does not manifest itself primarily in the record of individual events, but rather as the memory of entire epochs of history, from the Middle Ages up to the liberation wars in the 19th century' (Deretić 1994: 84).

Lord similarly argued that there are two levels of historical reality. 'On a general level', he wrote, songs can reflect 'the atmosphere and morality' of a particular period (Lord 1972b: 56). Here he mentioned, for example, 'the Turkish Empire under Sulejman the Magnificent', where the 'prevailing mood is one of loyalty on the part of the Bosnian leaders to a sultan surrounded by traitors in high places in Istanbul and constantly prey to betrayal by provincial governors' (Lord 1972b: 56). The second order of reality consists of details such as battles, invasions, people and places from history (Lord 1972b: 59–60). C. M. Bowra also considered ways in which history is revealed in epic. He suggested tendencies by singers 'to shape [historical] material in the interests of artistic needs', arguing that 'poets tend to simplify'; they 'select themes that appeal to them' at the expense of others; and they falsify history for 'the simple needs of narrative' (Bowra 1952: 519, 525, 531). Ultimately, as Bowra noted, heroic poetry 'does not record truthfully what happened, but it shows what men believed and felt' (Bowra 1952: 535).

Vuk Karadžić

Vuk Stefanović Karadžić (1787–1864) was a giant in Serbian culture. He was most notably a grammarian who standardised literary Serbo-Croatian and a folklorist who systematically collected and published countless oral traditional and ethnographic texts. His goals were threefold: first, to display to the West the rich contributions of the South Slavs and thus to gain international favour; second, to preserve for the Serbian people the 'gems' of their own oral traditions; and finally, to promote connections between the Serbian epic tradition and not only the great events and heroes of the past but also the ongoing Serbian struggle against the Ottomans. Vuk succeeded in all three. His first volume of collected oral poetry – mainly lyric – was published in Vienna in 1814: *A Simple Little Slaveno-Serbian Songbook* (*Mala prostonarodna slaveno-serbska pesnarica*). It was followed by another volume in 1815, *A Serbian Book of Folk Songs* (*Narodna srbska pjesnarica*), which contained the first published heroic songs, including poems about the Battle of Kosovo, the hero Marko Kraljević, and the Serbian Uprisings of 1804–1813. Additional volumes were published in 1823–1833 in Leipzig and then in Vienna again in 1841–1866, not to mention numerous posthumous volumes. This was all very timely: Johann Gottfried Herder's ideas of romantic nationalism and the 'Volk' were at their height. Thus Vuk's attempts to create a national epic and effectively define Serbian history were totally in keeping with West European currents since 'folk tradition [was] perceived [there] as ... cultural evidence of a glorious historical past' (Voigt 1994: 186). His collections were publicised widely and made a strong impression on the most influential cultural figures of the day: the Brothers Grimm, Johann Wolfgang von Goethe, and many others.

A major role was also played by Vuk in rescuing and preserving the verbal 'treasures' of the folk. He decided not only what types of songs were sung and recorded for posterity, but how they were 'marketed' to the public. Nada Milošević-Djordjević notes that Vuk was 'really the first to seek and publish new songs, mostly those sung by the traditional singers of his time' (Milošević-Djordjević 1994: 58). In creating a Serbian national epic, Vuk was instrumental in determining what the canon of Serbian oral epic would be since he specified which songs would be included for publication. As Radmila Pešić noted, Vuk had 'his own specific criterion not only for aesthetic quality but also for the subject-matter of Serbo-Croat folk songs' (Pešić 1967: 49). Vuk was drawn to epic songs about earlier heroes and events; he also opted to publish songs in which historical inconsistencies would be more convincing and less dissonant.

Not only did Vuk search for songs that articulated the nationalist aspirations of the moment, but he also carved out a Serbian history through epic, one that began with the Battle of Kosovo and heralded a good number of 'historical' Serbs as freedom-fighters and national heroes, in particular Marko Kraljević. Moreover, the epic songs in the collections by Vuk were arranged in what he determined was chronological order, in a type of 'historical' sequence, thus setting the stage for a historical vision of the meaning and significance of South Slavic epic. The Battle of Kosovo stood out in the songs that Vuk presented as the single most decisive event of Serbian history. As Milica Bakić-Hayden points out,

> By necessity selective, epic memory created its own periodization of history, consisting of events and personalities who were perceived as the turning points in the history of the people. If there was more than one such turning point in the narrative memory of the Serbian people, the others certainly faded away in the luminous memory of the Battle of Kosovo ... Intentionally or not, Vuk's work posited the Kosovo tradition as being the heart of his people's life, perceiving it, in the light of the current Western and Central European *zeitgeist*, as a living expression of their 'national spirit'. (Bakić-Hayden 2004: 31)

Moreover, Kosovo and the struggle against the Ottomans resonated within the context of the First Serbian Uprising of 1804, in which Vuk participated. Vuk collected songs about the insurrections, many of them solicited. It is well known that he requested songs about the Serbian uprisings from one of his best singers, Filip Višnjić (Lord 1995: 224). And while the Battle of Kosovo was seen as the most hallowed event of Serbian history, Marko Kraljević was perceived as the most important hero, and so, thanks to Vuk's efforts, Kosovo and Marko delineated and framed 500 years of Serbian history. Indeed, as Bakić-Hayden goes on to say,

> [i]n the context of societies with limited written history, epic, now defined in terms of social and collective experiences in addition to aesthetic ones, provided a narrative of the historical record, something at once 'our own,' but also, fortuitously, in agreement with widely accepted views of epic in the West as a measure of the antiquity of peoples and their cultures. (Bakić-Hayden 2004: 31–32)

Vuk and many of his contemporaries espoused the notion that epic mirrored history and historical reality was woven into epic poetry. This is evident in collections made by Petar II Petrović Njegoš, Ivo Franjo Jukić, Grga Martić, and others (see Kleut 1994). Vuk was dedicated to promoting national consciousness through emblems of the past that would be accessible to and echo among the common people. Indeed, the primary advocates of this perspective on folklore were also the leading proponents of the emergent Serbian nation (e.g., Njegoš). Vuk's publications were extraordinarily influential in the nineteenth century as South Slavs began to see an end to the Ottoman rule under which they had lived for centuries and to work actively toward the creation of Serbian national consciousness, national unity, and cultural expression. Romantic nationalism was everywhere and nation-building was supreme. The 'trophies' of Serbian oral tradition, interpreted as history, seemed to spell out a past and a destiny that spoke to both the educated and uneducated folk and which they, along with the culture-planners such as Vuk, promoted passionately. Indeed, the Serbian uprisings against the Turks took place from 1804 to 1813, shortly before his first collections were published: resistance, nationhood, and folklore were in the air.

Vuk also devised the first classification of Serbian heroic songs, based on those that he had collected and published. He sorted out songs according to the broad historical eras from which the heroes and events in them derived and arranged them in a supposedly chronological order, designating them as heroic songs of the oldest period, the intermediate period, and the most recent times. Implicit in this way of categorising epic was, as Marija Kleut points out, an 'assumption that oral epic songs represent a kind of history in verse' (Kleut 1994: 77). Vuk thus fostered the notion that epic and history be seen as inseparably paired. His classification became the established typology, one that most other scholars have adhered to for almost two hundred years. Except for one category designated as 'non-historical', the songs are grouped in cycles according to the South Slavic Christian historical frame within the Ottoman Empire: medieval Serbia, the Battle of Kosovo, Marko Kraljević, outlaws and border raiders, liberation from the Turks, and so on. Deretić noted that

> the poems of South Slavic epic are classified in accordance with historical principles, according to a real or supposed chronology of events and personages portrayed in them. Vuk ... was the first to adopt this approach, and others followed suit. This principle is based on a view of Serbo-Croat epic as a special kind of history expressed in poetic form, 'oral folk history'. (Deretić 1994: 83)

Vuk did not intend the epic songs to be classified into cycles, but his organisation nevertheless led in that direction. Interestingly enough, in 1833 Vuk warned his contemporaries to not search for 'historical truth' in the epic songs he had collected, published, and catalogued; yet in many regards he paved the way for them to do exactly that; and his admonition certainly did not stop them or anyone else from assigning at times blatantly historical readings to them (Kleut 1994: 78). As for the implications of this, Kleut remarks that the

> chronological principle in the arrangement of the songs and, arising from this, the division of songs into cycles are an expression of a romantic concept of oral literature. The emphasis or over-emphasis on the similarity between an actual event and the poetic version, the playing down or disregarding of differences between the epic songs and historically verified reality was the price some scholars paid for a national-romantic view of the past and of oral literature. (Kleut 1994: 80)

Ultimately – even ironically – the separation of epic into cycles promoting a historical vision negates a key principle of such poetry: its oral traditional character, including the fluidity of performance. It reduces one single, exclusive performance to a status of 'the' epic, as opposed to one of many performances within the tradition. There is, of course, no one definitive version in oral tradition. Yet when epic is viewed as a type of historical document frozen within a cycle, it can well be seen as the only account of that event from the past.

The Battle of Kosovo: Historical Explanations or Traditional Readings?

Vuk's collections of Kosovo epic songs made an extraordinary mark on Serbian cultural history. They were publicised widely and helped pave the way for Serbia's liberation from foreign rule and the simultaneous creation of a national literature. As literature developed along these lines, Serbian poets fashioned literary pieces after the oral poetry in the Vuk collections, e.g. Sima Milutinović, Njegoš, Branko Radičević, and others. The narratives that comprised the 'myth of Kosovo' brought history and culture together in a powerful and inspiring way. The medieval Battle of Kosovo produced the core of the Serbian 'national myth'. The spin this event was given as the single most important moment of Serbian history was perpetuated primarily through oral epic. During the nineteenth century, as the Serbs experienced their long-awaited liberation from the Ottomans as well as their cultural revival, one of their biggest dilemmas was to make sense of the collapse of the medieval Serbian state and the centuries-long degradation associated with Ottoman rule. The epic songs of the 'Kosovo Cycle' presented by Vuk provided an interpretation of Serbia's darkest moment as acceptable and even favourable. The Kosovo myth(s) became the 'Kosovo canon', providing respectable, positive ways to deal with what were perceived as the devastating and demeaning events of the past.

The Battle of Kosovo took place on Kosovo Field on June 15, 1389.[3] The Serbs, under the leadership of Prince Lazar, were defeated by the advancing Ottoman army; both Lazar and Sultan Murad were killed. Kosovo was perceived as the beginning of the Turkish dominance over Serbia, yet historically speaking, it did not provoke either the collapse of the Serbian state nor immediate Ottoman domination. Turkish control over the Balkan peninsula actually took place over a relatively lengthy period of time. Ottoman rule was not established until after the Serbian losses at Smederevo in 1459 (Redjep 1991: 254). Nonetheless, the defeat at Kosovo came to exemplify the fall of Serbia and subsequent loss of its autonomy and glory. While historical accounts of the battle were minimal, a legend of Kosovo, preserved in various texts over the years, gradually expanded and proceeded to embody an augmented cast of characters and events not mentioned in the original historical documents. By the end of the eighteenth century, the Kosovo legend had reached its essential form. A sainthood cult of Lazar had likewise evolved, and elaborate plot developments were devised in order to reconcile the Serbs' bitter loss at Kosovo with their national pride.

Treason – largely fictional – serves in the legend to help rationalise the Serbian defeat: Lazar's son-in-law, Vuk Branković, betrays Lazar to Murad. As Redjep points out,

> A study of medieval Serbian literary texts and other sources reveals that at first there is vague reference to treason, that it is then linked to a group of people, and that only later, at the end of the sixteenth and at the beginning of the seventeenth century, is there specific mention of Vuk Branković. (Redjep 1991: 257)

Tensions between Miloš Obilić – another son-in-law of Lazar – and Branković were also invented to justify Serbia's failure and loss at Kosovo. This emerged as a theme in the legend starting in the mid-fifteenth century. Redjep points out that '[i]n later sources this story evolved into a tale about the quarrel between Vuk Branković and Miloš Obilić/Kobilić and their wives, Lazar's daughters' (Redjep 1991: 258). The dispute allegedly provoked Vuk to defame Miloš to Lazar as a type of Judas during their 'last supper' on the eve of the battle, thus spurring Miloš to attempt somewhat recklessly to assassinate the Sultan. Miloš pretends he is a defector in order to gain access to Murad while Branković is the one who defects and betrays Serbia by fleeing with thousands of troops from Kosovo Field.

Over the years, the legend of Kosovo was expanded and elaborated in the literary texts that narrated it. Yet it did not surface in oral epic form until significantly later. The first documented song that treated Kosovo was a *bugarštica* from Dubrovnik dating from the end of the seventeenth century. Coote notes that

> there is scant record of songs on the events of Kosovo before Vuk Karadžić, little even in Vuk's early publications; ... [the] bulk of the Kosovo cycle appears in Vuk's later collections as the result of deliberate search and solicitation of songs on a subject Vuk and his contemporaries were convinced must exist in heroic song. (Coote 1978: 263)

In other words, Vuk intervened to foster and disseminate the Kosovo legend. This contrasts significantly with the general conception that the Kosovo epics had seamlessly continued from soon after the actual battle until the nineteenth century when they were discovered by Vuk. André Vaillant held a mainstream position when he affirmed in the earlier twentieth century that the oldest songs of the Kosovo cycle derived from the fifteenth century, which places them shortly after the battle itself occurred (Vaillant 1932: 433). But not all scholars accepted that view. Writing 50 years ago, Svetozar Matić boldly suggested that the poems of the Kosovo cycle were composed in the eighteenth and nineteenth centuries in Vojvodina by Serbs who had taken flight from southern Serbia and that they were appropriated at that time to promote the burgeoning national movement and cult of Kosovo (Matić 1964). Other Serbian scholars since then have also offered persuasive readings of the events and cycle of oral poetry surrounding the Battle of Kosovo (see Petrović 2001).

It appears, then, that in order to serve the needs of an increasingly nationalist agenda that sought independence from the Ottomans, a legend commemorating the devastating and humiliating Serbian defeat in 1389 by the Ottoman Turks was created, perpetuated, and came to be perceived as the most decisive and venerated event in Serbian history. Not only did the Kosovo myth resonate through the decades of Serbian nation-building in the nineteenth century but it also served as a powerful emblem of the destiny of the Serbian nation through the years of Yugoslavia-building in the earlier twentieth century, not to mention the revivalist post-Yugoslavia Serbia-building of more recent times. Kosovo represented the 'other', in conflict with 'us', the Serbian nation. In the Kosovo myth centred on 1389, the Kosovo 'other' was the

Turks; yet as the centuries passed, this 'other' took a new form: by the twentieth century, it was the Albanians. Kosovo as a symbolically powerful trope – both the Battle of Kosovo in 1389 and Kosovo itself as a province – was exploited repeatedly in the 1990s during the Yugoslav wars of secession and the bitter war of 1999 in Kosovo in which, in response to the Serbian expulsion of around one million Albanians from the province of Kosovo, NATO bombed Serbia. Kosovo proved to be a strong, effective, and mobilising metaphor that epitomised the xenophobic and exclusive nationalist discourse that dominated late twentieth-century Serbia. In April of 1987 at Kosovo, Slobodan Milošević, then a Belgrade city official, gave an influential speech to an assembled crowd that invoked Kosovo as a Serbian symbol of nationhood and independence. He spoke of the 'injustice and humiliation they were suffering; their ancestral land [Kosovo]; of the proud warrior spirit of their forefathers; of their duty to their descendants' (quoted in Wachtel 1998: 255). Another famous rallying speech that also powerfully invoked the myth of Kosovo was delivered two years later, on June 15 1989, which marked the 600th anniversary of the Battle of Kosovo; by then Milošević was President of Serbia. Thus Kosovo as a topos served a number of purposes. It was a historical incident – a place and event of the past that resonated keenly in the present. It was also, as we shall see, a religious-nationalist symbol embracing an entire ideology of death and rebirth. Finally, it was a corpus of epic narratives, each of which told a somewhat different tale of the suffering and meaning of the fateful battle.

One might be surprised to learn that there are only nine Kosovo songs in what has so famously been called the Kosovo Cycle. Five of them are simply short fragments that Vuk remembered from his childhood when his father sang them; the shortest contains only six lines, while the longest has 64. The remaining four form the core of the Kosovo canon and are (in the order in which Vuk presented them): 1. *Tsar Lazar and Tsaritsa Milica (about the Kosovo battle)* (*Car Lazar i carica Milica o boju Kosovskom*), collected by Vuk from a blind female singer named Stepanija; 2. *The Fall of the Serbian Empire (Propast carstva srpskoga)*, 3. *The Death of the Mother of the Jugovićes (Smrt majke Jugovića)*; and 4. *The Kosovo Maiden (Kosovska djevojka)*, recorded for Vuk 'by Lukijan Mušicki from a blind woman from the village of Grgurevci in Srem' (Koljević 1980: 168). All of them are from Karadžić (1969 [1845], vol. 2: nos. 2, 3 and 4). These four core Kosovo songs are all brief (the shortest contains 84 verses; the longest 204) and strikingly poignant, at times seemingly literary. They are clearly more balladic than epic and, in any case, are certainly not heroic (not one of them relates what would seem to be the key event of the Battle of Kosovo – the slaying of Murat the Sultan by Miloš Obilić). And little is known about the performance and collecting of these songs or the degree to which Vuk edited them. Koljević argues that Vuk's 'editing was negligible, his arrangements simple and straightforward, basically chronological, with poems grouped round certain heroes and historical events' (Koljević 1994: 25).

One of the most celebrated narratives of the Kosovo cycle is *The Fall of the Serbian Empire*, a story that attributes the defeat of the Serbs by the Ottomans to the calculated choice made by Prince Lazar between an ephemeral victory and everlasting life.

A blind woman sang this relatively short song in Srem (Vojvodina) for Lukijan Mušicki, the abbot of a nearby monastery, who sent it to Vuk in 1817 (Pennington 1983: 17). Lazar is confronted, near the beginning of the poem, with a choice for the outcome of the Battle of Kosovo and consequently the fate of the Serbian people. He receives a message from 'the Holy Virgin' and is asked:

> which of the two kingdoms   will you embrace?
> Would you rather   choose a heavenly kingdom,
> or have instead   an earthly kingdom here?[4] (Mihailovich 1997: 147 ll. 12–14)

She explains his options and their consequences:

> If, here and now,   you choose the earthly kingdom, ...
> ... launch you then   assault against the Turks.
> Then their army,   all the Turks, shall perish.
> But if, instead,   you choose the heavenly kingdom,
> then you must build   a church at Kosovo....
> and give your host   orders to Holy Mass.
> For every man,   all soldiers, will perish,
> and you, their prince,   will perish with your host. (Mihailovich 1997: 147–48 ll. 15–26)

A religious-literary aura pervades this passage. The alternatives of 'heavenly' versus 'earthly' kingdom are a 'repetition and periphrasis of similar points made in Serbian historical literature in the Middle Ages' (Koljević 1980: 162). Upon contemplation of these options,

> Lazar chooses   the heavenly kingdom;
> he refuses   the earthly kingdom here.
> So he has built   the church of Kosovo. (Mihailovich 1997: 148 ll. 37–39)

Lazar beckons the Serbian patriarch and 'twelve great Serbian bishops', and the whole army comes to take communion (Mihailovich 1997: 148 l. 43).

Apparently communion 'on the eve of the battle was ... customary in the Byzantine and presumably in the Serbian army' (Koljević 1980: 162). In the meantime, the Turks arrive, after which the singer undertakes a catalogue of Serbian heroes (comprising more than a third of the verses in the 93-line song) bravely fighting and falling on the field of Kosovo. Lazar then successfully rallies his men around him as the drama mounts:

> Prince Lazar, then,   would overwhelm the Turks, (Mihailovich 1997: 150 l. 85)

Yet in an unexpected reversal in the last verses of the poem, we read:

> But may God's curse   be on Vuk Branković!
> For he betrays   his prince and his wife's father,
> and Lazar's host   is overwhelmed by Turks.
> Now Lazar falls,   the Serbian Prince Lazar,
> and with him falls   the whole of his brave host,
> his seventy   and seven thousand men. (Mihailovich 1997: 150 ll. 86–91)

A short blessing then brings the song to a close:

> All this is done with good grace and honor,
> before the eyes of God the Lord Almighty. (Mihailovich 1997: 150 ll. 92–93)

This song is arguably the most famous Kosovo 'epic'; it played a fundamental role in the myth of Kosovo as a type of cultural doctrine. It serves as a powerful metaphor for both Christian Serbs and Serbia the nation. Andrew Wachtel suggests that 'Lazar's choice of the heavenly kingdom not only "explains" the Serbian loss; it provides a paradigm for seeing the Serbs (and the South Slavs in general) as a people of God, who choose honor over mere victory, physical suffering over easy glory, martyrdom over conquest' (Wachtel 1998: 35).

The religious meanings in the poem are explicit: the 'heavenly kingdom', the building of the 'church at Kosovo' and Holy Mass that will follow; the Communion on the eve of the battle representing a symbolic Last Supper, not to mention the twelve Serbian bishops in attendance who symbolise the twelve disciples of Jesus. The Christian discourse of death and resurrection in 'The Fall of the Serbian Empire' is transposed to the nationalist discourse on war and rebirth of a nation, providing a compelling narrative. And as in the formative Christian narrative, it is the glory that matters in the Kosovo myth, not the loss. The intriguing symbolism of defeat and resignation within the song and, by extension, within the Serbian ethos is also significant. The choice that Lazar makes in the song (whether it accounts for the defeat or not) is central to how many Serbs understand their history and thus their fate. The poem clothes this defeat in hallowed terms. Based on the prominence that the Battle of Kosovo has played and continues to play as Serbs find a place for themselves in the world, Mattjis Van de Port suggests that 'the ultimate experience of being a Serb can only be achieved in total defeat' and that Serbs as a people 'are destined to suffer' (van de Port 1998: 123). He argues that the story of the defeat at Kosovo is central to the Serbian psyche: 'Lazar sacrificed his life and his kingdom to achieve higher spiritual ends' such that 'total defeat offers spiritual victory' (van de Port 1998: 124–25). From this viewpoint, Serbian liberation has been effected through sacrifice, yet another sub-text of the narrative. This conviction 'assigns a very positive role to war experiences' (Van de Port 1998: 125), bringing the Battle of Kosovo once again into the world of the 1990s and beyond when the brutal wars of secession and ethnic conflict took place.

In a chilling extension of how the epics of Kosovo have been exploited by late twentieth-century Serbian nationalists, the well-known war crimes suspect Željko 'Arkan' Ražnatović (leader during the Yugoslav Wars of Secession of the voluntary paramilitary unit, the Serbian Voluntary Guard) turned to an epic from the Kosovo cycle, reports Ivan Čolović, as 'the framework for the new heroic identity which [he] attributed to himself and his volunteers'. Čolović continues:

> This is shown in the text of the oath which the fighters in his private army, the Serbian Voluntary Guard, solemnly swore. In his wish to be connected with the celebrated Serbian

> heroic past, Arkan ... did not satisfy himself with an evocation of the *hayduk* [16th–18th century Balkan freedom fighter] tradition, but rather returned to the Kosovo tradition, much more valuable for the Serbian political 'imaginarium'. (Čolović 2004: 261)

The text I have italicised in the oath below paraphrases a famous call to battle by Prince Lazar in the shortest fragment of a Kosovo song that Vuk recalled from his childhood, 'Fragments of various Kosovo songs' ('Komadi od različnijeh kosovskijeh pjesama', Karadžić Vol. 2). The original fragment is:

> If but one man   were present there to hear how Knez Lazar uttered his bitter curse:
> 'He who does not   come to Kosovo field,
> may nothing grow   from the toil of his hands,
> nor may there grow   the white wheat in his field,
> nor on the hills   the vine in the vineyard!' (Mihailovich 1997: 135 II, ll. 18–23)

Arkan's oath became the following, proceeding from the 4-verse curse of Lazar in the previous excerpt:

> *Anyone who* is a Serb and of Serb descent, of Serbian blood and ancestry, and *does not go into battle to save the Serbian people*, may he have no offspring, neither male or female, *may nothing grow from his hand, neither red wine nor white wheat*, may he not cross himself, may he dig corrosion while he has knees, may honourable struggle change his evil blood for all future generations. I make this oath with three fingers, and for this holy cross, I give my life for the salvation of the Serbian people. (quoted in Čolović 2004: 261)

Here the unmistakable echo of the near-inviolate epic of Kosovo and its call to arms provided a powerful and binding covenant loaded with religious and national emblems that Arkan exploited fully and effectively.

Viewing the verses from an oral literary point of view, the significant amount of repetition (even in such a short poem) is conspicuous, as is the catalogue of warriors who battle on Kosovo Field. The couplet – like a benediction – that ends the poem is also 'one of the most quoted of traditional phrases, and [is] often used proverbially' (Zimmerman 1986: 188). Moreover, how do we read the ostensibly contradictory ending that reshuffles Lazar's and Serbia's crucial defeat, placing it now in the hands of Vuk Branković, who betrays Lazar and the army, instead of in Lazar's celebrated choice of outcome? Branković's deed may well be seen as God's will, given the divinely supervised choice that Lazar has just made. Furthermore, with the inventing and tampering that the legend of Kosovo endured over the years, including the addition of the treachery element long after the basic events of the battle had been established, there must have been contradictory and irreconcilable elements to the story that singers heard, considered, and even borrowed at times in their performances. The treachery as the most obvious reason for Kosovo's fate at the end of the poem was perhaps a by-product of oral transmission. Indeed, a problem with assigning such great importance to a single, apparently oral literary version of what was undoubtedly a well-known cultural narrative is that it is precisely that: only a single performance. If this song had been collected more than once – from the same as well as other singers, what stories and motifs would we have, and how many variants of them? Instead, this is one rendering of a narrative song about Kosovo gleaned from an anonymous singer and conveyed to Vuk. It then proceeded to become a metaphor for the fall of Kosovo, itself a metaphor for the tragedy of Serbia.

'The Death of the Mother of the Jugovićes' is likewise one of the most well-known and symbolically expressive of the Kosovo poems – less overtly nationalistic and religious than the previous one, but an effective poem rooted in oral tradition. It was 'sent to Vuk from Croatia by an anonymous collector' (Mihailovich 1997: 151). Though called epic by many Serbian scholars, this poem is even shorter than the previous one (84 verses) and is more balladic than epic. Although not stanzaic, the poem is balladic in other ways: it is structured on a pattern of incremental repetition and includes recurrent short passages (sometimes couplets) that function as a type of refrain. Its domestic, tragic theme, despite the backdrop of the battle, is also balladic; the eponymous mother comes to terms with the death at Kosovo of her husband and nine sons. She receives the 'eyes of an eagle and wings of a swan' from God to fly over Kosovo Field in order to find out how her sons and husband, who are at battle, are faring. She spies all nine sons, as well as her husband, dead on Kosovo field, their nine war-lances, nine gray falcons, nine fine battle steeds, and nine ferocious hounds deserted nearby. In a series of three repeated events in which she recognises her loss, the mother remains stoically strong and does not falter. The first section of the mother's drama is the view of Kosovo field, concluded by the poet's observation of the mother's response. The passage is followed by a recurrent couplet-refrain:

> But even then, the mother's heart is firm;
> her heart won't break; she sheds no tears at all. (Mihailovich 1997: 151, ll. 24–25)

The second section is a scene of the mourning at home by the sons' widows, the orphaned children, and the animals. Again, we hear the couplet-refrain that sends us back to the mother's stoic response. The third section is a scene of the grief felt by Damjan's (the youngest son's) horse; the mother's couplet-refrain is again invoked. Finally, the last section is the mother's direct confrontation with Damjan's death, a metaphor for the deaths at Kosovo writ large, viewed as the centuries of Ottoman rule in Serbia. When Damjan's severed hand is delivered to her by 'a pair of black ravens' (harbingers of death), she is grief-stricken and turns it over in her own hands, speaking to it:

> O you dear hand, my precious green apple,
> where did you grow, and where were you plucked off?
> On this my lap, you, Damjan's hand, grew up;
> you were plucked off on Kosovo's flat field. (Mihailovich 1997: 153 ll. 77–80)

The 'green apple' represents the son – a young man in his prime; apples are clearly fertility symbols. The apple is also traditionally used, in epic poetry, 'to express a mother's love for her son or a husband's love for his wife, usually in a tragic context of death' (Koljević 1980: 237–38). It is here that the mother finally breaks; she can endure it no longer. The earlier recurrent couplet is replaced by the final four verses:

> The mother's heart then, is swollen with grief,
> as her heart swells and at the last it breaks
> for her nine sons, the nine Jugovićes,
> and for the tenth, the old man Jug Bogdan. (Mihailovich 1997: 153 ll. 81–84)

The symbolism of the number nine (3 × 3) is clearly informed by the Christian trinity. Moreover, the rhythmic invoking of nine over and over, especially as the mother views the Kosovo field, is repetitive and ritualistic. Kosovo as the backdrop for this tragic message furnished a powerful context that worked effectively in nineteenth-century Serbia: the intense pain of Kosovo was stirred and implicitly transposed to Serbia where it surely moved minds and inflamed nationalist fervor. The point of this song is of course a mourning of Kosovo, but it also transcends Kosovo and is a universal lament for the loss of loved ones at war.

Marko Kraljević: Historical Figure or Oral Traditional Hero?

Marko Kraljević and heroes like him are found throughout Balkan oral epic tradition and beyond. Contrasting with the more balladic nature of the Kosovo 'epics', the songs about Marko are heroic. Marko was not only an epic hero but also a historic figure: the son of King Vukašin, King of Prilep (Slavic Macedonia). He was born c. 1335 and succeeded his father as King of Prilep in 1371; in 1385 he became a vassal of the Sultan (a vassal system for Serbian princes was implemented in the early Ottoman years). He died at the Battle of Rovine in 1395. The historical Marko had an 'anomalous nature as Christian knight and Turkish vassal' and has always been somewhat ambiguous (Mihailovich 1997: 162). He is both historical and non-historical, serving both the Porte and Christian Serbia. He is surrounded in many of the epic songs by historically verifiable personages, places, and events, yet these details are presented in a jumbled and confused chronology. Marko is even associated in some of the songs with the Battle of Kosovo, yet there is no evidence that he actually fought in it.

Vuk collected numerous heroic songs about Marko Kraljević, which, added to the collections of subsequent folklorists, comprised what became known as a Marko cycle, containing at least 60 poems. Taking the entire South Slavic regions into consideration, Marko songs (found also in Bulgarian, Macedonian, and Slovenian) number about 200 (Popović 1988: 12). The first reference to Marko was from Dalmatia (Split) in 1547: a blind soldier sang in public about him (Koljević 1980: 177). Several years later (1556), a *bugarštica* that told of Marko and his brother Andrija was published in Petar Hektorović's *Fishing and Fishermen's Conversation*, mentioned earlier. Marko lore proliferated in the eighteenth century, and by Vuk's generation, a significant body of heroic songs about him circulated. Marko became a repository for some of the oldest patterns and symbols in Balkan epic and certainly in Christian Balkan epic. He was a special hero in a rich oral tradition, characterised by his connections with the Other World, extraordinary strength, special weapons, and a special horse. As a quintessential oral traditional hero, he became attached to diverse stories, including many that extended over a large cultural continuum, from the Balkans to Central Asia.

As a traditional hero, Marko is semi-divine. His connections with the Other World – already from birth – include his lineage as the offspring of a mortal father (King Vukašin) and Mandalina, a *vila* (the *vila*, or fairy, is an Otherworldly female helper or mischief-maker of South Slavic folklore) (see *King Vukašin and Mandalina the Fairy* [*Vukašin Kralj i Vila Mandalina*] in *Hrvatske narodne pjesme*, vol. 1; also *The Birth of Marko Kraljević* [*Rodjenje Marka Kraljevića*] in *Hrvatske narodne pjesme*, vol. 2). Marko has associations with *vilas* in several songs, underscoring his position within the semi-divine realm (e.g., *Marko Kraljević and the* Vila [*Marko Kraljević i vila*] in Karadžić 1969 [1845]). His extraordinary strength is also typical of oral-traditional heroes; he is a phenomenal warrior, and his deeds of prowess are pure hyperbole, even caricatures. Marko's special weapons are his mace and his sabre, and he has a special horse, Šarac ('Piebald'). Marko's close relationship with Šarac connects him to ancient hero-and-horse patterns. Lord maintained that the role Šarac played 'in Marko's life ... has cultic overtones' (Lord 1991: 223). Šarac is present at Marko's death, augured by his own stumbling (*The Death of Marko Kraljević* [*Smrt Marka Kraljevića*] in Karadžić 1969 [1845]).

Marko also has a crazy, wild streak. He is at times enormously exuberant, over-energised, temperamental and, of course, forever drinking wine. These are not features of his personality, however, but oral traditional heroic qualities. They are what Lord referred to as Heraklean traits, pointing out that Marko's colossal strength and 'irrational, frenzied behavior [are] a mark of special powers, of an otherworldliness' (Lord 1991: 204). Marko and other traditional heroes like him have roots in the deep past. After the Slavs settled in the Balkans (sixth–seventh centuries) and before the Ottoman period commenced (fourteenth century), stories and episodes about heroes were no doubt generated among the local inhabitants. Lord was convinced that at this time 'traditional songs and stories were being formed and reformed. It must have been a creative period for epic' (Lord 1991: 204). Heroic narratives that later came to be associated with the name Marko Kraljević would have been circulating over both time and space. This, of course, is a markedly different appraisal of Marko Kraljević from those that Serbian nationalist thinking has perpetuated and contrasts with historical readings, such as the following thoughts by Tatyana Popović:

> In the absence of more reliable sources, Prince Marko's epic life, replete with countless exploits and heroic deeds, serves as a viable means for tracing medieval events of South Slavic history. Through the interaction of epic and history, national ethical values were formulated, creating a central national ideal embodied in the heroic person of Prince Marko. (Popović 1988: 13)

Traditional story patterns found among poems of the Marko Kraljević 'cycle' are ubiquitous. To point out just a few of the most representative examples, Marko confronts and defeats the ferocious road-blocker and dragon substitute, Musa, in

Marko and Musa the Robber (*Marko Kraljević i Musa Kesedžija* in Karadžić 1969 [1845]), collected by Vuk in 1815 from one of his finest singers, Tešan Podrugović in Sremski Karlovci (Koljević 1980: 196). A classic example of the 'return-song' pattern is found in *Marko and Mina of Kostur* (*Marko Kraljević i Mina od Kostura* in Kraljević 1969 [1845]), which Vuk recorded from an anonymous singer (Mihailovich 1997: 182). While Marko the soldier is absent, his home comes under attack by Mina of Kostur, and his wife is abducted. When Marko returns, he kills Mina, wins back his wife, and restores order to his household. Yet another typical Marko song – a narrative wedding song – is *The Wedding of Marko Kraljević* (Ženidba Marka Kraljevića in Karadžić 1969 [1845]), an ethnographically colourful tale of the obtaining of a bride and the eventful journey to her husband-to-be's home; Vuk's informant again was Podrugović.

Such are traditional readings of Marko; they are informed by comparative analyses and draw their meanings from their connections to other traditional narrative and heroic patterns. Read historically, Marko is presented somewhat differently. He is a local champion and symbol of Serbian national culture: a source of inspiration for the oppressed, and a powerful symbol of heroism and hope in Serbia's strength as a nation. Indeed, sometimes Marko and Kosovo are combined for a particularly forceful message. Bowra related that in the First Balkan War, '[w]hen the Serbian armies entered the field of Kosovo in 1912, they fell on their knees, said prayers, and kissed the soil, or even thought that they saw Marko Kraljević on his famous horse, Šarac, and rushed after him' (Bowra 1952: 509).

In today's world too, in the aftermath of the wars of secession and the Kosovo conflict, it has been said that Marko continues to inspire the Serbs and lead them to victory.

* * * * *

I have examined how history has been employed in the creation, production, and interpretation of South Slavic Christian epic, especially since the nineteenth century, and how historical orientations of oral epic have been exploited especially in the construction of Serbian national identity. The role of Vuk Karadžić in this process was seminal. He actively determined how oral epic was collected, arranged for publication and perceived. History was seen by him and his cohort as a means for validating culture. The Battle of Kosovo and the heroic Marko Kraljević served as potent symbols for Serbs during the latter years of Ottoman rule, as liberation, nationhood and culture became fervent aspirations and then realities. Oral narrative songs – epic – provided a remarkably effective and compelling means by which nationalist emblems and their messages could be disseminated and embraced throughout Serbia, reaching all corners of society. The songs about Kosovo were – and are – metaphors for explaining the defeat, shame, yet underlying hope of the Serbs, who endured 500 years of Turkish rule. And the epic poems about Marko Kraljević, although drawing from a rich oral tradition, also offered a means by which an awe-inspiring, national hero and the vision, promise and sense of strength that he generated could animate the Serbian nation at various junctures in its history.

The power and influence of historical readings of South Slavic epic must be recognised, as well as how the leading voices, particularly of the nineteenth century, exploited these readings in their quest to build a Serbian nation and national culture. Alternative readings based on in-depth and comparative observations of traditional culture and expression also offer meaningful levels of understanding of these narrative songs and the heroes within them. A full and fair appreciation of South Slavic epic and the context in which it was promoted entails a critical examination of both historical and oral traditional processes and perspectives.

Notes

1. 'Pseudo-historical' refers to songs that contain references to historically identifiable names, places, and events, yet whose stories are not historical per se (Lord 1972a: 299).
2. Before the advance of the Ottomans in the fourteenth century, it is believed that there was a vibrant oral narrative poetic tradition (ballads and short songs) containing stories that dealt with ahistorical characters, mythological elements, and aspects of the supernatural – the materials of ancient story-making. By contrast, songs that have a more 'historical' imprint (containing events, names, and places that connect somehow to history) reveal a more recent lineage. As Lord explained, the ahistorical Muslim songs 'preserved and developed some of the mythic patterns more elaborately than the Christian tradition, which turned its sights more and more to ... history' (1972a: 299).
3. Formerly a province in southern Serbia, Kosovo declared its independence from Serbia in February 2008 and enacted a new constitution in June. Kosovo is inhabited primarily by Albanians.
4. Mihailovich has translated the Serbian epic texts into English as decasyllabic lines, in which there is a word break after the fourth syllable, just as in the original.

Bibliography

Bakić-Hayden, M.
2004 National memory as narrative memory. In M. Todorova (ed.), *Balkan Identities: Nation and Memory*: 25–40. New York: New York University Press.

Bowra, C. M.
1952 *Heroic Poetry*. London: Macmillan.

Čolović, I.
2004 A criminal-national hero? But who else? In M. Todorova (ed.), *Balkan Identities: Nation and Memory*: 253–68. New York: New York University Press.

Coote, M. P.
1978 Serbocroatian heroic songs. In F.J. Oinas (ed.), *Heroic Epic and Saga: An Introduction to the World's Great Folk Epics*: 257–85. Bloomington & London: Indiana University Press.

Deretić, J.
1994 Poems and events: historicity in Serbo-Croat oral epics. In M. Branch and C. Hawkesworth (eds.), *The Uses of Tradition*: 83–95. London: School of Slavonic and East European Studies.

Hrvatske narodne pjesme (Croatian Folk Songs).
1896–1942 *Hrvatske narodne pjesme* (10 vols.). Zagreb: Matica Hrvatska.

Karadžić, V. S.
1969 [1845] *Srpske narodne pjesme skupio ih i na svijet izdao Vuk. St. Karadžić: Knjiga druga u kojoj su pjesme junačke najstarije*. Vol. 2. Belgrade: Nolit.
Kekez, J.
1991 *Bugaršćice*: a unique type of archaic oral poetry. *Oral Tradition* 6: 200–24.
Kleut, M.
1994 The classification of Serbo-Croat oral epic songs into cycles: reasons and consequences. In M. Branch and C. Hawkesworth (eds.), *The Uses of Tradition*: 75–81. London: School of Slavonic and East European Studies.
Koljević, S.
1980 *The Epic in the Making*. Oxford: Clarendon Press.
1994 Vuk Karadžić and the achievement of his singers. In M. Branch and C. Hawkesworth (eds.), *The Uses of Tradition*: 23–36. London: School of Slavonic and East European Studies.
Lord, A. B.
1960 *The Singer of Tales*. Cambridge, MA: Harvard University Press.
1972a The effect of the Turkish conquest on Balkan epic tradition. In H. Birnbaum and S. Vryonis, Jr. (eds.), *Aspects of the Balkans: Contintuity and Change*: 298–318. The Hague: Mouton.
1972b History and tradition in Balkan oral epic and ballad. *Western Folklore* 31: 53–60.
1991 *Epic Singers and Oral Tradition*. Ithaca, NY: Cornell University Press.
1994 The impact of Vuk Karadžić on the tradition: the importance for Homer. In M. Branch and C. Hawkesworth (eds.), *The Uses of Tradition*: 3–21. London: School of Slavonic and East European Studies.
1995 The transitional text. In A.B. Lord, *The Singer Resumes the Tale*: 212–37. Ithaca, NY: Cornell University Press.
Marešić, T.
1966 *Naša narodna epika*. Belgrade: Nolit.
Matić, S.
1964 *Naš narodni ep i naš stih: Ogledi i studije*. Novi Sad: Matica Srpska.
Mihailovich, V. D. and M. Holton
1997 *Songs of the Serbian People: From the Collections of Vuk Karadžić*. Pittsburgh: University of Pittsburgh Press.
Milošević-Djordjević, N.
1994 The poetics of the Serbian oral tradition of Vuk Karadžić. In M. Branch and C. Hawkesworth (eds.), *The Uses of Tradition*: 51–67. London: School of Slavonic and East European Studies.
Pennington, A. and P. Levi (transl.)
1983 *Marko the Prince: Serbo-Croat Heroic Songs*. London: Duckworth.
Pešić, R.
1967 Stariji sloj pesama o uskocima. *Anali Filološkog fakulteta* 7: 49–65.
Petrović, S.
2001 *Kosovska bitka u usmenoj poeziji*. Belgrade: Gutenbergov Galerija.
Popović, T.
1988 *Prince Marko: The Hero of South Slavic Epics*. Syracuse, NY: Syracuse University Press.
Redjep, J.
1991 The Legend of Kosovo. *Oral Tradition* 6: 253–65.
Vaillant, A.
1932 Les chants épiques des Slaves du Sud: II. *Revue des cours et conférences* 33: 431–46.
Van de Port, M.
1998 *Gypsies, Wars and Other Instances of the Wild: Civilization and its Discontents in a Serbian Town*. Amsterdam: Amsterdam University Press.

Voigt, V.
1994 *Primus inter pares*: why was Vuk Karadžić the most influential folklore scholar in South-Eastern Europe in the nineteenth century? In M. Branch and C. Hawkesworth (eds.), *The Uses of Tradition*: 179–93. London: School of Slavonic and East European Studies.

Wachtel, A. B.
1998 *Making a Nation, Breaking a Nation: Literature and Cultural Politics in Yugoslavia*. Stanford: Stanford University Press.

Zimmerman, Z. D.
1986 *Serbian Folk Poetry: Ancient Legends, Romantic Songs*. Columbus, Ohio: Kosovo Publishing Company.

Chapter 10

'The National Epic of the Modern Greeks'? – *Digenis Akritis*, the Homeric Question, and the Making of a Modern Myth

Roderick Beaton

On 14 January (according to the Old Calendar), 1907, the founder of Greek folklore studies, Nikolaos Politis, gave his inaugural lecture as professor at the National and Capodistrian University of Athens. The subject that he chose was 'The national epic of the Modern Greeks' (Politis 1920). The 'modern Greeks' do not in fact have a 'national epic,' as Politis was honest enough almost to admit. This paper is about how they created one – the building blocks that existed to make the edifice possible, how and why it was done, and how effective was the result. Its relevance to the subject of the present volume can therefore only be by way of analogy. But the story of the epic about a hero called by the composite name of 'Digenis Akritas', an epic that never quite existed, can perhaps be instructive for the comparative study of epic traditions and their modern reception.

The story begins in 1869, when a schoolmaster of Trebizond, Savvas Ioannidis, discovered in the nearby monastery of Panagia Soumela a manuscript of a Byzantine poem in some three thousand lines. The manuscript itself disappeared when the monastery was ransacked in 1922. It lacked a beginning, and therefore a title for the work it contained. But its importance was quickly recognised, and the text was published six years after its first discovery, in Paris, by the formidable Franco-Greek team of Byzantinists, Konstantinos Sathas and Emile Legrand. The title they gave it was, *Les Exploits de Digénis Akritas* (Sathas and Legrand 1875).

In that edition, the previously unknown poem was for the first time hailed as an 'epic', but not yet a 'national' one. 'Digenis Akritas' is the name of the poem's hero, whose exploits it narrates. But actually not quite. It sounds at first like no more than a trivial philological quibble, but the name of the hero as it appears in this manuscript and in the five others that would subsequently come to light is not 'Digenis Akritas' (Διγενής Ακρίτας) but 'Digenis Akritis' (Διγενής Ακρίτης). The reason for the change is that Sathas and Legrand had recognised, with appropriate excitement, that some very similar 'exploits' to those narrated in their Byzantine poem are also found in oral folk songs that were very much part of the living tradition of their day. Not only that, but in the very same region in which Ioannidis had made his discovery of the manuscript – Pontos – and as it has since turned out, only there, some of these songs give to their hero the name 'Akritas.' Ever since 1875, in the popular Greek imagination and in the works of many reputable scholars and literary writers too, the hero of the Byzantine poem and the hero of these folksongs has been known by the hybrid, composite name 'Digenis Akritas' – a name which so far as I have been able to discover is attested in no known oral or manuscript source before Ioannidis' discovery and its subsequent publication by Sathas and Legrand.[1]

The excitement was justified, however. And it only increased as successive further manuscript versions of the Byzantine poem came to light, the latest in 1920. The manuscripts date from the mid-twelfth century to the late seventeenth, and there are significant divergences in style, language and even content among them. The folksongs, as might be expected, present an even greater variety. The hero's name may appear as 'Digenis', 'Akritis', 'Akritas', the more everyday 'Yannis', and very often he has no name at all. Some of his exploits are more or less recognisable from the Byzantine poem. These include: bride-snatching, defending his bride from rival snatchers, crossing impassable mountains and deserts, massacring human enemies, wild beasts and fantastic monsters in implausible numbers, and dying young. But sadly, the most famous of all the exploits of 'Digenis Akritas', known in many variants from the folk songs, is not to be found in any surviving version of the Byzantine poem. This is the heroic single combat in which the hero confronts the personification of Death, Charos, challenges him to a duel as man-to-man, they wrestle on the marble (or bronze, or iron) threshing floor, and the hero holds his own until his adversary is forced to cheat, thereby leaving the moral victory to his victim.[2]

Despite this not quite perfect fit between the different components of the hybrid hero, there were two main reasons for excitement. The first was that here, on the ground, in the Greek-speaking world, was confirmation of the position on the perennial 'Homeric Question' taken by the 'Analysts'. Songs similar to the ones that could still be heard in the oral tradition – and particularly in Pontos and Cyprus – must surely have been assembled together in Byzantine times, perhaps between the tenth century and the twelfth, in much the manner proposed by Wolf and his successors for the Homeric poems. And although there is no seriously plausible direct link between the tradition that produced the Byzantine and modern versions of *Digenis*, on the one hand, and the Homeric tradition on the other, the very fact of a similar process of composition and collation being common to both periods gave a boost to the self-presentation of the Greek élites at that time as the direct heirs to the ancients. (All this, of course, was several decades before the 'oral-formulaic' theory of the composition of the Homeric poems was first proposed by Milman Parry, based on observation of a living oral tradition.)

The second reason for excitement was more obviously political, and again had to do with the concurrently evolving national identity and ambitions of many Greeks. The last decades of the nineteenth century, when most of the known manuscripts of *Digenis Akritis* came to light, were the period when the 'Great Idea' (*Megali Idea*) was at its height – the irredentist ideology of reclaiming for the Greek state territories in the east that had once belonged to the Byzantine empire and where the Greek nation was still to some extent present at the beginning of the twentieth century.[3] This of course included Pontos and Cyprus, while the Byzantine poem clearly, and the contemporary folk songs to some extent also, preserved clear traces of historical memories from places even further to the east – the deserts of Arabia and the banks of the Euphrates. By its very existence, and still more thanks to its affinities to a still living tradition, the Byzantine poem gave substance to Greek territorial claims in the east, based on ideas of 'national tradition' and 'national memory' derived ultimately from Herder.

It is on those grounds, though this is not explicitly stated, that Politis in 1907 could describe the Byzantine poem as 'national', and indeed could claim a text approximately eight centuries old for the '*modern*' Greeks. Ever since then, the 'epic of Digenis Akritas' – note the hybrid title, though to be fair to Politis he himself avoids it – has taken its honoured place in the Greek literary and cultural tradition, exactly as has *Beowulf* in England, the *Song of Roland* in France, the *Nibelungenlied* in Germany, the *Poem of the Cid* in Spain. All of these epic poems came to acquire canonical status at about the same time, the later nineteenth century. Other nations, less favoured, had to resort to more complex expedients, as the Greeks did: such is the case, I understand, with the Finnish *Kalevala* and the Russian *Prince Igor*.

In order to try to get 'under the skin' of this process of 'creating tradition' and 'constructing epic' in the modern Greek case, I propose to look more closely at that inaugural address of a hundred years ago, and also at another which directly takes up some of the same issues in a different register – the published commentary on it by the poet Kostis Palamas, that appeared later the same year (Palamas n.d.). Then I shall conclude by sketching in some highlights from the later dissemination of this constructed tradition, which has been enormously influential.

Politis' lecture is the work of a well-informed and generally scrupulous scholar. By its nature, it is also a speech given at a formal public occasion. Close reading of what Politis actually says suggests that even for him, the 'epic of the modern Greeks' was more of an aspiration to be wished for than a given reality. A problem emerges early on with the characterisation 'national'. In none of the manuscript versions of the Byzantine 'epic' does the term 'Hellenes' appear. The hero's feats are performed on the borders of what the text calls 'Romania', by which is meant the Christian empire known to modern scholarship as 'Byzantium', but whose inhabitants normally referred to themselves as 'Romans' (*Romaioi*). In discussing his text, Politis imports an anachronistic sense of the term 'national', which clearly is that of his own time, not that of any Byzantine century. He writes of:

> a national epic ... in which we follow the historical development of the Hellenic soul, and which treats of the clash between the Hellenic and Muslim worlds and of the superiority of the Hellenic ... it embraces the ideals and aspirations of the Hellenic *genos*. (Politis 1920: 260)

In reality, in all the surviving versions of the Byzantine poem, as well as in a great many of the folksongs, the major exploits of the hero have nothing to do with Muslims. Usually his adversaries are either wild beasts, rivals in love, or the bands of truculent irregulars that the texts know as *apelatai*, whose names, if not much about their behaviour, are obviously Christian. There are relatively few passages, some of them demonstrably due to the copyists or redactors of particular manuscripts, in which we find Digenis overcoming specifically Saracen enemies or laying claim to Muslim lands (cf. Jeffreys 1998: 3). If there is an anti-Muslim element at all in the Byzantine texts, it is curiously understated, and in them (though not in any of the more recent folk songs) the hero is called 'Digenis' precisely because he is born of a Christian mother and a father who was a Saracen *emir* until he converted to Christianity – and for love. This aspect was well summed up by John Mavogordato, whose introduction to the Grottaferrata version of the poem takes issue with Politis precisely on this point:

> It is difficult to see how anybody capable of reading the poem from beginning to end could be expected to swallow this, seeing that the hero is *ex hypothesi* a happy fusion of Christian and Mohammedan blood. There is little religious fanaticism in the poem, and only the most perfunctory expressions of orthodox Christianity. (Mavrogordato 1956: lxv–lxvi)

Politis has even greater difficulty with the term 'epic'. Entirely correctly, if we compare what he wrote a hundred years ago with the most recent scholarship on the Byzantine texts, he concedes that 'any hope of reconstructing the archetype of the epic would be in vain'. This is because of the substantial divergences among the surviving manuscript witnesses. And he continues, 'It seems more probable that the first draft of the epic, if it were to come to light, would not be shown to be any more complete or artistically satisfying than the surviving versions' (Politis 1920: 239; cf. Ricks 1989). Politis believed, as many specialists have done since and still do, that the source for the Byzantine material must have lain in the oral tradition, but he does not make the mistake of assuming that these unrecoverable oral sources for the 'epic' would necessarily have been the same as the folksongs of the so-called 'acritic cycle', as they have been recorded since the nineteenth century. Entirely understandably, as a folklorist, Politis declares his preference for the oral versions, and does not shirk the (quite true) observation that generically modern Greek folk songs are quite different from the epic tradition (Politis 1920: 242). This leads him to the curious conclusion that 'this epic tradition is available to us in its fullest and most integral form possible, in the folksongs' (Politis 1920: 244).

A close reading of Politis' text then suggests that the epic claimed by his title for the 'modern Greeks' does not in fact exist. Not unfairly, he argues that the written versions preserved in the manuscripts can be described as 'epic' in character, but each one represents no more than an unskilful redaction of traditional material that may never have found its definitive form in writing. In this way, the 'national epic of the modern Greeks' seems destined, for Politis, to remain forever unrealised, incomplete, a masterpiece that might have been fashioned, as he puts it, only 'if some poet of genius had appeared, capable of assembling all this material and integrating it into a broad whole'. Such a poet, had he existed, Politis goes on, 'would have bequeathed to mankind an epic to compete with the *Iliad*'. But this did not happen. At least, it has not happened *yet*. Politis concludes, perhaps rather wistfully, 'From the influence of the acritic epic upon our renascent literature we have many benefits to expect. ... there may be no surer starting point for modern Greek poetry than to draw upon the national epic' (Politis 1920: 244, 259–60).

Precisely this challenge seems to have been recognised immediately by Palamas, far and away the most admired and influential Greek poet of the period. Writing in his preferred demotic Greek, rather than the academic *katharevousa* obligatory for the professor of folklore, Palamas commented, in a long letter to the demoticist periodical *Noumas* a few months later:

> And now with his speech on the national epic he [Politis] gives us to ponder an *Iliad* that was never put together, an *Iliad* that never saw the light of day ... because the Poet was lacking. Sleeping Beauty stayed asleep, because the Prince never turned up to wake her. (Palamas n.d.: 499)

Writing in blatantly more poetic mode, Palamas has no qualms about conflating the Byzantine *Digenis Akritis* with the folkloric *Akritas*, and refers to an undifferentiated 'Digenis Akritas'. For Palamas, the hero of this composite, if unrealised, epic poem is at once the scourge of enemy races and Islam, the quasi-kleftic hero of the Byzantine frontiers, and the popular hero of the folksongs who fights with Charos to the death.

This epic, the true 'epic of the modern Greeks', had never been written, as Politis in more cautious terms had conceded, and as Palamas well knew. But it still need not be too late. In Palamas' words, 'Digenis Akritas is an epic hero above all others made to reappear here and now, before our eyes'. The poem that Politis wistfully thought would have rivalled the *Iliad*, if only it had existed, according to Palamas: 'the poem that the Byzantines never gave us, perhaps has been given us, perhaps will be given us, perhaps is being given us at this moment, by our contemporaries?' (Palamas n.d.: 504–5).

Palamas never wrote that epic either, but at the time when he wrote these words he *had* almost finished the long poem that has perhaps the greatest claim of any to be regarded as the 'national epic of the modern Greeks': *Η φλογέρα του Βασιλιά*, whose title has been rendered alternatively as *The King's Flute* or *The Emperor's Reed Pipe* (Palamas 1982; cf. Beaton 1994: 86 n.). Published in 1910, this poem exploits the traditional fifteen-syllable verse, also used in *Digenis Akritis* and the folk songs, and blends together elements of Byzantine history with the later folk tradition, to create a vision of a new Greek national identity as the double heir to the legacies respectively of classical Athens and of Byzantine Constantinople. Characteristically, Palamas puts into the mouth of his protagonist, the emperor Basil II, the declaration: 'For I am Digenis [doubly-born], for I am Akritas [the frontiersman]' (Palamas 1982: 272).

Since then, even though the 'epic of Digenis Akritas' has never fully materialised, either as a real discovery from the past or as a new imaginative work, a modern myth came to be created by the first discoverers of the Byzantine poem, and consolidated by Politis and Palamas in 1907, by close analogy with the model proposed by the 'Analysts' for the Homeric poems. We cannot tell, now, to what extent the syncretism of disparate elements was ever fully deliberate. But it certainly was effective. The unrealised 'national epic' described by Politis was in part actualised, although in a quite different way, by Palamas in *The Emperor's Reed-Pipe*.

Its influence in Greek life and letters for most of the following century can be briefly summarised in tabular form:

1928.	Nikos Kazantzakis, *Ασκητική: Salvatores Dei* (translated as *The Saviors of God*). Among the final words of this post-Nietzschean, 'metacommunist' Credo are: I BELIEVE IN ONE GOD, A BORDERER, DOUBLE-BORN ...) (Kazantzakis 1971: 94).
1929.	Giorgos Theotokas publishes his literary manifesto for a new generation, *Free Spirit*, under the pseudonym 'Orestes Digenis' (Theotokas 1973).
1942.	Angelos Sikelianos, in Athens under German and Italian occupation, circulates a small collection of poems clandestinely, with the title *Akritika* (Sikelianos 1965).
1947.	Angelos Sikelianos: *The Death of Digenis*. The hero of this drama in verse is a heretic who dies defying the authority of the Orthodox church and of the emperor of Byzantium (Sikelianos 1955: 23–109).
1940s–1950s.	Nikos Kazantzakis projects a sequel to his epic poem *The Odyssey: A Modern Sequel*, to be called *Digenis Akritas*.
1955–1959.	The commander-in-chief of the armed struggle against British rule in Cyprus, Col. George Grivas, adopts the codename 'Digenis' and is still often referred to in Cyprus (e.g. in street-names) as 'Grivas-Digenis'.
1979.	Patrick White (Australian novelist, Nobel Prize for Literature 1973), *The Twyborn Affair*. A novel set in twentieth-century France, Australia and Britain, based on a different interpretation of the name 'Digenis' (Twyborn), in a transsexual sense, with allusions to the medieval Greek versions (White 1979).
1990.	Thanasis Papathanasopoulos, *Digenis Akritis*. Described as 'a Kazantzakian philosophical mishmash of 24 books and over 24,000 verses recently [1993] garlanded by no less a body than the Academy of Athens' (Kechagioglou 1993: 130).

Conclusion

There has been no archaeology in this paper. But the Homeric poems, and more immediately the 'Homeric Question', lie at the basis of everything I have been discussing. Had it not been for the 'Analyst' proposition about Homer, the discovery of the Byzantine poem, *Digenis Akritis*, would surely not have had the impact it did, either in the development of Greek literary and folkloric studies, or in the subsequent course of 'national imagining' in Greece throughout the twentieth century. The Homeric Question provided a model by which the concurrent existence of an old epic poem and of contemporary oral songs could be understood, but in turn lent enormous prestige and cultural significance to the new discovery. I hope that by trying to unpick something of the process by which this particular 'epic tradition' came to be consolidated in the late nineteenth and early twentieth centuries, I have been able to offer some comparative insights that may, even if tangentially, shed light on the primary theme of the present volume.

Notes

1. For an authoritative and up-to-date edition of the most important manuscripts, with English translation and an excellent introduction, including much background material, see Jeffreys 1998. For a cross-section of the scholarly debate, see the essays collected in Beaton and Ricks 1993.
2. Most twentieth-century anthologies of Greek folk songs include a section called *Akritika*, in which this material is represented. The most influential of these anthologies, although the methods of its editor were called into question as long ago as the 1930s, remains Politis 1914. Among the most scholarly of its successors are Academy of Athens 1963 and Petropoulos 1958.
3. For historical background see, for example, Clogg 2002: 95–103.

Bibliography

Academy of Athens [Ακαδημία Αθηνών]
1963 *Ελληνικά δημοτικά τραγούδια (εκλογή)*, vol. 1. Athens: Academy of Athens.
Beaton, R.
1994 *An Introduction to Modern Greek Literature.* Oxford: Oxford University Press.
Beaton, R. and D. Ricks (eds.)
1993 *Digenes Akrites: New Approaches to Byzantine Heroic Poetry* (Publications of the Centre for Hellenic Studies, King's College London, 2). Aldershot: Ashgate.
Clogg, R.
2002 *A Concise History of Greece.* Cambridge: Cambridge University Press.
Jeffreys, E. (ed. and transl.).
1998 *Digenis Akritis: The Grottaferrata and Escorial Versions* (Cambridge Medieval Classics 7). Cambridge: Cambridge University Press.
Kazantzakis, N.
1971 *Ασκητική: Salvatores Dei.* Athens: Ekdoseis Kazantzaki.
Kechagioglou, G.
1993 *Digenes Akrites* in prose. In Beaton and Ricks (eds.) 1993: 116–30.
Mavrogordato, J.
1956 *Digenes Akrites, Edited with an Introduction, Translation and Commentary.* Oxford: Clarendon Press.

Palamas, K.
1982 *The King's Flute* (transl. Theodore Ph. Stephanides and George C. Katsimbalis, preface by Charles Diehl, introduction by E. P. Papanoutsos). Athens: Idryma Kosti Palama.
n.d. Από την αφορμή ενός λόγου για το εθνικό έπος των νεώτερων Ελλήνων. In K. Palamas, Άπαντα, vol. 6: 487–511. Athens: Idryma Kosti Palama.
Petropoulos, D. (ed.)
1958 *Ελληνικά δημοτικά τραγούδια*, vol. 1 (Vasiki Vivliothiki 46). Athens: Zacharopoulos.
Politis, N.
1914 *Εκλογαί από τα τραγούδια του ελληνικού λαού*. Athens: n.p. (and reprints).
1920 Περί του έπους των νεωτέρων Ελλήνων. In N. Politis, *Λαογραφικά Σύμμεικτα*, vol. 1: 237–62. Athens: n.p.
Ricks, D.
1989 Is the Escorial *Akrites* a unitary poem? *Byzantion* 59: 184–207.
Sathas, C. and E. Legrand
1875 *Les exploits de Digénis Akritas: épopée byzantine du dixième siècle.* Paris: Maisonneuve.
Sikelianos, A.
1955 *Θυμέλη*, vol. 3. Athens: Ikaros.
1965 *Λυρικός βίος*, vol. 5 (ed. G.P. Savidis). Athens: Ikaros.
Theotokas, G.
1973 *Ελεύθερο πνεύμα* (ed. K.Th. Dimaras). Athens: Ermis.
White, P.
1979 *The Twyborn Affair.* London: Jonathan Cape.

Ο Γκιλγκαμές στην Τροία/Gilgamesh at Troy (a very short epic)

Paul Halstead

Ξεκίνησαν οι Έλληνες
Μενέλαος και σία
και μπήκαν στα καράβια τους
να κάψουνε την Τροία.

Ο Πρίαμος σαν το 'μαθε
το κινητό του πιάνει
ζητεί από τον Γκιλγκαμές
χατήρι να του κάνει.

'Αμέσως' του απάντησε,
'θα φέρω κι ένα φίλο'.
Τροχάδην με τον Εγκιντού
ξεκίνησε για ξύλο.

Ο δρόμος όμως μακρινός,
τα ήπιανε στα χάνια
και τους καθυστερήσανε
γυναίκες στα λιμάνια.

Και δέκα χρόνια για να δουν
της Τροίας τ' ακρογιάλι,
δεν πρόλαβαν τον Πρίαμο
μα ούτε και τον Πάρι.

Ώσπου να δουν το Βόσπορο,
η Τροία ήταν στάχτη
κι οι δυο τους ψάχναν θύματα
για να τους βγει το άχτι.

The Hellenes they set out one day –
the troops of Menelaos –
and got on board their hollow ships
to burn down Troy in chaos.

But Priam, when he learnt of this
an urgent text was sending,
he asked his old pal Gilgamesh
a favour to extend him.

'Immediately', he answered him,
'I'll bring a mate to back you.'
And quickly then with Enkidu
he set off for some aggro.

The road, alas, was very long.
they tippled in the arbours,
and they were seriously delayed
by women in the harbours.

It took ten years before they saw
the shore of windy Ilion.
They could not rescue Priam old
nor Paris, his most dear son.

At last they saw the Bosporos
and Troy consumed by burning.
These two for some poor victim sought,
their rage to action turning.

Αρχίσανε να ερευνάν
στης Τροίας το παλάτι,
επιάσαν έναν ποιητή
και τού 'βγαλαν το μάτι.

Ο Όμηρος πλέον τυφλός,
αλλά παρηγοριόταν -
τους Γκιλγκαμές και Εγκιντού
ευθύς θα εκδικιόταν.

Στο Έπος, για τον Πόλεμο
της Τροίας ούτε λέξη,
Ο Γκιλγκαμές τον Εγκιντού
πως ήθελε να μπλέξει.

They searched all through Troy's ruins black,
with the palace as its highlight.
They found and seized an ancient bard
and then removed his eyesight.

Poor Homer, they had left him blind.
But comfort he extracted;
from Gilgamesh and Enkidu
swift vengeance he exacted.

And thus, in Homer's Trojan War,
no word of epic glory
that Gilgamesh wished Enkidu
to take part in the story.